Jung's
Map of the Soul

Jung's
Map of the Soul

An Introduction

MURRAY STEIN

Open Court
Chicago and La Salle, Illinois

To order books from Open Court, call toll free 1-800-815-2280, or visit www.opencourtbooks.com.

Cover illustration: "Accent en Rose" by Wassily Kandinsky, 1926, Musée Nationale d' Art Moderne, Centre de Creation Industrielle/Centre Georges Pompidou. Used by permission.

Open Court Publishing Company is a division of Carus Publishing Company.

First printing 1998
Second printing 1998
Third printing 1999
Fourth printing 2001
Fifth printing 2003
Sixth printing 2004
Seventh printing 2004
Eighth printing 2005
Ninth printing 2006
Tenth printing 2007
Eleventh printing 2009
Twelfth printing 2010

Printed and bound in the United States of America.

Library of Congress Cataloging-in-Publication Data

Stein, Murray, 1943—
    Jung's map of the soul : an introduction / Murray Stein.
      p. cm.
    Includes bibliographical references and index.
    ISBN 0-8126-9376-0
    1. Psychoanalysis.   2. Jungian psychology.   3. Jung. C.G. (Carl Gustav), 1875–1961   I. Title
    BF173.S   1998   97-51485
    150.19'34—dc21   CIP

For Sarah and Christopher

Contents

Acknowledgments

This book would not have been possible without the patient typing and editorial assistance of Lynne Walter. I want to thank her for her dedication and unflagging optimism. I would also like to thank Jan Marlan for her encouragement and enthusiastic support. Those who have sat through my lectures over the years will recognize their contributions in the many points of detail that would not be in this text but for their questions and observations. Thanks to all of you.

Introduction

You could timidly explore the
coasts of Africa to the south,
but going west there was nothing
except fear, the unknown, not
"our sea" but the Sea of Mystery,
Mare Ignotum.

> Carlos Fuentes
> *The Buried Mirror*

The summer Jung died, I was preparing to go to college. It was 1961. Humans were beginning to explore outer space, and the race was on to see who would be the first to reach the moon, the Americans or the Russians. All eyes were focused on the great adventure of space exploration. For the first time in human history, people were succeeding in leaving *terra firma* and traveling toward the stars. What I did not realize at the time was that our century has been marked just as decisively by the journeys inward, the great explorations of the inner world undertaken by the likes of Carl Jung in the decades before Sputnik and Apollo. What John Glenn and Neil Armstrong have meant to us as explorers of outer space, Jung signifies with regard to inner space, a courageous and intrepid voyager into the unknown.

Jung died peacefully in his house just outside Zürich, in a room that faced the calm lake to the west. To the south one could see the Alps. The day before he passed away he asked his son to help him to the window to take a last look at his beloved mountains. He had spent a lifetime exploring inner space and describing what he found there in his writings. By coincidence it happened that the

1

year Neil Armstrong stepped onto the surface of the moon I embarked on a journey to Zürich, Switzerland to study at the Jung Institute. What I am sharing in this volume is the distillation of nearly thirty years of studying Jung's map of the soul.

The aim of this book is to describe Jung's findings as he presented them in his published writings. First discovering Jung can itself be something like plunging into that "Sea of Mystery" written about by Fuentes in his account of earlier explorers who ventured across the Atlantic from Spain. It is with a sense of excitement, but also fear, that one launches out into these far-reaching places. I remember my first attempts. I was swept away by so much excitement at the prospect that I anxiously sought the advice of several of my university professors. I wondered if this was "safe." Jung was so attractive that he seemed too good to be true! Would I become lost, confused, misled? Luckily for me, these mentors gave me the green light, and I have been journeying and finding treasures ever since.

Jung's own original journey was even more frightening. He literally had no idea if he was going to find a treasure or fall over the edge of the world into outer space. The unconscious was truly a *Mare Ignotum w*hen he first let himself into it. But he was young and courageous, and he was determined to make some new discoveries. So away he went.

Jung often referred to himself as a pioneer and explorer of the uncharted mystery that is the human soul. He seems to have had an adventuresome spirit. For him—as for us still—the human psyche was a vast territory, and in his day it had not yet been much studied. It was a mystery that challenged the adventuresome with the prospect of rich discovery and frightened the timid with the threat of insanity. For Jung the study of the soul also became a matter of grave historical importance, for, as he once said, the whole world hangs on a thread and that thread is the human psyche. It is vital that we all become more familiar with it.

The great question is, of course: Can the human soul ever be known, its depths plumbed, its vast territory charted? It was perhaps some leftover nineteenth-century scientific grandiosity that led early pioneers of depth psychology like Jung and Freud and

Adler ever to undertake this effort and to think that they could define the ineffable and the supremely inscrutable human psyche. But set out into this *Mare Ignotum* they did, and Jung became a Christopher Columbus of the inner world. The twentieth century has been an age of scientific breakthroughs and technological wonders of all kinds; it has also been an age of deep introspection and probing into our common human subjectivity, which have resulted in the field broadly known today as depth psychology.

One way to familiarize ourselves with the psyche is to study the maps of it that have been drawn up and made available by these great pioneers. In their works we can find many points of orientation for ourselves, and perhaps we too will be stimulated to carry out further investigations and to make new discoveries. Jung's map of the psyche, as preliminary and perhaps unrefined and open-ended as it is—as are all first attempts at charting unknown territories—can still be a great boon to those who want to enter inner space, the world of the psyche, and not lose their way completely.

In this book, I accept Jung in his self-designated role of explorer and mapmaker, and I let this image guide me in presenting this introduction to his theory of the human psyche. The psyche is the territory, the unknown realm he was exploring; his theory is the map he created to communicate his understanding of the psyche. So it is Jung's map of the soul that I will attempt to describe in this book by leading you, the reader, into and through the territory of his writings. In doing so, I am presenting a map of a map, but one that I hope will be useful to you in your own further journeys into Jung's life and work.

Like all mapmakers, Jung worked with the instruments and evidence available to him in his time. Born in 1875, he completed his basic medical studies at the University of Basel in Switzerland by 1900 and his psychiatric training at the Burghölzli Klinik in Zürich by 1905. His important association with Freud extended from 1907 to 1913, after which he spent some years in a deep self-analysis and then emerged with his own distinctive psychological theory—called analytical psychology—which he presented to the world in 1921 in the book *Psychological Types*.[1] By 1930, aged 55, he had created most of the basic features of his theory but had not yet detailed a number of important items. The details would be presented in the years following 1930 and would continue to flow from Jung's pen until he died in 1961.

The project of exploring the human psyche scientifically was begun early in Jung's adult life. His first official expedition is described in his doctoral study, *On the Psychology and Pathology of So-Called Occult Phenomena.*[2] This gives a psychological account of the inner world of a gifted young woman whom we now know was actually his own cousin, Helene Preiswerk. As a teenager, she had the unusual ability to act as a medium for spirits of the dead, who would speak through her in remarkably accurate historical voices and accents. Jung was fascinated and set out to understand and interpret this puzzling psychological phenomenon. Pressing ahead, he used the word association test to uncover hidden features of the psychic landscape that had not been classified before. These were published in numerous papers, which are now housed in Volume 2 of his *Collected Works.* The newly discovered features of the unconscious he named "complexes," a term that would stick and make him famous. After that, he took up two burning psychiatric problems of the day, psychosis and schizophrenia, and produced a book, *The Psychology of Dementia Praecox,*[3] which he sent to Freud as an example of his work and as a suggestion for how some of Freud's ideas could be applied in psychiatry (Freud was a neurologist). After receiving Freud's warm and enthusiastic response, he entered into a professional relationship with him and quickly became the leader of the fledgling psychoanalytic movement. With this he began his study of the shadowy regions of neurotic conditions, landing finally on the discovery of more or less invariant universal fantasies and patterns of behavior (the archetypes) in an area of the deep psyche that he called the "collective unconscious." The description and detailed account of the archetype and the collective unconscious would become his signature, a mark that sets his map apart from those of all other explorers of the deep psyche, the unconscious.

The year 1930 divides Jung's professional life almost exactly in half: in 1900 he began his training and psychiatric studies at the

Burghölzli Klinik, and in 1961 he died a wise old man in his home at Küsnacht on Lake Zürich. In retrospect, one can see that Jung's first thirty years of professional activity were profoundly creative. During these years, he generated the basic elements of a monumental psychological theory as well as addressed major collective issues of the day. The second thirty years were perhaps less innovative of new theoretical constructs, but the output of books and articles was even greater than it had been earlier. These were the years of deepening and validating earlier hypotheses and intuitions. He extended his theories further to include studies of history, culture, and religion and to create a key link to modern physics. Jung's clinical work with psychiatric patients and with analysands was more consuming and intense in the first half of his professional life; it tapered off to a minimum after 1940, when the war interrupted normal collective life in Europe and Jung himself shortly thereafter also suffered a heart attack.

Jung's investigation of the psyche was also highly personal. His exploration of the unconscious mind was not only carried out on patients and experimental subjects. He also analyzed himself. In fact, for a time he became his own prime subject of study. By carefully observing his own dreams and developing the technique of active imagination, he found a way to enter ever more deeply into the hidden spaces of his inner world. To understand his patients and himself, he developed a method of interpretation that drew upon comparative studies in human culture, myth, and religion; in fact, he used any and all materials from world history that had a bearing on mental processes. This method he called "amplification."

The many sources and origins of Jung's thought have not yet been clearly worked out in detail. In his writings, he acknowledges a debt to many earlier thinkers, among them Goethe, Kant, Schopenhauer, Carus, Hartmann, and Nietzsche; most importantly, he places himself in the lineage of the ancient Gnostics and the medieval alchemists. His philosopher of choice was Kant. The influence of Hegel's dialectic is also apparent in his theorizing. And Freud left a mark. While Jung's thought can be shown to have developed and grown over the years that span his career, however, there is a remarkable continuity in his basic intellectual orientation. Some of Jung's readers have found seeds of his later psychological theories already apparent in some college papers delivered at his fraternity and published as *The Zofingia Lectures.* These were composed before 1900 while he was still an undergraduate at the University of Basel. The historian Henri Ellenberger goes so far as to claim that the "germinal cell of Jung's analytical psychology is to be found in his discussion of the Zofingia Students Association and in his experiments with his young medium cousin, Helene Preiswerk."[4] The Zofingia lectures show Jung's early struggles with issues that would occupy him throughout his life, such as the question of exposing religion and mystical experience to scientific, empirical investigation. Even as a young man, Jung argued that such subjects should be opened up to empirical research and approached with an open mind. When he met William James in 1909 at Clark University, it was a high point, because James had adopted the same position and had produced his classic study, *Varieties of Religious Experience,* using precisely this type of method.

From all of this study and experience, then, Jung drew up a map of the human soul. It is a map that describes the psyche in all of its dimensions, and it also tries to explain its internal dynamics. But Jung was always careful to respect the psyche's ultimate mystery. His theory can be read as a map of the soul, but it is the map of a mystery that cannot be ultimately captured in rational terms and categories. It is a map of a living, Mercurial thing, the psyche.

In reading Jung, also, one needs to keep in mind that the map is not the territory. Knowledge of the map is not the same as an experience of the deep psyche. At best, the map can be a useful tool for those who want orientation and guidance. For some who are lost, it can even be a lifesaver. For others, it will stimulate a powerful urge to experience what Jung is talking about. I began to write down my dreams when I first read Jung. Later I even journeyed to Zürich and studied for four years at the Jung Institute. Through analysis and personal experience of the unconscious, I have gained firsthand knowledge of many of Jung's findings. And yet my inner world is not identical to his. His map can show the way and can indicate general outlines, but it does not offer specific content. This must be discovered for oneself.

For many features of the map, Jung relied on scientific intuition and an amazingly vigorous imagination. The methods of science in his day could not confirm or disprove his hypothesis about the collective unconscious, for instance. Today we are closer to being able to do that. But Jung was an artist who used his creative thoughts to fashion a picture of the inner world of the mind. Like those beautifully illustrated maps of Antiquity and the Renaissance—drawn before mapmaking became scientific—the map that Jung created is gorgeous, not only abstract. Here one can find mermaids and dragons, heroes and evil characters. As a scientific investigator, of course, he was obliged to test his hunches and hypothetical constructs empirically. But this still left plenty of room for mythic imagination.

Jung worked in the discipline of psychiatry, or medical psychology as he sometimes refers to it. His chief teacher in the early years of his apprenticeship at the Burghölzli Klinik in Zürich was the well-known Swiss psychiatrist Eugen Bleuler, who coined the term "schizophrenia" to refer to one of the most severe of mental illnesses and wrote a great deal about the psychological issue of ambivalence. As much as possible, Jung searched for evidence and verification for his theories and hypotheses from sources outside of himself and his own immediate experience. His range of reading and study was vast. His claim was that as an empirical investigator of the psyche he was drawing a map that described not only the territory of his own inner world but one that referred to the features of the human soul in general. Like other great artists, the pictures he painted would have the power to speak to people of many generations and cultures.

My view is that this Swiss psychologist, whose name is today so widely known and highly regarded but whose own work is often not carefully read and frequently criticized for being inconsistent and contradictory, actually produced a coherent psychological theory. I think of it as a three-dimensional map that shows the levels of the psyche as well as the dynamic interrelations among them. It is a self-consistent work of art that appeals to some and not to others. Its postulates are cast as scientific propositions, and yet many of these are extremely hard to prove or disprove empirically. Important work is going on in this area, but whatever the outcomes may show, Jung's body of work will continue to attract attention and admiration. Works of art never become outdated, although maps may lose their relevance with the progress of time and changes in methodology.

To describe Jung's map of the psyche in a brief book is not a completely novel project, and others, notably Jolande Jacobi and Frieda Fordham, have produced similar introductory works in days of yore. What my work adds, I hope, is an emphasis on the overarching coherence within the theory and its subtle network of interconnections. As the theory is often presented, there is a bit of this and a bit of that, and the point that all the pieces stem from a single unified vision—which I see as a sublime vision of the soul—is not so obvious. It is also the case that a considerable number of years have passed since these earlier introductions to Jung's theory were offered, and the time is ripe for a new one.

My aim is to show that while gaps and inconsistencies do exist in Jung's map, there is a more profound underlying unity of vision that far outweighs the occasional lapses from logical precision. My main interest in this account is not to show the development of Jung's thought or to consider at any length its practical applications in psychotherapy and analysis. It is rather to expose the underlying intellectual unity beneath the welter of commentary and detail that constitute his complete *oeuvre*. The careful reader will, I hope, come away from this book with a general picture of the theory of analytical psychology as Jung himself expounded it, as well as a grasp on the most important details and how they belong to a single whole.

The reason for the remarkable unity in Jung's account of the psyche stems, I believe, from a feature of his thought that did not grow out of his empirical methodology. Jung was an intuitive creative thinker, after the fashion of oldtime philosophers like Plato and Schopenhauer. He created his map of the psyche from the ideas available in the general scientific and intellectual community of his day, but he gave these ideas a unique twist. He did not come up so much with radical new notions as take what was generally available and fashion a new and highly distinctive pattern out of it. Like a great artist working in a tradition of painting, he used the images and materials that were available to him and made something new which had not been seen before in quite the same combination of elements.

Jung was also a visionary in the tradition of Meister Eckhart, Boehme, Blake, and Emerson. Many of his most important intuitions originated in his experiences of the sublime, which came to him in dreams, visions, and active imagination. He confesses this openly in his autobiography, where he writes that his prime teacher about the "reality of the psyche" was the figure Philemon, who first appeared to him in a dream and whom he then engaged for years in active imagination.[5] Direct experience of the soul is the ultimate source of Jung's theory, and this accounts for its deep internal unity and self-consistency.

But Jung was also a dedicated scientist, and this sets his work apart from the writings of poets and mystics. He worked with the scientific method, which meant that he held his work accountable to the scientific community and subjected it to empirical tests. His visions, intuitions, and inner realizations were not simply allowed to rest on their own merit; they were checked against the evidence of human experience in general. Jung's strong need to be scientific and empirical accounts for the unbeveled edges in his theory, for the rough approximations that could have been made much smoother by pure intellect and imagination. The empirical world—life as it is experienced—is messy and does not fit neatly into the boxes made by human thought and imagination. Because Jung was both a visionary intuitive thinker and an empirical scientist, his map of the human psyche is both coherent and yet only loosely systematic and self-consistent.

One reason I have continued to appreciate Jung's writings and have read him steadily for over twenty-five years is that he is not compulsively consistent. When I have studied truly systematic thinkers such as Tillich or Hegel, I have always squirmed in the tight jaws of their steely minds. Their thoughts are too highly organized for me. Where is the messiness, the juiciness of life? This has led me to look to artists and poets for wisdom rather than primarily to philosophers and theologians. I am suspicious of rigid systems. They feel paranoid to me. Jung's writings have never affected me in this way.

Reading Jung, I have always sensed his deep respect for the mysteries of the human psyche, and this attitude allows the horizons to go on expanding. His map opens vistas up rather than closes them off. I hope I will be able to communicate this same impression to you, the reader.

This is an introductory work. Although I do hope that even advanced students of Jung's psychology will benefit from reading it, my true audience is those who would like to know what Jung said but have not yet found the right entry into his massive writings and complex thinking. Each chapter of this book is focused on one theme in his theory. I look at specific passages from his *Collected Works* that lay out that piece of his map. The especially motivated and diligent reader can consult those references later at leisure. My text-centered presentation will, I hope, offer a friendly invitation to become immersed in the primary documents and to face the challenge of teasing out Jung's sometimes obscure meaning and reflecting upon its implications.

The selection of these readings is my own personal choice. Other equally valuable texts could have been cited and used just as well. I have tried to choose the clearest and most representative essays and passages from Jung's work to demonstrate the essential coherence of his vision. Jung's map of the psyche is a massive achievement of intellect, observation, and creative intuition. Few modern thinkers have come close to equaling this towering work, which is housed in the eighteen volumes of the *Collected Works*, the three volumes of *Letters*, the various collections of interviews and occasional writings, and his autobiography (written with Aniela Jaffe). From this mountain of material I have selected the topics that belong most essentially to his theory and have left out those that have to do with analytical practice and interpretation of culture, history, and religion.

I come back to the question I asked before: Is there really a system in Jung's works? Is he a systematic thinker? The answer is probably a guarded yes. The theory is coherent, in the same way that Switzerland is a coherent country although the population speaks four different languages. The whole hangs together even though the parts look as if they could stand alone and function quite independently. Jung did not think systematically in the way a philosopher does, building on basic premises and making certain that the parts fit together without contradiction. He claimed to be an empirical scientist, and so his theorizing matches the disorderliness of the empirical world. An intuitive thinker, Jung lays out big concepts, elaborates them in some detail, and then proceeds to other big concepts. He backtracks frequently, repeats himself, and fills in gaps as he goes along. This quality makes for difficulty in reading him. One has to know all of his work in order to get the picture. If you read more or less randomly in his works for a while, you begin to suspect that the pieces fit together somehow in Jung's own mind, but only after reading his whole work and considering it for a long time can you see how they really do.

I think Jung felt that, having become aware of the profundity and far reaches of the human psyche through his clinical work and his own experience, he had to work patiently over a considerable length of time in order to formulate responsibly this sublime vision of the human soul. He would not rush it, and often he delayed publishing for years while he worked at building the structures that could support his thought in the intellectual community. As we try to grasp this vision in its full magnitude, we need to bear in mind that he elaborated it over a period of some sixty years. We should not be overly obsessed with exact consistency in a work this large and in one that is attuned to empirical reality.

A story is told of Jung by his students in Zürich. Once when he was criticized for being inconsistent on some point of theory, he responded: I have my eye on the central fire, and I am trying to put some mirrors around it to show it to others. Sometimes the edges of those mirrors leave gaps and don't fit together exactly. I can't help that. Look at what I'm trying to point to!

I take it as my task to describe as accurately as possible what Jung shows in these mirrors. It is a vision that has sustained many people in our generation and may be a vision for the foreseeable future. Above all, his writings provide us with images of a great mystery, the human psyche.

1

Surface:
(Ego-Conconscious)

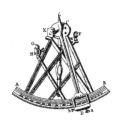

I will begin unrolling Jung's map of the psyche by looking at his description of human consciousness and its most central feature, the *ego*. "Ego" is a technical term whose origin is the Latin word meaning "I." Consciousness is the state of awakeness, and at its center there is an "I." This is an obvious starting point, and it is the entrance to the vast inner space that we call the psyche. It is also a complex feature of the psyche, one that still holds many puzzles and unanswered questions.

Although Jung was more interested in discovering what lay beneath consciousness in the hinterlands of the psyche, he also took on the task of describing and explaining human consciousness. He wanted to create a complete map of the psyche, so this was unavoidable: ego-consciousness is a prime feature of the territory he was exploring. Jung cannot really be called an ego psychologist, but he did place a social value on the ego. He offered an account of the ego's functions, and he recognized the critical importance of greater consciousness for the future of human life and for culture. Moreover, he was acutely aware that ego-consciousness is itself the prerequisite for psychological investigation. It is the tool. Our knowledge as human beings about anything at all is conditioned by the capacities and limitations of our consciousness. To study consciousness, therefore, is to direct attention to the instrument that one is using for psychological investigation and exploration.

Why is it so important, especially in psychology, to understand the nature of ego-consciousness? It is because one needs to make adjustments for distortion. Jung said that every psychology is a personal confession.[1] Every creative psychologist is limited by his or her own personal biases and unexamined assumptions. Not all that seems true to even the most earnest and sincere investigator's consciousness is necessarily accurate knowledge. Much that passes for knowledge among human beings is actually, upon closer and more critical inspection, merely prejudice or belief based on distortion, bias, hearsay, speculation, or pure fantasy. Beliefs pass as knowledge and are clung to as reliable certainties. "I believe in order that I may understand," a famous remark from St. Augustine, may sound strange to our modern ears today, and yet this is often the case when people begin to speak about psychological reality. Jung seriously sought to examine the foundations of his own thinking by critically examining the instrument he was using to make his discoveries. He argued strongly that a critical understanding of consciousness is essential for science, just as it has been for philosophy. Accurate understanding of the psyche, or of anything else for that matter, depends upon the state of one's consciousness. Jung wanted to offer a critical understanding of consciousness. This was his primary objective in writing the key work, *Psychological Types*, which describes eight cognitive styles that distinguish human consciousness and process information and life experience differently.

The Relation of Ego to Consciousness

Jung therefore writes a great deal about ego-consciousness throughout his published works. For my purposes here, I will discuss primarily the first chapter of the late work *Aion*, entitled "The Ego," as well as some related texts and passages. These summarize his position adequately and represent his mature thinking on the subject. At the end of this chapter I will also include some references to *Psychological Types*.

Aion can be read on many different levels. It is a work of Jung's later years and reflects his profound engagement with Western intellectual and religious history and their future, as well his most detailed thoughts about the archetype of the self. The first four chapters were added to the book later to provide the new reader with an introduction to his general psychological theory and to offer an entry point into the vocabulary of analytical psychology. While these introductory pages are not detailed or particularly technical, they do contain Jung's most condensed discussions about the psychic structures called ego, shadow, anima, animus, and self.

Here Jung defines the ego as follows: "It forms, as it were, the centre of the field of consciousness; and, in so far as this comprises the empirical personality, the ego is the subject of all personal acts of consciousness."[2] Consciousness is a "field," and what Jung calls the "empirical personality" here is our personality as we are aware of it and experience it firsthand. The ego, as "the subject of all personal acts of consciousness," occupies the center of this field. The term ego refers to one's experience of oneself as a center of willing, desiring, reflecting, and acting. This definition of the ego as the center of consciousness is consistent throughout all of Jung's writings.

Jung continues this text by commenting on the function of the ego within the psyche: "The relation of a psychic content to the ego forms the criterion of its consciousness, for no content can be conscious unless it is represented to a subject."[3] The ego is a "subject" to whom psychic contents are "represented." It is like a mirror. Moreover, a connection to the ego is the necessary condition for making anything conscious—a feeling, a thought, a perception, or a fantasy. The ego is a kind of mirror in which the psyche can see itself and can become aware. The degree to which a psychic content is taken up and reflected by the ego is the degree to which it can be said to belong to the realm of consciousness. When a psychic content is only vaguely or marginally conscious, it has not yet been captured and held it in place upon the ego's reflective surface.

In the passages that follow this definition of the ego, Jung makes a crucial distinction between conscious and unconscious features of the psyche: consciousness is what we know, and unconsciousness is all that we do not know. In another text, written at about the same time, he makes this a little more precise: "The unconscious is not simply the unknown, it is rather the *unknown psychic;* and this we define . . . as all those things in us which, if they came to consciousness, would presumably differ in no respect from the known psychic contents."[4] The distinction between conscious and unconscious, so fundamental in Jung's general theory of the psyche, as it is in all of depth psychology, posits that some contents are reflected by the ego and held in consciousness, where they can be further examined and manipulated, while other psychic contents lie outside of consciousness either temporarily or permanently. The unconscious includes all psychic contents that lie outside of consciousness, for whatever reason or whatever duration. Actually, this is the vast bulk of the psychic world. The unconscious was the major area of investigation in depth psychology, and Jung's most passionate interest lay in exploring that territory. But more of that later.

Often in his writings Jung refers to the ego as a "complex," a term that will be discussed extensively in the next chapter. In the *Aion* passage, however, he simply calls it a specific content of consciousness, stating by this that consciousness is a broader category than the ego and contains more than only the ego.

What is consciousness itself, this field in which the ego is located and where it occupies and defines the center? Most simply, consciousness is awareness. It is the state of being awake, of observing and registering what is going on in the world around and within. Humans are not, of course, the only conscious beings on earth. Other animals are conscious as well, since obviously they can observe and react to their environments in carefully modulated ways. Plants' sensitivity to their environment can also be taken as a form of consciousness. By itself, consciousness does not set the human species apart from other forms of life. Nor is consciousness something that sets human adults apart from infants and children. In the strictest sense, human consciousness does not depend for its essential quality upon age or psychological development at all. A friend who observed the birth of his daughter told me how moved he was when, after the placenta was removed and her eyes were cleaned, she opened them and looked around the room, taking it in. Obviously this was a sign of consciousness. The eye is an indicator of the presence of consciousness. Its aliveness and movement is the signal that an aware being is observing the world. Consciousness depends not only on sight, of course, but on the other senses as well. In the womb, before the infant's eyes are functioning to see, it registers sounds, reacts to voices and to music, and indicates a remarkable degree of responsiveness. We do not yet know exactly when the embryo first attains a level of awareness and reactiveness that could definitely be called conscious, but it is early and it is certainly in the prenatal period.

The opposite of consciousness is deep dreamless sleep, the total lack of responsiveness and sentient awareness. And the permanent absence of consciousness from a body is practically a definition of death, except in cases of longterm coma. Consciousness, even if it is only the potential for future consciousness, is the "life factor"; it belongs to living bodies.

What development does to consciousness is add specific content. In theory, human consciousness can be separated from its contents—the thoughts, memories, identity, fantasies, emotions, images, and words that crowd its space. But in practice this is almost impossible. In fact, only advanced spiritual adepts seem able to make this distinction convincingly. It is truly a sage who can separate consciousness from its contents and keep them apart, whose consciousness is not defined by identifications with selected thoughts and images. For most people, consciousness without a stable object to ground it seems to be an exceedingly ephemeral and transient thing. The substantiality of consciousness and the feeling of solidity are typically provided by stable objects and contents such as images, memories, and thoughts. Substance and continuity in consciousness are made of these. Yet, as evidence from stroke victims attests, the contents and even the ego functions of consciousness—thinking, remembering, naming and speaking, recognizing familiar images and persons and faces—are actually more transient and fragile than is consciousness itself. It is possible to lose one's memory entirely, for example, and still be conscious. Consciousness is like a room that surrounds the psychic contents that temporarily fill it. And consciousness precedes the ego, which becomes its eventual center.

The ego, like consciousness, also transcends and outlasts the particular contents that occupy the room of consciousness at any particular moment. The ego is a focal point within consciousness, its most central and perhaps most permanent feature. Against the opinion of the East, Jung argues that without an ego, consciousness itself becomes questionable. But it is true that certain ego functions can be suspended or seemingly obliterated without destroying consciousness completely, and so a sort of ego-less consciousness, a type of consciousness that shows very little evidence of a willful center, an "I," is a human possibility at least for short periods of time.

For Jung, the ego forms the critical center of consciousness and in fact determines to a large extent which contents remain within the realm of consciousness and which ones drop away into the unconscious. The ego is responsible for retaining contents in consciousness, and it can also eliminate contents from consciousness by ceasing to reflect them. To use Freud's term, which Jung found useful, the ego can "repress" contents it does not like or finds intolerably painful or incompatible with other contents. It can also retrieve contents from storage in the unconscious (i.e., from the memory bank) so long as (a) they are not blocked by defense mechanisms, such as repression, which keep intolerable conflicts out of reach, and (b) they have a strong enough associative connection to the ego—they are "learned" strongly enough.

The ego is not fundamentally constituted and defined by the acquired contents of consciousness such as momentary or even chronic identifications. It is like a mirror or magnet that holds contents in a focal point of awareness. But it also wills and acts. As the vital center of consciousness, it precedes the acquisition of language, personal identity, and even awareness of a personal name. Later acquisitions of the ego, such as recognition of one's own face and name, are contents that cluster closely around this center of consciousness, and they have the effect of defining the ego and enlarging its range of executive command and self-awareness. Fundamentally, the ego is a virtual center of awareness that exists at least from birth, the eye that sees and has always seen the world from this vantage point, from this body, from this individual point of view. In itself it is nothing, that is, not a thing. It is therefore highly elusive and impossible to pin down. One can even deny that it exists at all. And yet it is always present. It is not the product of nurture, growth, or development. It is innate. While it can be shown to develop and gain strength from this point onward through "collisions" with reality (see below), its core is "given." It comes with the infant.

As Jung describes the psyche, there is a network of associations among the various contents of consciousness. All of them are linked directly or indirectly to the central agency, the ego. The ego is the center of consciousness not only geographically but also dynamically. It is the energy center that moves the contents of consciousness around and arranges them in orders of priority. The ego is the locus of decisionmaking and free will. When I say, "I am going to the post office," my ego has made a decision and mobilizes the physical and emotional energy necessary to do the job. The ego directs me to the post office and gets me there. It is the executive who sets the priorities: "Go to the post office, don't get distracted by your wish to go for a stroll in the park." While the ego can be regarded as the center of selfishness (*ego*-ism), it is also the center of altruism. In and of itself, the ego, as Jung understood and described it, is morally neutral, not a "bad thing" as one hears it referred to in common parlance ("oh, he's got such an ego!") but a necessary part of human psychological life. The ego is what sets humans apart from other creatures of nature who also possess consciousness; it also sets the individual human being apart from other human beings. It is the individualizing agent in human consciousness.

The ego focuses human consciousness and gives our conscious behavior its purposefulness and direction. Because we have an ego, we possess the freedom to make choices that may defy our instincts for self-preservation, propagation, and creativity. The ego contains our capacity to master large amounts of material within consciousness and to manipulate them. It is a powerful associative magnet and an organizational agent. Because humans have such a force at the center of consciousness, they are able to integrate and direct large quantities of data. A strong ego is one that can obtain and move around in a deliberate way large amounts of conscious content. A weak ego cannot do very much of this kind of work and more easily succumbs to impulses and emotional reactions. A weak ego is easily distracted, and as a result consciousness lacks focus and consistent motivation.

It is possible for humans to remain conscious while suspending much of normal ego functioning. By will we can direct ourselves to be passive and inactive and simply to observe the world within or without, like a camera. Normally, though, it is not possible to maintain a volitionally restrained observational consciousness for a great length of time, because the ego and the wider psyche usually become quickly engaged by what is being observed. When we watch a movie, for example, we may begin by simply observing and taking in the people and scenery. But we soon begin to identify with one character or another, and our emotions become activated. The ego readies itself to act, and if one has difficulty distinguishing between movie images and reality (another ego function) one may be tempted to engage in physical behavior. The body then becomes mobilized, and the ego aims at and intends a particular course of action. Indeed, movies are structured so that viewers will take sides emotionally and support whatever a particular character is doing or feeling. Engaged in this way, the ego becomes activated as a center of wishing, hoping, and perhaps even intending. It is conceivable that one would make a major life decision while watching a movie as a consequence of the feelings and thoughts generated in consciousness by these images. People have been known to leave a movie theater and become violent or lustful as a direct result of the impact of the movie. The ego has become enlisted by emotion, identification, and desire, and uses its directive function and energy to act.

As becomes evident, the ego's freedom is limited. It is easily influenced by both internal psychic and external environmental stimuli. The ego may respond to a threatening stimulus by taking up arms and defending itself; or it may be activated and stimulated by an interior urge to create, or to love, or to seek revenge. It may also respond to an ego impulse—that is, narcissistically. It may in this way be seized by a need for revenge, for example.

Waking consciousness is focused, then, by the ego's registering of internal and environmental stimuli and phenomena and putting the body into motion. The origins of the ego, to say it again, extend back before earliest childhood and infancy. Even a very young infant notices shapes in its environment, some of which seem pleasurable, and it reaches out for them. These very early signals of an organism's intentionality are evidence for the primordial roots of the ego, one's "I-ness."

Reflecting on the nature and essence of this "I" leads to profound psychological questions. What is the ego fundamentally? What am I? Jung would simply say that the ego is the center of consciousness.

The "I" feels, perhaps naively, that it has existed forever. Even notions of earlier lifetimes sometimes take on a feeling of truth and reality. It is an open question whether the "I" changes essentially in the course of a lifetime. Is not the "I" that cried for mother at two the same one that cries for a lost love at forty-five or over a lost spouse at eighty? While many features of the ego clearly do develop and change, particularly with regard to cognition, self-knowledge, psychosocial identity, competence, etc., one also senses an important continuity at the heart of the ego. Many people have been moved to find the "child within." This is nothing less than the recognition that the person I was as a child is the same person I am as an adult. Probably the essential core of the ego does not change over a lifetime. This could also possibly account for the strong intuition and conviction of many people that this core of the ego does not disappear with one's physical death but either goes to a place of eternal rest (heaven, nirvana) or is reborn in another life on the physical plane (reincarnation).

A child first says "I" at about two. Until then it refers to itself in the third person or by name: "Timmie want" or "Sarah go." When a child is able to say "I" and to think self-referentially, placing itself consciously at the center of a personal world and giving that position a specific first-person pronoun, it has made a great leap forward in consciousness. But this is by no means the birth of the primordial ego. Long before this, consciousness and behavior have been organized around a virtual center. The ego clearly exists before one can refer to it consciously and reflectively, and the process of coming to know it is gradual and continues throughout a lifetime. Growing into self-consciousness is a process that passes through many stages from infancy to adulthood. One of these Jung describes in some detail in *Memories, Dreams, Reflections*, when he speaks of walking out of a cloud at about the age of thirteen and realizing for the first time: "Now I am myself."[5]

By virtue of this capacity to achieve a high level of self-knowledge and self-awareness—that is, a self-reflective ego—human consciousness differs from animal consciousness, at least so far as we presently know. This difference is attributable not only to human verbal capacity, which gives us the ability to talk about the "I" that we know we are and thereby to enrich its complexity, but to the sheer self-mirroring function present in human consciousness. This function is prelinguistic and postlinguistic. It is knowing that one is (and later, that one will die). By virtue of having an ego—this built-in mirror within consciousness—we can know that we are and what we are. Other animal species also clearly want to live and to control their environments, and they show evidence of emotion and consciousness as well as intentionality, reality testing, self-control, and much else that we associate with an ego function. But animals do not have, or have much less of, this self-mirroring function within consciousness. They have less of an ego. Do they know that they are, that they will individually die, that they are separate individuals? It is doubtful. The poet Rilke held that animals do not face death the way humans do, and that gives them the advantage of living more fully in the present moment. Animals are not self-conscious in the same way that humans are, and without language they cannot express whatever self-consciousness they do have with any degree of sophistication nor differentiate themselves from others with the kind of linguistic tools humans possess.[6]

After a certain point in development, the human ego and human consciousness become largely defined and shaped by the cultural world in which a person grows up and becomes educated. This is a layer, or wrapping, of ego structure that surrounds the central ego. As a child grows into a culture and learns its forms and habits through family interactions and educational experiences in school, this ego wrapping becomes thicker and thicker. Jung refers to these two features of the ego as "Personality No. 1" and "Personality No. 2."[7] Personality No. 2 is the innate core ego, and Personality No. 1 is the culturally acquired layer of the ego that grows up over time.

Some specific contents of a person's ego-consciousness can show a great deal of stability over time. One's own name is ordinarily a stable feature of consciousness. It may even seem after a certain point to be permanently welded to the ego. While a name is an impersonal handle and belongs to the public arena as part of one's *persona* (see chaper 5), when it is spoken by a parent or a child or a lover it touches our most intimate places of self-feeling. Yet it must still be recognized that a name is a cultural artifact and as such is less securely fixed to the ego than is, for instance, the body. People have changed their names and remained the same people. So far no one has changed complete bodies to see if this is still the case; if (or when) this comes to pass, we will find out if the ego also transcends the body. I suspect the answer will be that it does indeed transcend the body, even though its relation to the body seems to us so completely fused.

One might be tempted to define the ego as the body's consciousness of itself as a willing, individual, limited, unique entity. If one had been named differently, it could be argued, one's essential "I" would not be different than it is. But if one had a different body, would the ego be essentially other? The ego is deeply rooted in a body, more so even than it is in culture, but just how deep this connection goes is open to debate. Nevertheless, the ego is profoundly fearful of the body's death. It is a fear that the ego's extinction will follow upon the body's demise. According to Jung, however, the ego is not strictly limited to the somatic base. In *Aion* he states that the ego "is not a simple or elementary factor, but a complex one, which as such, cannot be described exhaustively. Experience shows that it rests on two seemingly different bases, the somatic and the psychic."[8]

In Jung's thinking, the psyche cannot be reduced to a mere expression of the body, the result of brain chemistry or some such physical process. For the psyche also partakes of mind or spirit (the Greek word *nous* captures best Jung's thinking on this point), and as such it can and occasionally does transcend its physical location. In later chapters, we shall see more precisely how Jung derives psyche from a combination of physical nature and transcendent spirit or mind, *nous*. But, for now, it is sufficient to note that psyche and body are not coterminous, nor is the one derived from the other. The ego, too, which is predominantly treated by Jung as a completely psychic object, rests only partially on a somatic base. The ego is based in the body only in the sense that it experiences unity with the body, but the body that the ego experiences is psychic. It is a body image. and not the body itself. The body is experienced "from the totality of endosomatic perceptions,"[9] that is, from what one can consciously feel of the body. These percepts of the body "are produced by endosomatic stimuli, only some of which cross the threshold of consciousness. A considerable proportion of these stimuli occur unconsciously, that is, subliminally . . . The fact that they are subliminal does not necessarily mean that their status is merely physiological, any more than this would be true of a psychic content. Sometimes they are capable of crossing the threshold, that is, of becoming perceptions. But there is no doubt that a large proportion of these endosomatic stimuli are simply incapable of consciousness and are so elementary that there is no reason to assign them a psychic nature."[10]

In this passage, we observe how Jung draws the line on the psyche's boundary to include ego-consciousness and the unconscious but not the somatic base as such. Many physiological processes never pass over into the psyche, even into the *uncon-scious* psyche. In principle, they are incapable of ever becoming conscious. It is evident that the sympathetic nervous system, for instance, is for the most part not accessible to consciousness. As the heart beats, blood circulates, and neurons fire, some but not all somatic processes can become conscious. It is not clear just how far the ego's capacity to penetrate into the somatic base can be developed. Trained yogis claim to be able to exercise very large control over somatic processes. They have been known to will their deaths, for example, and to have simply stopped their hearts at will. One yogi's ability to change the surface temperature in the palm of his hand by will was tested and verified: he could willfully alter it by ten or twenty degrees. This demonstrates a considerable psychic capacity to penetrate and control the body, but it still leaves much territory untouched. How far down into the cellular substructure can the ego penetrate? Can a trained ego shrink a cancerous tumor, for example, or effectively overcome hyperten-sion? Many questions remain.

One should keep in mind that there are two thresholds: the first separates consciousness from the unconscious, the second separates the psyche (both conscious and unconscious) from the somatic base. I will discuss these thresholds in greater detail in later chapters, but for now it should be noted that they are broad thresholds and should be conceived of as fluid boundaries, not fixed and rigid barriers. The psyche is, for Jung, inclusive of both consciousness and the unconscious, but it does not include all of the body in its purely physiological dimension. The ego, Jung holds, rests on the *psychic* soma, that is, on a body image, and not on the body per se. The ego is therefore essentially a psychic factor.

The Location of the Ego

The whole territory of the psyche is very nearly coterminous with the potential range of the ego. The psyche, as Jung defines it in this passage, is bounded by and limited to where the ego can in principle go. This does not mean that psyche and ego are identical, however, since the psyche includes the unconscious and the ego is more or less limited to consciousness. But the unconscious is at least potentially available to the ego, even if the ego does not ever actually experience much of it. The point here is that the psyche itself has a limit, and that limit is the point at which stimuli or extrapsychic contents can no longer, in principle, *ever* be experienced consciously. In Kantian philosophy, which Jung followed, this nonexperiencable entity is called the *Ding an sich,* the "thing in itself." Human experience is limited. The psyche is limited. Jung was not a pan-psychist, that is, someone who claims that the psyche is everywhere and makes up everything. The body lies outside of the psyche, and the world is far greater than the psyche.

We should avoid imposing too much precision on Jung's use of terminology, however, particularly on terms like *psyche* and *unconscious.* Otherwise we will create tight fits where Jung deliberately left gaps and openings. Psyche is not *precisely* co-extensive with the combined territory conscious-and-unconscious, nor is it *exactly* limited to the range of the ego. At the edges, where psyche and soma come together and where psyche and world meet, there are shadings of "inside/outside." These gray areas Jung calls *psychoid.* This is an area that behaves in a psyche-like way but is not altogether psychic. It is quasi-psychic. In these gray areas lie psychosomatic puzzles, for example. How do mind and body influence each other? Where does one leave off and the other begin? These questions have still not been answered.

Jung draws these subtle distinctions in the *Aion* passage, where he describes the psychic base of the ego this way: "on the one hand the ego rests on the total field of consciousness, and on the other, on the sum total of unconscious contents. These fall into three groups: first, temporarily subliminal contents that can be reproduced voluntarily (memory) . . . second, unconscious contents that cannot be reproduced voluntarily . . . third, contents that are not capable of becoming conscious at all."[11] This third group should, by earlier definitions, be left outside of the psyche, and yet Jung here places it inside the unconscious. Evidently he saw that the unconscious reaches a place where it is no longer psyche and extends into nonpsychic regions, that is, into the "world" beyond the psyche. And yet for a certain distance at least this nonpsychic world lies within the unconscious. Here we approach the borders of great mysteries: the basis for extrapsychic perception, synchronicity, miracle healings of the body, and others.

As a scientist, Jung had to provide arguments and evidence for such bold hypotheses as the existence of the unconscious, both its personal and collective aspects. Here he merely alludes to these arguments, which in other writings are developed in great detail: "Group two can be inferred from the spontaneous irruption of subliminal contents into consciousness."[12] This describes how complexes affect consciousness. "Group three is hypothetical; it is a logical inference from the facts underlying group two."[13] Certain consistent patterns in the complexes led Jung to hypothesize the archetypes. If certain effects are sufficiently strong and persistent, a scientist formulates a hypothesis which, it is hoped, will account for the effects and lead to further investigation.[14]

The ego, Jung goes on in the *Aion* text, rests on two bases: a somatic (bodily) and a psychic. Each of these bases is multilayered and exists partially in consciousness but mostly in the unconscious. To say that the ego rests on them is to say that the ego's roots reach into the unconscious. In its upper structure, the ego is rational, cognitive, and reality-oriented, but in its deeper and more hidden layers it is subject to the flux of emotion, fantasy, and conflict, and to intrusions from the physical and psychic levels of the unconscious. The ego can be easily disturbed, therefore, both by somatic problems and by psychic conflicts. A purely psychic entity, a vital center of consciousness, the home of identity and volition, the ego in its deeper layers is vulnerable to disturbances from many sources.

As I pointed out above, the ego must be distinguished from the field of consciousness in which it is nested and for which it forms the focal point of reference. Jung writes: "When I said that the ego 'rests' on the total field of consciousness I do not mean that it consists of this. Were that so, it would be indistinguishable from the field of consciousness as a whole."[15] Like William James who distinguished between the "I" and the "me,"[16] Jung draws a difference between the ego and what James called "the stream of consciousness." The ego is a point or a dot that dips into the stream and can separate itself from the stream of consciousness and become aware of it as something other than itself. Consciousness is not fully under the ego's control even if it gains distance from it sufficient to observe and study its flow. The ego moves around within the field of consciousness, observing, selecting, directing motor activity to an extent, but also ignoring a good deal of material that consciousness is otherwise attending to. If you drive a car on a familiar route, the ego's attention will frequently wander and attend to matters other than driving. You arrive safely at your destination, having negotiated traffic lights and numerous hazardous traffic situations, wondering how you got there! The focus of attention was elsewhere, the ego had wandered off and left the driving to non-egoic consciousness. Consciousness, meanwhile, aside from the ego, is constantly monitoring, taking in, processing, and reacting to information. Should a crisis occur, the ego returns and takes charge. The ego often focuses on a memory, on a thought or feeling, or on plans which it has plucked out of the stream of consciousness. It leaves other routine operations to an habituated consciousness. This separability of the ego from consciousness is a mild and non-pathological form of dissociation. The ego can dissociate from consciousness, to a degree.

Although a rudimentary or primitive ego seems to be present from the earliest moments of consciousness as a sort of virtual center or focal point, it does grow and develop in important respects during the early phases of infancy and later childhood. Jung writes: "Although its bases are themselves relatively unknown and unconscious, both psychic and somatic, the ego is a conscious factor par excellence. It is even acquired, empirically speaking, during the individual's lifetime. It seems to arise in the first place from the collision between the somatic factor and the environment, and, once established as a subject, it goes on developing from further collisions with the outer world and the inner."[17] What makes the ego grow, according to Jung, is what he calls "collisions." In other words, conflict, trouble, anguish, sorrow, suffering. These are what lead the ego to develop. The requirements made upon a person to adapt to physical and psychic environments draws upon a potential center in consciousness and strengthens its capacity to function, in order to focus consciousness and to mobilize the organism in a specific direction. As a virtual center of consciousness, the ego is innate, but as an actual and effective center it owes its stature to those collisions between the psycho-physical body and an environmental milieu that demands response and adaptation. A moderate amount of conflict with the environment and some frustration are, therefore, according to Jung, the best conditions for ego growth.

These collisions may be catastrophic, however, and lead to severe damage to the psyche. Then the nascent ego is not strengthened but rather injured and so severely traumatized that its later functioning is radically impaired. Infant abuse and childhood sexual trauma are examples of such psychic catastrophes. From these the ego is often permanently impaired in its lower psychic registers. Cognitively it may be able to function normally, but in its less conscious parts the emotional turmoil and absence of cohesive structure create severe character disorders and dissociative tendencies. Such egos are not merely vulnerable in a normal fashion—as all egos are—but they are fragile and hyperdefensive. They fragment easily under stress and therefore tend to resort to primitive (but very powerful) defenses to wall off the world and to protect the psyche from intrusions and possible injury. Such people cannot trust others. Paradoxically, they are also constantly let down and seriously disappointed by others and by life in general. Gradually these people isolate themselves from the environment, which is perceived as overwhelmingly threatening, and they live out their lives in defensive isolation.

The nascent ego might be described as an infant's cry of anguish signaling a discrepancy between need and satisfaction. From there it begins to develop and eventually it becomes more complex. By the time a two-year-old child's ego is saying "no" to everybody, it is not only coping with environmental challenges, but it is already trying to change or to control many aspects of its environment. That little person's ego is very busy strengthening itself by creating numerous collisions, and that "no!" and "I won't!" are exercises that strengthen the ego as a separate entity and as a strong inner center of will, intentionality, and control.

An ego that has achieved autonomy in childhood feels also that consciousness can be harnessed and directed at will. The guardedness characteristic of the overly anxious person is an indication that the ego has not fully achieved this level of confident autonomy. More openness and flexibility is possible when the ego has acquired a degree of control sufficient to insure survival and basic need-gratification.

Jung's notion of ego development arising from collisions with the environment offers a creative way of viewing the potential in all of those inevitable human experiences of frustration in the face of an ungratifying environment. As the ego tries to apply its will, it meets a certain measure of resistance from the environment, and if this collision is handled well the result will be the ego's growth. This insight also cautions us against trying to provide too much insulation for a child against the onslaughts of a challenging reality. For stimulating ego growth, a constant-climated overprotective environment is not particularly useful.

Psychological Types

A brief discussion of Jung's theory of psychological types also belongs in this chapter on ego-consciousness. The editors of Jung's *Collected Works* quote Jung in their introductory note to *Psychological Types* as viewing this work to be "a psychology of consciousness regarded from what might be called a clinical angle."[18] The two major *attitudes* (introversion and extroversion) and the four *functions* (thinking, feeling, sensation, and intuition) have a strong influence upon the ego's orientation as it undertakes its adaptive tasks and requirements. The core ego's innate disposition toward assuming one of these attitudes and functions forms its characteristic stance toward the world and toward assimilating experience.

Collisions with reality awaken the nascent ego's potentiality and challenge it to relate to the world. Such collisions also

interrupt the psyche's *participation mystique*[19] with the surrounding world. Once aroused, the ego must adapt itself to reality by
whatever means are available. Jung theorized that there are four
such means or functions of the ego, each of which could be oriented by either an introverted (i.e., inward-looking) or extroverted
(outward-looking) attitude. After a certain amount of ego development has taken place, the person's innate tendency to orient to
the world, both within and without, will reveal itself in certain
definite ways. Jung argued that the ego has an inborn, genetic tendency to prefer one particular *type* of attitude and function combination and to rely secondarily on another complementary
combination for balance, with a third and fourth remaining less
used and consequently less available and developed. The combinations make up what he called "psychological types."

For example, a person is born with an innate tendency to
assume an introverted attitude toward the world. This first manifests itself as shyness in the infant, and later it develops into a preference to pursue solitary interests such as reading and studying. If
this is combined with an innate tendency toward adapting to the
environment by using the function of thinking, this person will be
naturally inclined to adapt to the world by seeking out activities,
such as science or scholarship, which match these tendencies. In
such arenas this person does well, feels confident, and finds satisfaction functioning in a way that comes naturally. In other areas,
such as socializing or selling newspaper subscriptions door to
door, this introverted thinking orientation is much less useful, and
the person feels at a loss often with considerable discomfort and
stress. If this person is born into a culture that rewards the extroverted attitude more than the introverted one, or into a family that
negatively reinforces introversion, the ego is forced to adapt to the
environment by developing extroversion. This comes at a high
price. The introverted person must assume a good deal of chronic
psychological stress in order to make this work. Since this ego
adaptation does not come naturally, it will also strike the observer
as artificial. It does not work very well, and yet it is necessary. Such
a person functions with a handicap, just as a natural extrovert
would take on a handicap in an introverted culture.

Typological differences between people lead to a great deal of conflict within families and groups. Children who are typologically different from their parents are often misunderstood and may be coerced into adopting a false typology that conforms to parental preferences. The child with the "correct" typological profile will be preferred and become the favorite. This sets the stage for sibling rivalry and envy. Each child in a large family will be somewhat different typologically, as the parents usually are also. The extroverts may gang up on the introverts, and the introverts are not as good at forming gangs and teams. On the other hand, introverts are better at hiding. If the differences of type can be recognized as a positive value and appreciated, there can be a great enrichment in family life and group politics. What one person can contribute, others will find to be beneficial precisely because they are not tuned into the same wavelength. Recognition and positive appreciation of typological differences can form the basis for creative pluralism in familial and cultural life.

This combination of a superior function and a preferred attitude make up the ego's single best tool for adapting to and interacting with the inner and outer worlds. The inferior fourth function, on the other hand, is the least available for ego utilization. The secondary function is, next to the superior function, the most useful to the ego, and the superior and secondary functions in combination are most frequently and effectively used for orientation and accomplishment. As a rule one of these two best functions is extroverted and the other is introverted, the extroverted function giving a reading of external reality and the introverted function providing information about what is going on within. The ego uses these tools to control and to transform both inner and outer worlds to the best of its ability.

Much of what we experience of other people, and indeed much of what we come to recognize as our own personalities, does not belong to ego-consciousness. The vitality a person communicates, the spontaneous reactions and emotional responses to others and to life, the burst of humor and the moods and spells of sadness, the puzzling complications of psychological life—all of these qualities and attributes will be assigned to other aspects of the larger psyche, not to ego-consciousness as such. So it is incorrect to think of the ego as being equivalent to the whole person. The ego is simply an agent, a focus of consciousness, a center of awareness. We can attribute either too much or too little to it.

Personal Freedom

Once the ego has achieved sufficient autonomy and a measure of control over consciousness, the feeling of personal freedom becomes a strong feature of subjective reality. Throughout childhood and adolescence, the range of personal freedom is tested, challenged, and expanded. Typically a young person lives with an illusion of much greater self-control and free will than is psychologically true. All the limitations on freedom seem to be imposed from the outside, from society and external regulations, and there is little awareness of how the ego is just as much controlled from within. Closer reflection reveals that one is as enslaved to one's own character structure and inner demons as to external authority. Often this is not realized until the second half of life, when there is typically a dawning awareness that one is one's own worst enemy, harshest critic, and severest taskmaster. Fate is spun from within as well as dictated from without.

Jung has some thought-provoking reflections to offer on the question of how free the will actually is. As we will see in the chapters to come, the ego is only a small part of a much larger psychological world, like the earth is a small part of the solar system. Learning that the earth revolves around the sun is similar to becoming aware that the ego revolves around a greater psychic entity, the self. Both insights are disturbing and destabilizing to the person who has put the ego at the center. The freedom of the ego is limited. "Inside the field of consciousness [the ego] has, as we say, free will," Jung writes. "By this I do not mean anything philosophical, only the well-known psychological fact of 'free choice', or rather the subjective feeling of freedom."[20] Within its own domain, ego-consciousness has an amount of apparent freedom. But what is the extent of this? And to what degree do we make our choices on the basis of conditioning and habit?

Choosing a Coke rather than a Pepsi reflects a measure of freedom, but in fact this choice is limited by previous conditioning such as advertising and by the availability or lack of other alternatives. A child may be encouraged to practice free will and to make discriminations by being given a choice among three kinds of shirts, for example. The child's ego feels gratified, for it is free to choose the one it wants. Yet the child's will is limited by many factors: the subtle wish to please the parent, or contrarily the wish to rebel against the parent; by the range of possibilities offered; by peer group pressures and requirements. Our actual range of free will is, like the child's, limited by habit, pressure, availability, conditioning and many other factors. In Jung's words, "just as our free will clashes with necessity in the outside world, so it also finds its limits outside the field of consciousness in the subjective inner world where it comes into conflict with the facts of the self."[21] The outside world inflicts political and economic limitations, but subjective factors limit us equally much from exercising free choice.

Broadly speaking, it is the contents of the unconscious that curtail the free will of the ego. The Apostle Paul expressed this classically when he confessed: "I do not understand my own actions. For I do not do what I want, but I do the very thing I hate . . . I can will what is right but I cannot do it."[22] Demons of contrariness conflict with the ego. Jung concurs: "just as circumstances and outside events 'happen' to us and limit our freedom, so the self acts upon the ego like an objective occurrence, which free will can do very little to alter."[23] When the psyche takes over the ego as an uncontrollable inner necessity, the ego feels defeated and has to face the requirement of accepting its inability to control inner reality just as it has to come to this conclusion regarding the larger surrounding social and physical worlds. Most people in the course of their lives come to realize that they cannot control the external world, but fairly few become conscious that inner psychic processes are not subject to ego control either.

With this discussion we have begun to enter the territory of the unconscious. In the next chapters I will describe Jung's vision of the unconscious areas of the human psyche, which make up by far the vast majority of its territory.

2

The Populated Interior
(The Complexes)

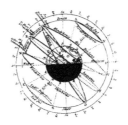

In the previous chapter, we saw that ego-consciousness—the surface of the psyche—is subject to disturbances and emotional reactions that are created by collisions between the individual and the external environment. Jung felt that these collisions between psyche and world have a positive function. If not too harsh, they tend to stimulate ego development because they demand greater focusing capacity on the part of consciousness and eventually this leads to stronger problem-solving ability and greater individual autonomy. Forced to make choices and take stands, a person develops the capacity to do more of the same and to do it better. This is like building a muscle by applying isometric tension. The ego grows through many such vigorous interactions with the world. Dangers, attractions, annoyances, threats, and frustrations from other people and various environmental factors all arouse a certain level of focused energy in consciousness, and the ego is mobilized to deal with these aspects of the impinging world.

There are other disturbances of consciousness, however, that are not clearly linked to environmental causes and are out of all proportion to the observable stimuli. What causes these disturbances are not primarily outer but inner collisions. People sometimes go crazy for little apparent reason. Or they have bizarre internal imaginary experiences that lead to inexplicable forms of behavior. They become psychotic, they hallucinate, they dream, or they just plain get mad or fall in love or run amuck. Humans do not always act rationally and behave according to clear calculations of personal interest. The "rational man," on whom so much economic theory is based, is at best only a partial description of human beings as they actually function. Humans are driven by psychic forces, motivated by thoughts that are not based on rational processes, and subject to images and influences beyond those that can be measured in the observable environment. In short, we are emotion- and image-driven creatures as much as we are rational and environmentally adapted ones. We dream as much as we cogitate, and we feel probably a lot more than we think. At the very least, a lot of thinking is colored and shaped by emotions, and most of our rational calculations are servants of our passions and fears. It was to understand this less rational side of human nature that led Jung to take up the tools of scientific method and spend his life investigating what shapes and motivates human emotion, fantasy, and behavior. This inner world was a *terra incognita* in his day. And he discovered that it is populated.

Reaching the Unconscious

Imagine for a moment that the psyche is a three-dimensional object like the solar system. Ego-consciousness is the earth, *terra firma;* it is where we live, at least during our waking hours. The space around the earth is filled with satellites and meteorites, some large, some small. This space is what Jung called the unconscious, and the objects that we first come across as we venture out into this space are what he called the *complexes.* The unconscious is populated by complexes. This is the territory that Jung explored initially in his career as a psychiatrist. He later called it the *personal* unconscious.

He began to map this area of the psyche even before he looked very closely at the ego complex or at the nature of consciousness.

He undertook this initial exploration by using a scientific instrument that was highly regarded at the turn of the century, the Word Association Experiment.[1] Later he also employed some insights gleaned from the early writings of Sigmund Freud. Armed with the notion of unconscious determination of mental processes and the Word Association Experiment, Jung led a team of researchers on the scientific project of conducting carefully controlled laboratory experiments to see if such unconscious psychological factors could be verified empirically.

The results of this project were assembled in the book *Diagnostische Assoziationstudien (Studies in Word Association)*, edited by Jung. These studies were carried out at the Psychiatric Clinic of the University of Zürich with the support and encouragement of his teacher, Eugen Bleuler.[2] The project was conceived in 1902 and continued over the next five years. The results were singly published between 1904 to 1910 in *Journal für Psychologie und Neurologie*. It was in the course of these experimental studies that Jung began to use the term "complex," which he borrowed from the German psychologist Ziehen but expanded and enriched with a great deal of his own research and theorizing. This term was later also adopted by Freud and was used widely in psychoanalytic circles[3] until Freud and Jung ended their relationship, after which it was more or less completely deleted, along with Jung and everything "Jungian," from the Freudian lexicon.

The theory of complexes was Jung's most important early contribution to the understanding of the unconscious and its structure. Partially it was Jung's way of conceptualizing what Freud had been writing about up to that point on the psychological results of repression, on the enduring importance of childhood for the structure of character, and on the puzzle of resistance in analysis. It continues to be a useful concept in analytic practice to this day. How did he first come to discover and map this feature of the unconscious?

The question was how to penetrate into the mind beyond the barriers of consciousness. Consciousness can be investigated by simply asking questions and noting responses, or by introspecting. But how could one go deeper into the subjective world and explore its structures and workings? To get at this problem, Jung and a team of fellow psychiatric residents set up a series of experiments with human subjects to see if, by bombarding the psyche with verbal stimuli and observing the responses in consciousness—the "tracks," so to speak, of subtle emotional reactions—they could find evidence of underlying structures. Working closely with his colleagues Bleuler, Wehrlin, Ruerst, Binswanger, Nunberg, and most importantly Riklin, Jung first refined the Word Association Experiment for their purposes and settled on 400 common, everyday, seemingly neutral stimulus words—words like table, head, ink, needle, bread, and lamp.[4] Scattered among these words were more provocative ones—war, faithful, to strike, to stroke. This number was later reduced to 100. These stimulus words, read one by one to a subject who had been instructed to respond with the first word that came to mind, elicited a wide variety of reactions. There would be long pauses, nonsensical responses, rhymes and "klang" responses, and even physiological reactions that could be measured using a device called a psychogalvanometer.[5]

The interesting question for Jung was, what is happening in the psyche of the test subject when the stimulus word is spoken? He looked for emotion, and in particular for signs of stimulation of anxiety and its effects upon consciousness. The response times were clocked and recorded along with the verbatim responses. Then all the stimulus words were repeated a second time, and the subject was asked to repeat each earlier response. Again the results were noted. The test was then analyzed, first by calculating the subject's average response time, to which all other response times were compared. Some words might take one second to elicit a response, others ten seconds; others might produce no response at all as the subject blocked completely. Then other types of responses were noted. Some words would be met with idiosyncratic responses such as rhymes, nonsense words, or uncommon associations. Jung considered these responses to be *complex indicators*—signs of anxiety and evidence of defensive reactions against unconscious psychological conflicts. What could they tell him about the nature of the unconscious?

The Complexes

Jung assumed that the disturbances of consciousness, which were registered and measured as responses to these verbal stimuli, were due to unconscious associations to the words read. Here his thinking was congruent with Freud's as expressed in *The Interpretation of Dreams,* where Freud had argued that dream images could be linked up with thoughts and feelings from the previous day (or even from previous years, including the time all the way back to early childhood). Such associations, however, are extremely obscure and hidden. The associations exist, Jung reasoned, not between the stimulus and response words, but rather between the stimulus words and hidden, unconscious contents. Some stimulus words activate unconscious contents, and these are associated with yet other contents. When stimulated, this network of associated material—made out of repressed memories, fantasies, images, thoughts—produces a disturbance in consciousness. The complex indicators are the signs of disturbance. Precisely what causes the disturbance still needs to be ferreted out, and this was done through further questioning of the subject and then through more analysis if that was needed. But the disturbances registered by this experiment provided the key sites for further exploration and offered evidence that unconscious structures were indeed located beneath the level of awareness. Often subjects did not at first know why certain words caused these reactions.

Jung observed that measurable disturbances in the stream of consciousness are sometimes related to seemingly innocuous stimulus words like "table" or "barn." Analyzing the patterns of response, he found that the words showing disturbance can be clustered thematically. These clusters point to a common content. When the subjects were asked to talk about their associations to these clusters of stimulus words, they gradually were able to tell him about highly charged emotional moments in their past. Usually traumas were involved. The stimulus words, it turned out, had aroused painful associations that had been buried in the unconscious, and these stressful associations were what had disturbed consciousness. The unconscious contents responsible for the disturbances of consciousness Jung called "complexes."

Having established that complexes exist in the unconscious, Jung was interested in examining them further. With tools such as the Word Association Experiment he could measure them rather precisely. Exact measurement could transform vague intuitions and speculative theories into data and into science, a fact very pleasing to Jung's scientific temperament. Jung found that he could measure the emotional charge held by a particular complex if he simply added up the number of complex indicators it generated and the severity of these disturbances. This indicated to him the relative quantity of psychic energy bound up in that complex. Investigation of the unconscious could thus be quantified. This information would also become important for therapy, as a guide to where the most severe emotional problems of a patient were located and what work needed to be done in the treatment. It is especially useful for short-term psychotherapy.

The results of his experiments convinced Jung that there are indeed psychic entities outside of consciousness, which exist as satellite-like objects in relation to ego-consciousness but are able to cause ego disturbances in a surprising and sometimes overwhelming way. They are the gremlins and inner demons that may catch a person by surprise. The disturbances caused by complexes must be differentiated, understandably, from disturbances brought about by stressors originating in the external environment, even though they may and often do relate intimately to one another.

When Jung sent his *Diagnostischen Assoziationstudien* to Freud in April 1906, Freud immediately recognized a kindred spirit and wrote him a warm letter of thanks. The two men met a year later, and from that moment until they finally ended their correspondence early in 1913, their relationship was emotionally and intellectually filled with high purpose and intensity. One might say that they succeeded in stimulating core complexes in each other. Certainly they connected profoundly around their shared interest in the unconscious. For Jung, the personal connection with Freud had enormous implications for his career in psychiatry and also for the later development of his own psychological theory. Both his career and his theory took their early shape in the shadow of Freud's growing cultural presence. And yet, for all that, Jung's final map of the inner world is remarkably independent of Freudian influence. Jung's mind was fundamentally non-Freudian, and so his map of the psyche is vastly different from Freud's. For readers who are familiar with Freud's work, this will become evident in the remainder of this book. These two men lived in different intellectual universes.

By 1910, Jung's theoretical work on the complexes was largely complete. In later years he would continue to elaborate it a bit, but he did not add much new material or change his mind about the basic concept of the complex except to add that every complex contains an archetypal (i.e., innate, primitive) component. His paper, "A Review of the Complex Theory,"[6] published in 1934, offers an excellent summary. Written long after his break with Freud, Jung makes some highly complimentary references to his former teacher and colleague and to psychoanalysis generally as he acknowledges Freud's significance for his own work on the theory of complexes. If Freud's influence is to be found importantly anywhere in Jung's theories, it is here.

It is worth noting that Jung delivered "A Review of the Complex Theory" in May 1934 in Bad Neuheim, Germany at the 7th Congress for Psychotherapy. At the time, Jung was president of the International Medical Society for Psychotherapy, which sponsored this conference. The political situation in Germany was at the time fraught with conflict and confusion. The Nazis, having recently taken power, were attacking Freud, a Jew, as a poisonous influence to be expunged from German culture. Freud's books were burned and his ideas violently opposed. Jung, who had been vice president of the organization and had accepted the presidency in 1933, was faced with a complicated and dangerous set of political options. On the one hand, it was a terrible time to be the leader of any type of organization in German-speaking lands. The Nazis watched like hawks for the least sign of departure from their racist doctrines. This medical society was no exception. Jung was heavily pressured to say what the German officials wanted to hear and to conform to their program. On the other hand, it was a moment when a non-German psychiatrist could possibly make a difference in this international association. It was Jung's intent to preserve the organization as an international medical society. One of his first acts as president was to modify the constitution so that German Jewish doctors could maintain their membership as individual members even though they were excluded from all German medical societies. In 1933 there was no way to know how effective and all-consuming the evil impulse of the Nazi leaders would turn out to be.

On the shadow side of the ledger, however, this was also a moment of professional opportunity for Jung. Freud had been pre-eminent among psychiatrists and psychologists in Germany for the past decade, and now Jung's ideas had a chance to come to the fore. Jung was walking a moral tightrope. The world was watching, and every move he made during this period influenced public opinion. Jung's decision to accept the presidency of this medical organization in 1933 and his subsequent role in it until 1940 have been the cause for a great deal of heated discussion then and now. Charges that Jung was sympathetic to Hitler's policies and to the Nazi program of "purifying" the German *Volk* have an important source in the things he actually, perhaps inadvertently and under severe political pressure, said and did in his first years as president.[7]

One item in Jung's favor is that he did present this particular paper, "A Review of the Complex Theory," at Bad Neuheim in 1934, for in this presidential address he does not discount the importance of Freud. In fact, he credits him with as much influence as he could reasonably be expected to give to an early mentor with whom he had broken and to whom he had not spoken for twenty years. In 1934, it was courageous to speak in even mildly positive tones about Freud in Germany. Jung was if anything protecting Freud's international reputation by giving him so much credit in this paper.

The paper begins with a discussion of the word association work Jung sponsored and carried out in the early years of his career. Having learned a great deal in the meantime about how human beings react to one another in clinical and other intimate settings, he starts by focusing on the psychological dimensions of the experimental situation. He points out that in and of itself this testing situation already leads to the constellation of complexes. Personalities affect each other, and when they begin to interact a psychic field is set up between them which stimulates the complexes.

The term "constellation" appears frequently in Jung's writings and is an important one in the Jungian lexicon. It is a word that often mystifies readers at first. Usually it refers to the creation of a psychologically charged moment, a moment when consciousness either already is, or is about to become, disturbed by a complex. "This term simply expresses the fact that the outward situation releases a psychic process in which certain contents gather together and prepare for action. When we say that a person is 'constellated' we mean that he has taken up a position from which he can be expected to react in a quite definite way."[8] Complex reactions are quite predictable once one knows what the specific complexes of an individual are. We refer to the complex-laden areas of the psyche colloquially as "buttons," as in "She knows how to press my buttons!" When you press such a button, you get an emotional reaction. In other words, you constellate a complex. After you have known a person for a while, you know where some of their buttons are and either avoid these tender areas or go out of your way to touch them.

Experientially everyone knows what it means to be constellated. It occurs on a spectrum from being slightly anxious to losing it and going over the top into madness. When a complex is constellated, one is threatened with loss of control over one's emotions and to some extent also one's behavior. One reacts irrationally and often regrets it or thinks better of it later. For the psychologically-minded, there is the depressing knowledge that one has been here many times before, has reacted in just this way on many occasions, and yet is utterly helpless to refrain from doing the same thing again this time. When constellated, one is as though in the grip of a demon, a force stronger than one's will. This creates a feeling of helplessness. Even as one watches oneself

becoming the witless victim of an inner compulsion to say or do
something one knows should better be left unsaid or undone, the
scenario unscrolls as predicted and the words are said, the deeds
done. An intrapsychic force has been called into action by a constellating situation.

The architects of these constellations "are definite complexes
possessing their own specific energy."[9] The complex's "energy"
(this term will be discussed more thoroughly in the next chapter)
refers to the precise amount of potential for feeling and action
that is bound up in the magnet-like core of the complex. The complexes have energy and manifest a sort of electronic "spin" of their
own, like the electrons surrounding the nucleus of an atom. When
they are stimulated by a situation or an event, they give off a burst
of energy and jump levels until they arrive in consciousness. Their
energy penetrates the shell of ego-consciousness and floods into
it, thereby influencing it to spin in the same direction and to discharge some of the emotional energy that has been released by
this collision. When this happens, the ego is no longer altogether
in control of consciousness or, for that matter, of the body. The
person becomes subject to energic discharges that are not under
the ego's control. What the ego can do, if it is strong enough, is to
contain some of the complex's energy within itself and to mini-
mize emotional and physical outbursts. But, to a degree, none of
us is wholly responsible for what we say and do while in the grip
of a complex. Needless to say, this does not constitute an effective
defense in a court of law. Sometimes society demands a higher
standard than the psyche will allow.

The complexity (pardon the pun) of the psyche is becoming
apparent. In fact, Jung's theory was sometimes called complex
psychology (rather than the more usual name for it, analytical
psychology): both complexity and the concept of complexes are
fundamental to his view of the psyche. The psyche is made up of
many centers, each of them possessing energy and even some consciousness and purpose of their own.

In this conceptualization of the personality, the ego is one
complex among many. Each has its own specific quantum of
energy. When we speak of the ego's energy, we call it "free will." If

we wish to refer to the amount of energy tied up in a complex, we can speak of the power of our inner demons. These are the irrational compulsions that can seize us and do with us more or less what they want. A complex generally creates its effects within the domain of consciousness, but this is not always so. Sometimes the disturbances occur outside of the psyche altogether. Jung observed that a complex can affect objects and other people in the surrounding world. It can act as a poltergeist or a subtle influence on other people.

Jung made another interesting observation about complexes. A person can sometimes block the effects of a stimulus and fend off the constellation of a complex: "subjects with strong wills can, through verbal-motor facility, screen off the meaning of a stimulus word by short reaction times in such a way that it does not reach them at all, but this only works when really important personal secrets have to be protected."[10] This means that people can control their unconscious reactions by deliberately screening out stimuli. To overcome this obstacle in the testing situation, Jung cooked up what is the precursor of the lie detector test. It was an ingenious extension of the Word Association Experiment.

By measuring the skin's electrical conductivity with a psychogalvanometer, Jung showed that changes in conductivity correlate with complex indicators. In other words, when a person lies or tries to hide the evidence of a complex-charged reaction, the ego may be able to cover up some of the indicators, but it has a much more difficult time suppressing the more subtle physiological responses. In response to a complex-stimulating word or question a person might get sweaty palms or begin shivering or experience dryness of the mouth. By measuring skin conductivity, Jung introduced a more refined method of collecting complex indicators. By using this device, Jung was able to solve a case of robbery in his psychiatric hospital.[11] Needless to say, this method is not infallible.

Most people's egos will normally be able to neutralize the effects of complexes to some degree. This ability serves the interests of adaptation and even survival. This is akin (or perhaps identical) to the ability to dissociate. If one could not do this, the ego would become dysfunctional just at the moment of greatest danger when keeping a cool head is most desperately needed. In professional life, it is essential to put one's personal complexes to the side for the sake of carrying on with one's job. Psychotherapists have to be able to bracket their own emotions and personal conflicts when they are seeing patients. In order to be present for a patient whose life is in shambles, the therapist must stay calm even though this may be a moment of chaos in the therapist's own life. All professions demand that the job get done no matter what is going on in personal life. As they say in theater, the show must go on. This requires the ability to override the effects of complexes upon ego-consciousness to at least some degree. In discussing this ability to contain one's own personal anxieties and complex reactions, Jung refers to a consummate master of this art, the diplomat Talleyrand. Diplomats operate on instruction from heads of state and use a vocabulary that betrays little of their own feeling or preference. They prize the art of speaking in terms that conceal emotion and hide complex indicators. And they have the advantage of not being hooked up to psychogalvanometers.

Levels of the Unconscious

Usually one considers complexes to be "personal." And it is true that most complexes are generated in a person's own specific life history and belong strictly to the individual. But there are also family and social complexes. Such complexes belong no more to the individual than a disease belongs to an individual. It belongs to a collective, and the individual "catches" it. This means that in society many people are similarly wired, psychologically speaking. People who grow up in the same families or extended kinship groups or traditional cultures share a great deal of this common unconscious structure. Even in a large and diverse society like America, many typical experiences are shared throughout the entire population. Nearly every child begins school at the age of five or six, experiences the same stress of tests and trauma of failures and humiliations, then goes through the anxiety of applying to colleges for further education or to businesses for jobs. All of these common experiences at the hands of similarly disposed persons in authority create socially based psychological patterns through a kind of subtle programming of the personal unconscious. Shared traumas make for shared complexes. Sometimes these are generational. Earlier, one often spoke of a "depression mentality" characteristic of people who came of age in the 1930s and shared the trauma of the Great Depression. Today we speak of the "Vietnam veteran" and assume that all who participated in this war share more or less the same type of complex-formation from the traumas of fighting in that war.

We can think here of a cultural layer of the unconscious, a sort of cultural unconscious.[12] It is personal in the sense that it is acquired in the individual's lifetime, but it is collective because it is shared with a group. The unconscious, at this level, is structured by larger cultural patterns and attitudes, and these end up influencing the individual's conscious attitudes and the more unique complexes within a nexus of unconscious cultural assumptions. (The cultural unconscious is different from the collective unconscious, which I will discuss in chapter 4.)

This raises the interesting question of how complexes are formed. The usual answer is by trauma. But this must be put into a wider social context. Some of Jung's studies in word association looked at the question of family influences on the formation of unconscious contents in children. Through the Word Association Experiment he found strong evidence of strikingly similar patterns of complex formation among family members—between mothers and daughters, fathers and sons, and mothers and sons, for example. Of these combinations, the closest were mothers and daughters. Their responses to the stimulus words revealed nearly identical anxieties and conflicts. From this Jung concluded that the unconscious is importantly patterned by close relationships in the family environment. Exactly how this takes place is not clear from his work. Is it by some sort of transmission? Is it by repetition of similar traumas passed along through the generations? This is not answered.

Later in a child's development these early psychic structures are modified significantly by exposure to the wider culture. The psyche's constant exposure to social and cultural stimuli, from TV and school, becomes a factor in later stages of childhood, and this reduces the psychological influence of ethnic and family cultures, at least in a pluralistic society like America's. When the peer group becomes central, it generates important new structural elements, many of them based, however, on commonly available cultural patterns. And yet the early family-induced complexes do not disappear from the psyche. The mother and father complexes continue to dominate the scene in the personal unconscious.[13] They are the giants.

Psychic Images

To get at the basic structure of the complex, it must be broken down into its parts. "What then, scientifically speaking, is a 'feeling-toned complex'?" Jung asks. "It is the image of a certain psychic situation which is strongly accentuated emotionally and is, moreover, incompatible with the habitual attitude of consciousness."[14] The word "image" is key here. It is an extremely important term for Jung. Image defines the essence of psyche. Sometimes Jung uses the word Latin *imago* rather than image to refer to a complex. The "mother imago" is the mother complex, as distinguished from the actual mother. The point is that the complex is an image and as such belongs essentially to the subjective world; it is made of pure psyche, so to speak, although it also represents an actual person, experience, or situation. It should not be mistaken for objective reality—for another actual person or a material body. The complex is an inner object, and at its core it is an image.

Surprisingly, there may be a close correspondence between a psychic image and external reality, even when no chance exists that the psyche has been imprinted by it or recorded it from experience. Konrad Lorenz, a famous ethologist, studied innate reflex responses in some animals in reaction to specific stimuli. For example, chicks who had never been exposed to chicken hawks knew to run for cover when a chicken hawk flew overhead and its shadow appeared on the ground. Using devices that ran on wires overhead and cast shadows resembling the chicken hawk, ethologists have shown that untutored chicks, seeing the shadow, will run for cover. The defensive response to a predator is built into the chick's system, and the image of the predator is innate and recognized without having to be learned.

Complexes operate in a similar way, only in humans they seem to be only quasi-instinctive rather than truly instinctive. They act like instincts in that they produce spontaneous reactions to particular situations or persons, but they are not purely innate in the same way that instincts are. Mostly they are products of experience—trauma, family interactions and patterns, cultural conditioning. These are combined with some innate elements, which Jung called archetypal images, to make up the total package of the complex. Complexes are what remain in the psyche after it has digested experience and reconstructed it into inner objects. In human beings, complexes function as the equivalent of instincts in other mammals. Imagoes, or complexes, are, in a manner of speaking, constructed human instincts.

Dreams are made out of these unconscious images, the complexes. Jung speaks in various places of complexes as being the architects of dreams. Over a period of time, dreams present images, patterns, repetitions, and themes that give us a picture of what a person's complexes look like.

"This image has a powerful inner coherence, it has its own wholeness and, in addition, a relatively high degree of autonomy, so that it is subject of the control of the conscious mind to only a limited extent, and therefore behaves like an animated foreign body in the sphere of consciousness."[15] Each of these features of the image—its inner coherence, its wholeness, and its autonomy—are important aspects of Jung's definition of the complex. A complex possesses psychic solidity; it is stable and endures through time. Left in its own space without intervention or challenge by ego-consciousness, a complex tends not to change very much. One can witness this in repetitions of the same patterns of emotional reaction and discharge, the same mistakes, the same unfortunate choices made over and over again in a person's life.

Analysis tries to uncover the complexes and expose them to the conscious reflection of the ego. This intervention can alter them somewhat. In analysis a person learns how the complexes function, what triggers their constellation, and what can prevent their endless repetition. Without such intervention on the part of the ego, a complex will behave like an animated foreign body or an infection. In the grip of a complex, a person can feel quite helpless and emotionally out of control.

Generally, the psychological effects of complex constellations perseverate over an extended period of time after the stimulus has left off impacting the psyche. "Certain experimental investigations seem to indicate that [the complex's] intensity or activity curve has a wavelike character with a 'wavelength' of hours, days, or weeks."[16] The stimulus that provokes the complex may be slight or great, of long or short duration, but its effects on the psyche can continue for extended periods of time and can come into consciousness in waves of emotion or anxiety. One of the signs of effective psychotherapy is that the complex-induced disturbances perseverate for shorter lengths of time than they did before. A more rapid recovery from complex-induced disturbances indicates increased ego strength and integration of psychic material, as well as decreased power in the complexes. A shortened perseveration time means that the complex's power has diminished. Nevertheless, it must be recognized that a complex can never be completely eliminated. The wavelike effects of complex "aftershock" are exhausting and draining. The discharge of a powerful complex can consume an enormous amount of psychic and physical energy.

Personality Fragments

The complexes can be thought of, too, as personality fragments or subpersonalities. Every adult's personality is somewhat vulnerable to disintegration because it is constructed of large and small fragments. These can come unglued. "My findings in regard to complexes corroborate the somewhat disquieting picture of the possibilities of psychic disintegration, for fundamentally there is no difference in principle between a fragmentary personality and a complex. They have all the essential features in common, until we come to the delicate question of fragmented consciousness. Personality fragments undoubtedly have their own consciousness, but whether such small psychic fragments as complexes are also capable of a consciousness of their own is a still unanswered question."[17] Jung is here raising an important but extremely subtle question about the differences between normal dissociation, more severe dissociative disorders, and multiple personality disorder.

Every human being can and does from time to time dissociate, in the sense of experiencing mild altered states of consciousness or splitting off from traumatic experience in order to keep functioning. Being "in complex" is itself a state of dissociation. Ego-consciousness becomes disturbed and, depending upon the extent of the disturbance, can be thrown into a state of considerable disorientation and confusion. Since complexes possess a type of consciousness in their own right, a person who is "in complex" is in a sort of state of possession by an alien personality. In the multiple personality disorder, these various states of consciousness are not held together by a unifying consciousness, and the ego is not able to bridge the psychic space among the pieces. In this case, the ego is restricted to fragments of consciousness, while each other complex possesses a sort of ego of its own, each operating more or less independently. Each has its own identity and even its own type of control over somatic functions. Some studies of multiple personalities have indicated surprising psyche-soma connections in each of the subpersonalities, to the extent that one personality may show physical capacities or difficulties not displayed by others. One personality may be allergic to tobacco smoke, another can be a chain smoker.

The multiple personality represents an extreme form of personality dissociation. The integration processes normally active in the psyche have been thwarted by severe (usually sexual) childhood trauma. But to a lesser degree, everyone has multiple personalities, because everyone has complexes. The difference lies in the fact that complexes are as a rule subordinated to an integrated ego, and ego-consciousness is maintained when a complex is constellated. In general, the complexes have less energy than the ego has, and they show only minimal consciousness of their own. The ego, in contrast, has considerable energy and will at its disposal, and it is the primary center of consciousness.

While the ego is responsible for much of what we call motivation and purpose, the other complexes also seem to have a separate purpose and will. Often this is in conflict with what the ego complex wants at a particular moment. Jung describes complexes as "the actors in our dreams, whom we confront so powerlessly; they are the elfin beings so aptly characterized in Danish folklore by the story of the clergyman who tried to teach the Lord's prayer to two elves. They took the greatest pains to repeat the words after him correctly, but at the very first sentence they could not avoid saying: 'Our Father, who are not in heaven'. As one might expect on theoretical grounds, these impish complexes are unteachable."[18] The moral of this story is that complexes cannot be made to do what the ego wants them to do. They are intractable. They are like frozen memory images of traumatic experiences. And they are not experienced only in dreams but in everyday life as well, where they leave the ego feeling equally powerless.

The Structure of Complexes

Further on the structure of the complex, Jung describes it as being made up of associated images and frozen memories of traumatic moments that are buried in the unconscious and not readily available for retrieval by the ego. These are repressed memories. What knits the various associated elements of the complex together and holds them in place is emotion. This is the glue. Furthermore, "the feeling-toned content, the complex, consists of a nuclear element and a large number of secondarily constellated associations."[19] The nuclear element is the core image and experience on which the complex is based—the frozen memory. But this core turns out to be made up of two parts: an image or psychic trace of the originating trauma and an innate (archetypal) piece closely associated to it. The dual core of the complex grows by gathering associations around itself, and this can go on over the course of an entire lifetime. If, for example, a man reminds a woman of her harsh, abusive father by his tone of voice, by his way of reacting to life, by his intensity of emotional response, and so on, he will understandably constellate her father complex. If she interacts with him over a period of time, material will be added to that complex. If he abuses her, the negative father complex will be further enriched and energized, and she will become all the more reactive in situations where the father complex is constellated. Increasingly she may avoid such men entirely, or on the other hand she may find herself irrationally drawn to them. In either case, her life becomes more and more restricted by this complex. The stronger the complexes, the more they restrict the range of the ego's freedom of choice.

That complexes can be modified by later experience is of course to the benefit of the individual, and the healing potential of psychotherapy depends upon this. Therapy involves a kind of thawing out of the frozen memory images. It can restructure the personality to some extent because transference allows the therapist to stand in for (among other figures of the psyche) the parents, both mother and father, at different stages of therapy. When a parental complex is constellated by the therapist, the patient's experience of a different kind of parent figure adds material to the old complex and builds a new layer into, or over, it. This new structure does not entirely replace the old, but it can importantly modify it, to the point where the complex no longer restricts a person's life in such a debilitating way. The harshness of an abusive parent imago may be softened—thawed out—or offset by new structures.

The other piece of the complex's nuclear core is "a factor innate in the individual's character and determined by his disposition."[20] This piece is archetypal. In the case of parental complexes, for instance, it is an archetypal image of Mother or Father, an image derived not from personal experience but from the collective unconscious. The archetypal elements in the personality are innate dispositions to react, behave, and interact in certain typical and predictable ways. They are similar to the innate release mechanisms of animals. They are inherited and not acquired, and they belong to each human being by virtue of being born human. They are what make us uniquely and characteristically human. Not only the body but also the soul—the psyche—is specifically human and creates the preconditions for all later experience, development, and education. I will expand upon Jung's theory of archetypes in later chapters. For now it is sufficient to recognize that the archetypal elements of the psyche are experienced in everyday life through the experience of the complexes.

Generally speaking, complexes are created by trauma. Prior to the trauma, the archetypal piece exists as an image and a motivating force but does not have the same disturbing and anxiety-producing qualities of the complex. The trauma creates an emotionally charged memory image that becomes associated with an archetypal image, and together these freeze into a more or less permanent structure. This structure contains a specific amount of energy, and with this it can tie in other associated images to create a network. Thus a complex becomes enriched and extended by later experiences of a similar sort. But not all traumas are of an external nature or are inflicted by abrasive collisions with the environment. There are traumas that occur mostly internal to the individual psyche. Jung indicates that complexes may also be created or supplemented by a "moral conflict, which ultimately derives from the apparent impossibility of affirming the whole of one's nature."[21] Everchanging moral attitudes in our society make it impossible to affirm our wholeness completely in many situations. We have to deny our true feelings and refrain from expressing them in order to get along or, occasionally, even to survive. Making such social adjustments for the sake of adaptation creates a social mask, a "persona," that excludes essential parts of oneself. In general, people prefer to be included in their social groups, and those who bluntly speak their minds or do not conform to group standards tend to be ostracized or marginalized. This social dilemma puts a person into what Jung calls a moral conflict. At the deepest level, the imperative is to be whole. Human nature rebels against the strictures of society and culture if they too severely inhibit this innate drive toward wholeness, and this is a further source of complexes.

This was the issue that Freud took up in Vienna, a society that was officially sexually inhibited but also quite blatantly hypocritical about its sexual mores. Freud demonstrated how the conflicts around sexuality become rooted in psychological patterns and produce neurosis. Sexuality, which is built into the innate make-up of the human being, becomes socially incompatible and is therefore split off from consciousness and repressed. This creates a sexual complex around which related traumas cluster. Fundamentally, what makes the repression of sexuality the source of pathology is the insistent imperative of the human organism to pursue its innate wholeness, which includes uninhibited sexuality. It is not the conflict between the individual and society per se that produces the neurotic problem, as Freud argued, but the moral conflict that comes about in a psyche that wants to deny itself on the one hand but is forced to affirm itself on the other.

The Eruption of Complexes

Complexes have the ability to erupt suddenly and spontaneously into consciousness and to take possession of the ego's functions. What appears as utter spontaneity, however, may not be so pure. Often there is a subtle triggering stimulus that can be detected if one looks carefully enough into the recent past. A neurotic depression, for instance, may look endogenous until one finds the tiny insult that set it off. When the ego is possessed in this fashion, it becomes assimilated to the complex and the complex's purposes, and the result is what we call "acting out." People who are acting out are often not aware that this is what is going on. They are simply "in a mood," and the behavior seems congruent with the ego. But this is the nature of possession: the ego is deceived into thinking that it is freely expressing itself. Only in retrospect does one realize, "Something got into me and made me do it. I didn't know what I was doing!" If another person tries to point out that one is acting out of character, the usual response is angry defensiveness. The person in a state of possession does not take such feedback kindly. Jung says that in the Middle Ages this identification with a complex "went by another name; it was called possession.

Probably no one imagines this state as being particularly harm-
less, and there is in it no difference in principle between a slip of
the tongue caused by a complex and the wildest blasphemies."[22]
The difference is a matter of degree. There are degrees of possession, from the momentary and slight ones to the psychotic and
chronic ones. What we see in possession is that features of personality that are usually not a part of the ego's character and style
become blatantly manifest. These unknown features have been
built up in the unconscious over a period of time, and suddenly
the ego is overcome by this inner opposite. Now the person is possessed by the devil and curses the things that consciousness had
formerly held most sacred.

People with Tourette's Syndrome do this openly on a continual
basis. For a person blessed with so-called normal psychology, the
splinter personalities show themselves in a multitude of much
more subtle ways, some so slight as to be nearly undetectable—
slips of the tongue, forgetfulness. In the course of an hour one
may pass through several states of consciousness, moods, subpersonalities, and barely notice the shifts. This subtlety passes into
more gross forms as we approach the level of true possession.
Possession has a more extreme and distinctive quality. It is hard
to miss, and it often even acquires the features of a specific character type. A Savior complex, for example, typically develops from
painful experiences of abandonment in childhood, and then
shows itself in behavior that passes for kindness and helpfulness.
These features do not, however, belong to the ego in an integrated
way; rather they tend to wax and wane because they are rooted in
an autonomous complex over which the ego has little control.
These are the people who cannot refrain from being helpful and
enabling no matter how destructive it may be to themselves or to
others. The behavior is actually controlled by a complex and is
therefore not under ego control. It also tends to fluctuate more or
less arbitrarily. There are sudden inconsistencies that cannot be
anticipated or explained. Sometimes this person will be excessively thoughtful and caring, at other times ruthless, indifferent,
or even abusive. Other splinter psyches (complexes) are compet-
ing for the ego's sponsorship. When a possession-prone ego leaves

off identifying with one complex, it shifts to another. This other is more often than not a sort of shadow brother or sister of the first. A Christ-like complex with its spiritual, upward-oriented, giving, altruistic features is matched by a Devilish complex with an attitude of materialism and selfishness. The two may alternate in taking possession of the ego, Jekyll-and-Hyde-like. The one will function as the official persona in many public social situations, and the other will dominate the conscious personality in private, intimate settings. This ego is vulnerable to what Jung called "enantiodromia," a reversal into the opposite.

The complexes are objects of the inner world. "It is on them that the weal and woe of personal life depends. They are the *lares* and *penates* [the household gods] who await us at the fireside, and whose peaceableness it is dangerous to extol."[23] Such deities are not to be taken lightly.

3

Psychic Energy
(Libido Theory)

Thus far I have described two basic structures of the psyche—ego-consciousness and the complexes—as Jung conceived and wrote about them. Now I will consider the force that animates these structures and gives them life, namely *libido*. This is desire and emotion, the life blood of the psyche. Jung called libido *psychic energy*. In the previous two chapters, I have frequently used the term energy. This is the dynamic feature of the psyche. Jung's theory of libido conceptualizes, in an abstract way, the relationships among the various parts of the psyche. To use the metaphor of the psyche as solar system, this chapter is about physics and the forces that affect the various objects in this universe.

In a general philosophical sense, the subject of psychic energy has been investigated by thinkers throughout the ages. It is not something new and modern to reflect upon questions of life force, the will, passion and emotion, the ebb and flow of interest and desire. Philosophers in the West have considered such matters since Heraclitus and Plato, and in the East since Lao-tsu and Confucius. In recent centuries, philosophers like Schopenhauer, Bergson, and Nietzsche have given these questions central attention. Physicians, too, like Anton Mesmer with his theory of a

psychic fluid in the body, began to pursue the subject of psychological movement and motivation in more empirical and quasi-
scientific ways. The famous nineteenth-century German
physician-philosopher C.G. Carus speculated extensively and in
depth about the unconscious as a source of energy and noted its
extensive influences upon the conscious mind. Jung cites such figures as these, as well as von Hartmann, Wundt, Schiller, and
Goethe, as precursors to his own thinking. Although Freud was
the modern psychological originator of the term libido and the
figure to whom Jung bows in his psychoanalytic discussions of
libido theory, he was not the only influence upon Jung or the single figure to whom he was responding in his extensive writings on
libido and psychic energy.

A position on the nature and flow of psychic energy is, in fact,
fundamental to every philosophy of human nature and the soul,
for this will contain the author's views on motivation and on the
dynamic elements in life that separate living beings from the
dead. The distinction between movement and stasis constitutes a
basic category of human thought, and it leads spontaneously to
wondering what accounts for the difference between these two
states of being. Why do physical bodies move in space, and why
do they move in one direction rather than in another? In physical
science these questions lead to theories of causation and the for-
mulation of laws of motion, like the law of gravity. The same is
true for philosophy and psychology, where questions of causation,
motivation, and the laws governing psychic bodies in movement
are equally important. In psychology it becomes a question of the
soul and its movement and of its power to move other objects.
Aristotle pondered this. Psychic energy is present in a living body
and not in a corpse; it is present in all waking life and in dream
life; it is what makes the difference between being "on" and being
"off," to use an electrical metaphor. But what is it?

Sexuality and Libido

What Schopenhauer called Will and presented as the primal motivator of human activity and thought, Freud chose to call libido.

With this choice of terminology, he emphasized the sensual, pleasure-seeking element in human nature. The soul for Freud is essentially qualified by sexual energy. The Latin word *libido* suited his purposes particularly well because of his conviction that the sexual drive lies at the base of psychic life and is the primary source of the psyche's movement. Freud's libido theory became, on the one hand, a polite way to talk about sexuality, giving sex a Latin name and making the conversation sound somewhat medical; on the other hand, it was a way to carry on a quasi-scientific and abstract discussion about how sexuality moves and motivates a person to engage in a variety of different activities and how it ends up in some instances causing neurotic attitudes and behavior.

It was Freud's contention that sexuality is the prime motivator of most, if not all, mental processes and behavior. Libido is the juice that turns the human machine on and makes it hum, even if the specific activities a person may be engaged in, like playing the violin or counting money, do not look particularly sexual. Sexuality is the primary motivator of even those human activities, as well as the primary cause of the psychological conflicts that end up ensnaring a person in the tangles of neurosis and severe mental illnesses such as paranoia and schizophrenia. In the final analysis, Freud wanted to show, all manifestations of psychic energy in individual and collective life can be assigned, at least in significant part, to the sexual drive and its sublimations or repressions. Freud was particularly intent on demonstrating that sexual conflict lay at the base of all neurotic and psychotic illnesses.

Early in his discussions with Freud about psychological theory and clinical practice, Jung showed grave reservations about the primacy of sexuality and suggested the obvious point that there might be other drives active in human life as well. For instance, there is a basic drive called *hunger:*

> As you have noticed, it is possible that my reservations about your far-reaching views are due to lack of experience. But don't you think that a number of borderline phenomena might be considered more appropriately in terms of the other basic drive, *hunger:* for instance, eating, sucking (predominantly hunger), kissing (predominantly sexuality)?

Two complexes existing at the same time are always bound to coa-
lesce psychologically, so that one of them invariably contains constellated aspects of the other.[1]

This note of disagreement appears already in Jung's second letter to Freud, dated October 23, 1906. From the very outset of this
collaboration, Jung evidently had doubts and reservations about
Freud's insistence on the centrality of sexual conflict in psy-
chopathology. In the years that followed, there were many more
letters and numerous published exchanges on the subject of
drives and the sources of psychic energy, and Jung went back and
forth in his adherence to Freudian doctrine. "Under the impress
of Freud's personality," Jung would write many years later in his
autobiography, "I had, as far as possible, cast aside my own judgments and repressed my criticisms. That was the prerequisite for
collaborating with him."[2] At times in his early writings, Jung
sounds like a true reductionist in the Freudian mold. And yet it is
also clear from the written record that he never became an uncrit-
ical disciple of Freud's, even though he may have held back in his
disagreement for the sake of smoothing over differences and
potential troublespots in the relationship.

As it turned out, the debate over how to conceptualize psychic
energy and what to name it became much more than a minor
technical point. While Jung's early divergent views may have
seemed somewhat trivial and vague, or based on misunderstand-
ings of what Freud meant to say, the implications ran deep and in
time these led to major philosophical, theoretical, and clinical dis-
agreements. In fact, their differences on the subject of libido
turned out to define the central theoretical point of division
between them. At issue was the conception of human nature and
the meaning of human consciousness. In the early years, this
could not be foreseen with the clarity that hindsight provides.
Jung was learning as he went—from Freud and also from his
patients and from many other sources.

In the masterful essay "On Psychic Energy,"[3] published in
1928, Jung spells out his fully considered position on the subject
of libido. This paper is the primary source for the present chapter.
By the time he wrote it in the mid-1920s, he had been separated

from Freud and the psychoanalytic movement for more than a decade. This essay has the quality of cool objectivity, whereas his earlier major work on the subject, *Wandlungen und Symbole der Libido* (1912–13) (translated into English in 1916 by Beatrice Hinkle as *Psychology of the Unconscious*, by which title I refer to it throughout this book), was hastily assembled and bears the marks of feverish creative thinking that has not quite settled into place. In that earlier work, composed while he was still in close communication with Freud and indeed was still Freud's crown prince and heir apparent as president of the International Psychoanalytic Association, he tackled libido theory as a kind of side-issue, but it became the centerpiece before he was finished. I will consider that work briefly here, as historical background, before going on to describe Jung's later essay on psychic energy.

In a letter to Freud, dated November 14, 1911, Jung wrote:

> In my second part [of *Psychology of the Unconscious*] I have got down to a fundamental discussion of the libido theory. That passage in your Schreber analysis where you ran into the libido problem (loss of libido = loss of reality) is one of the points where our mental paths cross. In my view the concept of libido as set forth in the *Three Essays* needs to be supplemented by the genetic factor to make it applicable to Dem[entia] praec[ox].[4]

Jung is referring here to his second chapter in Part II of *Psychology of the Unconscious*, "The Conception and the Genetic Theory of Libido." In this chapter he discusses the question, referred to in the letter quoted above, of the relationship between libido (as sexually defined by Freud in "Three Essays on the Theory of Sexuality" in 1905) and the *fonction du reel* (a term used by French psychiatrist Pierre Janet for ego-consciousness). Does the latter derive from the former? If ego-consciousness is a derivative of sexually determined attachments to objects, then it would follow that disturbances of sexuality would cause disturbances in the ego, and indeed that ego disturbances could be assumed to be rooted in sexual disturbances. What Freud (and Berlin psychoanalyst Karl Abraham) wanted to argue was that the severe disturbances in the ego, in psychosis and schizophrenia, are to be attributed to the loss of sexual interest in the object world, because the reality function and attachments to objects were created by sexual interest in the first place. This is a circular argument, however, and Jung cogently points this out.[5] In place of this, he offers another explanation for schizophrenia and psychosis, but one that would lead to a basic revision of libido theory.

Jung starts from what he calls a genetic instead of a descriptive position. He begins with a broad conception of libido as psychic energy, following Schopenhauer's conception of Will. "As you know," he writes somewhat apologetically to Freud, "I always have to proceed from the outside to the inside and from the whole to the part."[6] From this broad viewpoint, sexual libido is but one branch of the more general Will or life force. This general stream of psychic energy has several branches, and in the history of human evolution some of these branches are more prominent than others at certain points. At some stages of human development, both collective and individual, sexual libido is more prominent and fundamental; at others, it is less so.

Moreover, Jung writes, it can be argued that activities which were once closely related to sexuality and indeed could be clearly seen as derivative from the sexual instinct have become, through evolution of human consciousness and culture, separated from the sexual domain to such a great extent that they no longer have any relation to sexuality:

> Thus we discover the first instincts of art in animals used in the service of the impulse of creation, and limited to the breeding season. The original sexual character of these biological institutions became lost in their organic fixation and functional independence. Even if there can be no doubt about the sexual origin of music, still it would be a poor, unaesthetic generalization if one were to include music in the category of sexuality. A similar nomenclature would then lead us to classify the cathedral of Cologne as mineralogy because it is built of stones.[7]

It was obvious to Jung that not all expressions of psychic activity have a sexual origin or purpose, even though they may once have had such connections in the primordial history of the human race. Taking an evolutionary viewpoint, Jung then speculates about how activities that had once been sexual in meaning and intention have later become transformed into nonsexual activities, such as music and art.

The Transformation of Psychic Energy

How is psychic energy transformed from an expression of simple instinct, from the discharge of a powerful impulse (i.e., eating because one is hungry or copulating because one feels sexy) to cultural expressions and endeavors (i.e., haute cuisine or music making)? When do these activities leave off being "instinctual" in any meaningful sense of the word and become something else with quite different meaning and intention?

Jung argues in *Psychology of the Unconscious* that this transformation of energy may happen by virtue of the human mind's native capacity for creating analogies. Humans have the ability, and the need, to think in metaphors, and this may lie behind this process of transformation. Thus hunting, for instance, is like *(gleich wie)* finding a sexual mate, so this analogy can be applied and used in order to generate enthusiasm and excitement about hunting. In time the activity of hunting develops its own cultural meanings and motivations and takes on a life of its own. It does not need the sexual metaphor any longer, and so sexuality does not apply to it so concretely. Yet some residues of a strong analogy always remain, and these residues allow for the possibility of reductive sexual interpretations of contemporary cultural activities.

Due to the tendency to create analogies, the human world of consciousness and culture in time becomes vastly expanded:

> It appears as if, by this means of phantastic analogy formation, more libido would gradually become desexualized, because increasingly more phantasy correlates were put in the place of the primitive achievement of the sexual libido. With this an enormous broadening of the world idea was gradually developed because new objects were always assimilated as sexual symbols.[8]

The archaic world of human activity and consciousness thus became over millennia more sexualized, but was also de-sexualized at the same time: sexualized because more analogies to sexuality were continually being created, but de-sexualized because these analogies became more and more remote from their source.

Jung's insight was that sexual motives and thoughts are gradually replaced by metaphors, analogies, and symbols in the conscious and unconscious life of the human being. The sexual motive will reappear vividly during regressions in the patient's mental life, however, and this is what Freud's conceptions are based on. Up to this point in the argument, Jung is filling in detail and adding supporting arguments for the view that much of the modern human adult's mental life derives from sexual sources even if it no longer has much to do with sexuality per se. Such differences as he shows from Freudian orthodoxy to this point would not have constituted heresy. The more critical part was to come later, in the final chapter of *Psychology of the Unconscious* entitled "The Sacrifice," which dealt with the subject of incest.

In his autobiography, Jung recalls:

> When I was working on my book about the libido and approaching the end of the chapter "The Sacrifice," I knew in advance that its publication would cost my friendship with Freud. For I planned to set down in it my own conception of incest, the decisive transformation of the concept of libido . . . To me incest signified a personal complication only in the rarest cases. Usually incest has a highly religious aspect, for which reason the incest theme plays a decisive part in almost all cosmogonies and in numerous myths. But Freud clung to the literal interpretation of it and could not grasp the spiritual significance of incest as a symbol. I knew that he would never be able to accept any of my ideas on this subject.[9]

Why was Jung's conception of incest "the decisive transformation of the concept of libido"? It was because he deliteralized the incest wish. Freud saw in the incest wish an unconscious wish to have the actual mother sexually in a literal sense. Jung, on the other hand, interpreted the incest wish symbolically as a general longing to remain in the paradise of childhood. This longing becomes more pronounced when a person faces a daunting challenge in life, to grow up, to adapt to a stress-filled environment. One wants to climb in bed and pull the covers over one's head. The longed-for "mother" becomes, in Jung's symbolic interpretation, the desire to regress to infantile dependence, to childhood, to unconsciousness and irresponsibility. This is the motivation behind much drug and alcohol addiction. When incest fantasies appeared in the treatment of neurosis, therefore, Jung would interpret them as resistances to adaptation rather than as the appearance of actual unconscious wishes or of childhood memories of such wishes. The practice of literal incest among some ancient peoples, like the Egyptian pharaohs for example, was understood by Jung to be religiously symbolic, stating a privileged status and indicating the union with a divine source of energy. It was marriage to the Mother-as-origin-of-life, not a wish-fulfillment of literal sexual desire. Actually, Jung argued, sexuality has little to do with incest. Incest is symbolically significant, not biologically desired.

This kind of symbolic interpretation of psychological themes and images set Freud's teeth on edge. Over against his doctrines, Jung held that libido does not consist simply of sexual desire for specific objects, nor is it to be conceived as a kind of inner pressure that seeks to discharge itself by attaching to ("cathecting" is the pretentious psychoanalytic term) fixed-upon love objects. Libido is "will." Jung is bowing to Schopenhauer here. But, Jung continues, will is divided into two parts, a will to life and a will to death: "In the first half of life [the libido's] will is for growth, in the second half of life it hints, softly at first, and then audibly, at its will for death."[10] Amazingly, this reference to divided libido and to a death wish precedes Freud's theory of a death wish by roughly a decade and owes its source most probably to Jung's collaboration with Sabina Spielrein, who was his student at the time. It should be noted that Jung deleted this phrasing from his text when he revised it in 1952 in the work entitled *Symbols of Transformation.*[11] By that time, he had dropped Spielrein from his theory and no longer espoused the notion of a death instinct.

The theme of sacrifice that Jung dwells upon at length in *Psychology of the Unconscious* is a centerpiece in his thoughts about the growth of consciousness and the needs of the human personality to develop maturity. Were humans to stay in bondage to incestuous desire and behavior, symbolically speaking, there would be no psychic movement out of childhood. Paradise would be home. At the same time, the human species would fail to thrive because adaptation to harsh and demanding environments could not occur. The incest wish for eternal childhood had to be sacrificed collectively in primordial times, and it has to be sacrificed individually by every modern person, in order to promote movement in consciousness toward greater consciousness. And for Jung this movement toward psychological maturity comes about naturally through internal mechanisms and dynamics. It does not have to be induced by outer threats. The great sacrifice of incest is made voluntarily, not (as taught by Freudian theory) because of threats of castration. Freud's theory of patricide or atonement for guilt as the basis of conscience was alien to Jung's way of thinking. Humans develop conscience, morality, and culture naturally, as part of their nature. Culture is therefore natural to the human species.

In *Psychology of the Unconscious,* Jung argues the general point that the transformation of libido comes about not through a conflict between the sexual drive and external reality but rather through the intervention of a mechanism within human nature itself. This mechanism produces the sacrifice of incest for the sake of development. It can be seen at work in many religions, notably in Mithraism and Christianity, which Jung compares here at some length.

At this point in his career, Jung had not yet conceptualized the archetype as a force that structures the psyche and psychic energy. This would come later and would then allow him to achieve much greater specificity in tracing the various transformations within the instinctual base. When he produced the extensive revision of the 1912–13 text in 1952, published as *Symbols of Transformation,* he inserted archetypal theory in many places in order to achieve precisely this type of specification. In 1913, however, he was limited theoretically and could only speak vaguely about the notion that there is a natural movement toward sacrifice of instinctual gratification, innate to the human psychic system, without which culture and human consciousness as we know it would not be possible. Sacrifice accounts for the transformation of energy from one form of expression and activity to another, but it remained unclear at that time what motivates humans to make such extraordinary sacrifices.[12] Furthermore, there is the question of what directs energy along particular pathways to specific occupations and endeavors. A key insight would be the capacity for *symbols* to transform and direct libido.

In taking the position on instinct and libido that he did, Jung knew that his days as Freud's heir and crown prince were numbered. Freud was not one to tolerate wide differences of opinion among his followers. Authority was at stake here, and Freud would demand an intellectual kowtow. Jung balked on this point, and this was the psychological nub of their bitter separation.[13]

And so it did indeed come to pass that Jung's collegial relationship with Freud ended within months of the publication of Part II of *Psychology of the Unconscious*. The publication date was September 1912, when the material appeared in the sixth volume of *Jahrbuch für psychoanalytische und psychopathologische Forschungen*, of which Jung was the general editor. For Jung, the whole point of differing with Freud on the definition and conception of libido was to avoid his severe type of reductionism that considers every manifestation of conscious life and cultural activity to be assignable to sexuality in one or another of its variety of flavors. For Freud, the point of insisting on the centrality of sexuality was to retain the edge of psychoanalytic insight into how the civilized human being avoids truth and suffers from having to deal so deviously with sexuality. In addition, Jung was aiming for the creation of a general theory of energy and for a general psychology, while Freud was intent on burrowing ever deeper into the distortions and subterfuges of psychological life as regards sexuality and (later) destructiveness and the death wish.

By 1928, when he published "On Psychic Energy," Jung had been thinking about this subject for twenty years. His detailed argument and references to various authorities in this essay still reflect his disagreement with Freud and psychoanalysis, but they also represent his desire to present the strongest possible case for a general view of libido as psychic energy.

Physics as a Model

Physics, with which Jung was not technically familiar in any great detail but which was very much in the air around him in the Zürich of the early twentieth century, provided a model for thinking about psychic energy. For Jung it was a metaphor that offered possibilities for formulating a similar set of understandings for psychic energy. Physics had constructed an elaborate theory of energy, with laws of causality, entropy, conservation of energy, transformation, and so on. Looking to these laws of physics and leaving out the mathematical formulas and equations, Jung set out to conceptualize the psyche in a manner that reminds one somewhat of his earlier work in experimental psychology with the Word Association Experiment. Jung points out that when dealing with energy one is drawn to quantification.[14]

Energy is an abstraction from the object world, he writes. One cannot see, touch, or taste it. To speak of energy is to be concerned with the relation between objects rather than with the objects themselves. Gravity, for example, describes the way one object affects another but says nothing specifically about the quality of the objects in question. Similarly, Jung argues, a theory of psychic energy, or libido, should account for how objects in the psychic world affect one another.

Jung argues that energy is finalistic and has to do with the transfer of motion or momentum among (psychic) objects as they move irreversibly along a gradient and end up in a state of equilibrium. This resembles a description of a physical chain of events: as one object bumps into another, the first is slowed and the momentum of the second is increased. The law of conservation of energy is applied to this sequence, which says that energy can neither be created nor destroyed, so the amount of energy that leaves the first object must equal the amount of energy received by the second. This can be precisely measured. Thus, while energy is abstract and intangible, its effects are observable, as anyone who plays pool knows. Jung applied this model to the psyche, and this essay is about measuring psychic energy and thinking about psychic life in terms of energy transfers and movements.

"Empathy leads to the mechanistic view, abstraction to the energic view,"[15] Jung writes, and goes on to contrast a mechanistic with an energic view of physical and psychic reality. The perspectives are incompatible, yet both are true. "The causal-mechanistic view sees the sequence of facts, a-b-c-d, as follows: a causes b, b causes c, and so on,"[16] its focus being on causation. This ball hits a second one, which hits the third. The first collision causes an effect, which causes another effect, and so on. Effects are thus traced back to an initial cause. "Here the concept of effect appears as the designation of a quality, as a 'virtue' of the cause, in other words, as a dynamism."[17] Applying this perspective to psychological life, a complex is seen as caused by a trauma. The force of the trauma enters the psychic system, causing a series of effects that continue to manifest for many years in the form of symptoms. From a mechanistic perspective, the trauma is regarded as the causal origin of the complex. And this understanding leads to empathy for the traumatized one.

"The *final-energic* view, on the other hand," Jung writes, "sees the sequence thus: *a-b-c* are means towards the transformation of energy, which flows causelessly from *a*, the improbable state, entropically to *b-c* and so to the probable state *d*. Here a causal effect is totally disregarded, since only intensities of effect are taken into account. Insofar as the intensities are the same, we could just as well put *w-x-y-z* instead of *a-b-c-d*."[18] From a final-energic point of view, energy is transferred from a less probable to a more probable state by moving along a gradient of intensities until it ends up in equilibrium. Applying that perspective to psychological life—and here one comes to understand why Jung called this an abstract and not an empathic view— wherever one ends up in life, psychologically or emotionally speaking, is where the intensity of gradients has led in order to achieve a state of equilibrium. Equilibrium is the aim, and in that sense it is the cause, a final cause, that draws a chain of events to itself. It is a "just so" story. Causation seems like personal destiny.[19]

For whatever reason—whether pushed from the behind or drawn forward to a goal in the future—energy moves. According to the physical law of entropy, energy flows from higher to lower

levels, from less to more probable states of intensity; according to
the law of negentropy, on the other hand, it moves toward states
of greater complexity. The energic viewpoint sees the final state as
the most important fact, while the mechanistic-causal perspective
focuses on the initial impetus that sent energy into the system in
the first place. Neither perspective finds outcomes to be random
or unpredictable. And both are potentially scientific.

It should be noted that Jung is not dealing here with questions
of ultimate purpose or meaning. Often accused of being a mystic,
he was especially sensitive to the dangers of projecting purpose
and meaning into natural processes. He does not regard the final-
energic view as teleological, in the religious sense of natural and
historical processes aiming for and seeking a meaningful spiritual
conclusion. He is simply speaking here of a viewpoint that
observes the transfer of energy from less probable to more probable states. Questions like: Is there a designer behind the design?
Does God control and guide energy and lead it to preordained
conclusions and goals? are interesting metaphysically, but Jung
did not wish to address such issues here. He is merely speaking of
the transfer of energy from one level to another.

While his psychological theory is finalistic in important ways,
Jung also tried to create a synthesis between causal and final perspectives. He thought that the disagreement between Freud and
Adler could be attributed to the difference between a causal and a
finalistic psychology. While Freud's psychology (extroverted)
searches out causes, Adler's finalistic psychology (introverted)
looks at end points. Adler assumed that a person's present life situation, no matter what it might be, was constructed to fit the individual's personal needs and preferences in some way. Adler's
finalistic-energic view conflicted absolutely with Freud's mechanistic-causal position. Jung was looking for a middle ground, for
a position that could take both perspectives into account.[20]

Causal-mechanistic models and finalistic models begin with a
different premise concerning original energy states. The causal-
mechanistic model starts with an assumption of original stasis. At
the beginning nothing has happened yet, and nothing will happen

until something intervenes from outside the system and gives it a boost of energy. Someone gives a ball a shove, it hits another, and so a chain of events is set in motion. The finalistic-energic position, on the other hand, assumes a highly energized state at the beginning, and from this there emerge patterns of movement as energy seeks more probable states, finally achieving balance and stasis. Complexes—Jung would say, for example—possess a specific quantum of energy, and this can result in movement if the psychic system is in disequilibrium. Complexes are not only reactive, then, but at times they can also be creative. If complexes were not proactive and creative but only reactive, they could not be considered autonomous in any strong sense of the word. Under certain conditions, they will press into ego consciousness with a fantasy or a desire or thought that is quite unprovoked by the environment. The environmental stimulus simply invites or releases the energy that is bound up in the complex. Finalistically seen, the complex would be seen as seeking to discharge its energy and to return to a lower energy level. It does this by introducing into the conscious subject a thought, a feeling or mood, or fantasy, and this may lead the person to behave in a certain way. When the discharge of energy has been completed, it settles back to a more latent state in the unconscious and awaits either the build-up of more energy from within the intrapsychic system or constellation by an outer stimulus.

The Source of Energy

In the essay "On Psychic Energy," Jung does not go into detail on the specific sources of a complex's energy. He states only that psychic energy gets distributed among the various components of the psyche, and he is interested in studying how, using the energic viewpoint, one can track the distribution of energy from one state to another. His questions are: How does energy move about within the psyche? Why are some complexes more energized than others, or sometimes more energized than at other times? How does instinctual energy, which has its source in the biological base of the psyche, get transformed into other activities?

A complex collects new psychic energy to itself in two ways: from new traumas that become associated with it and enrich it with more material, and from the magnetic power of its archetypal core. This core attracts its energy from two sources. It is fed with energy on the one hand by the instinct with which it is affiliated. Instincts and archetypes are two sides of a single coin in the psyche, as I will discuss in detail in the next chapter. The archetypal image, therefore, acts as an attractor of energy as it becomes available to the psyche from the biological base (through a process that Jung calls *psychization*). On the other hand, archetypes also attract energy from other sources. They tune into culture, to exchanges with other people, even to spirit itself, as Jung will say in his later essay, "On the Nature of the Psyche." The psyche is by no means a closed system. Rather it is open to the world through the body and through the spirit.

The irruption of a complex into consciousness indicates that it has become temporarily more energized than the ego. Its energy flows from the complex into the ego system and may flood and possess it. Whether or not the ego can manage to contain this influx of energy is an important practical question. How can the ego channel and use what at times seems like a tremendous flood of unruly energy? The key lies with the ego, which can choose, if it is strong and determined enough, to direct this influx of energy into the creation of structure, boundaries, or projects, for example. Otherwise a person may simply become emotionally overwrought and dysfunctional.

For Jung, then, the psyche was not conceived as a closed energy system. Closed systems move toward entropy, and absolutely closed systems stabilize in a totally static final state. Jung believed that the psychic system is only relatively closed. The healthy psyche is somewhat closed and does show a tendency toward entropy, but it is also open in that it is fed and influenced by the surrounding world. Tightly closed psychic systems are pathological. Those are often so sealed off from outer influences that they do not yield to psychotherapy. Paranoid schizophrenia, for instance, is such a tightly locked psychic system, and it ends in total stasis with rigidly frozen ideas and attitudes and increased isolation. Only biological treatment can influence it.

In a healthy personality, psychic energy also follows the law of entropy to some extent. Over time there is a tendency toward conservatism and gradual stasis. Change becomes more difficult as one ages. The polarities in the psyche, which generate energy through their vigorous interaction, approach a position of stability and accommodation. This fact would indicate that the normal psychic system is only relatively open and somewhat closed. Energy distribution tends to move from high to lower levels, analogous to water falling to the lowest level it can reach.

Measurement of Psychic Energy

Jung wonders in this essay how such energy states could be measured scientifically. He suggests that this could be done by estimating *values*. The amount of value placed on an attitude or activity indicates the intensity level of energy. Quantifying that, however, presents difficulties. If one were to make an inventory of one's conscious contents and preoccupations—politics, religion, money, sex, career, relationships, family—and put an estimate of value on each item, using a scale of 1 to 100, one would have a sense of how energy is distributed among the contents of consciousness. Obviously this fluctuates day by day, year by year, decade by decade. And how does one really know how much something is valued by the psyche? It is easy to fool oneself. An inventory of conscious contents can be rated on a scale, but one cannot be certain of the accuracy of these ratings until they are put to the test. Only when choices are forced between two or more attractive things does a person actually become certain of what the relative values are. An alcoholic who is forced to choose between more boozing and a wife and family will be hard pressed to commit himself, but such a crisis will test his promise never to drink again. Spending habits can provide important clues to one's actual, as opposed one's supposed, values. The flow of money, which symbolizes energy, is a way of showing where value intensity lies. People voluntarily spend money for what they value highly.

These are some of the ways in which the energy values of conscious contents can be measured. But what about the values of unconscious contents? How can these be measured? This cannot be accomplished by introspection alone because the ego cannot ordinarily penetrate far enough into the unconscious depths. Complexes will make choices that the ego would not make. An indirect method of measurement is necessary, and for Jung the Word Association Experiment provided such a method. A complex's energy level is indicated by the number of complex indicators associated to it. Once this is known, an estimate can be made of its energy potential. Over time, too, one learns experientially which complexes generate the most intense emotional reactions. These sensitive areas are better not exposed in public and in polite society because of one's predictably intense reactions. Some collective complexes, circling around issues of sex, religion, money, or power affect almost everyone to some degree and can lead to fierce discharges of energy, even to war, if provoked severely enough. The intensity and frequency of disturbances in daily life are useful indicators of the energy levels of the unconscious complexes. The energy level of a psychic content may be indicated by either positive or negative emotions and reactions. From an energic point of view, this distinction in feeling makes no difference.

The Unity of Body and Mind

Psychic energy—Jung repeats in this essay what he said some fifteen years earlier in *Psychology of the Unconscious*—is a subcategory of life energy. Some people simply have a great deal of it, while others have less. It was said that Lyndon Johnson, for example, seemed to have more glands than anybody else around. He could overwhelm people with his sheer energy. As a senator, he wrote 250 letters a day to constituents while carrying out his regular duties as majority leader. Some people have a tremendous amount of raw energy while others can barely get from bed to the breakfast table. In a sense, the physical side of life strongly affects the psychological, and feeling healthy physically contributes to one's reservoir of psychic energy. But the relation between psyche and body is complex and often paradoxical. Nietzsche, for example, was extremely ill and in severe pain while writing his poetic masterpiece, *Also Sprach Zarathustra*. Heinrich Heine spent the last ten years of his life in bed in physical agony, and yet he composed hundreds of songs and poems and other literary works of the highest caliber during this period. The immense amounts of psychic energy needed for these efforts of genius cannot be accounted for by using the simple notion that a healthy body produces the psychic energy that is available for work. There is more going on than a simple transfer of calories from soma to soul and mind.

Because of conundrums such as these, some thinkers have regarded the physical and psychological as two relatively independent parallel systems. This has the virtue of preserving the integrity of each system and denying the reduction of psychic energy to physical energy. But Jung was not content with that model, even while he strongly opposed biological reductionism. He affirmed that there are two systems, but their interaction is so intricate and complex, and for the most part buried so deeply in the unconscious, that it is difficult to define where one begins and the other leaves off. In some ways they are independent, but in others they are deeply interconnected and seem dependent on one another. The mind/body issue appears many times in Jung's writings, and I will touch on it again in later chapters. In the essay "On Psychic Energy" he merely alludes to the problem.

Since the psyche-soma unity is only a relatively and not an absolutely closed system, neither entropy nor conservation of energy operates in it precisely. Practically speaking, however, there is a strong correlation. If one's interest in one thing diminishes or vanishes, that same amount of energy often appears somewhere else. The two objects of interest might not be related in any apparent way, but the total amount of energy in the system remains constant. On the other hand, a great deal of energy sometimes vanishes completely. A person becomes lethargic or depressed. In this instance, Jung says, the energy has gone into regression. It has drained out of consciousness and returned to the unconscious.

Energy, Movement, and Direction

Regression and *progression* of libido are important terms in Jung's theory. They refer to directions of energy movement. In progression, libido is utilized for adaptation to life and the world. The person uses it for functioning in the world and can spend it freely on chosen activities. This person is experiencing a positive flow of psychic energy. But suppose this person fails an important exam, or gets shunted aside in a corporate shake-up, or loses a beloved mate or a child. Progression of libido may come to a stop, life ceases its forward momentum, and the flow of energy reverses direction. It goes into regression and disappears into the unconscious, where it activates complexes. This may lead to splitting apart polarities that were once linked; they now become warring opposites. Now ego-consciousness may have one set of principles and values, while the unconscious takes up a contrary position. The person is torn by inner conflict and becomes paralyzed. During progression, the polarities within the self balance each other and generate energy that moves forward. One may be ambivalent, but in a way that is adaptive to reality. In regression, on the other hand, the flow of energy goes back into the psychic system and becomes unavailable for adaptation. When the polarities come apart, a severe kind of ambivalence develops that paralyzes life. A standstill ensues, yes and no cancel each other out, and one cannot move.

Jung noted that when energy is not spent adapting to the world and is not moving in a progressive way, it activates the complexes and increases their energy potential in the degree to which the ego loses available energy. This is the law of conservation of energy as it applies to the psyche. The energy does not disappear from the system but rather disappears from consciousness. And this results typically in states of depression, crippling ambivalence, internal conflict, uncertainty, doubt, questioning, and loss of motivation.

While progression fosters adaptation to the world, regression leads paradoxically to new possibilities for development. Regression activates the inner world. When the inner world has been activated, a person is forced to deal with it and later to make a new adaptation to life that takes the results into account. That movement toward inner adaptation eventually leads to a fresh outer adaptation when the libido once again begins moving in the direction of progression. But now the person is more mature precisely because of the confrontation with the unconscious—the complexes, personal history, foibles, faults, and all the other troublesome and painful issues that surface during regression. (I will discuss Jung's concept of individuation in greater detail in chapter 8.)

It should be noted that Jung makes a clear distinction between the progression and regression of libido on the one hand and the attitudes of extroversion and introversion on the other. It is easy for the beginner to confuse them. Introverts progress in their own way, adapting to the world in an introverted fashion, while extroverts progress in an extroverted way. The same holds true for regression. For example, an extroverted-thinking type person, who has habitually used thinking to deal with the world and to manipulate people, comes up against a situation in life where that function does not work very effectively and experiences defeat. Relationship problems cannot as a rule be solved by extroverted thinking. Here a totally different approach is needed. When this person's superior function is rendered useless, a sense of frustration and defeat takes over, for now suddenly other functions are demanded and these are not readily available. So the libido regresses and typically activates the inferior function, in this case the introverted-feeling function. As Jung pointed out, the inferior function is unconscious and carries the slime of the murky depths with it when it comes up into consciousness. An integrated-feeling function is a tool of the ego and is a refined, discriminating and rational function that orients one by establishing values. An inferior, undifferentiated feeling function surging up from the unconscious, however, provides only a small amount of guidance about values, but rather screams in bright red letters: "This is the most important thing in my whole life! I cannot live without it!" It is highly emotional. The inferior function's lack of adaptive skill is generally all too evident, but the ego is challenged to use the emotions and thoughts that come into consciousness in this fashion, and by doing so it begins the task of adapting to the hidden side of the personality, the unconscious.

By contrast, people who get a lot of mileage in the first half of their lives out of their ability to relate well to other people reach a point where this no longer satisfies them. The highly developed extroverted-feeling function does not feed the soul anymore. Other potentials demand to be realized. Perhaps introverted intuitive-thinking projects (studying philosophy or theology) beckon and seem more attractive than another luncheon with friends or one more family gathering over the holidays. The full human life span has many periods of significant transformation.

Transformations and Symbols

How such transformations occur was a deep and abiding concern of Jung's. In the essay "On Psychic Energy" he provides a formal theoretical account of transformation. In the section on *canalization of libido,*[21] he considers some natural *gradients* of energy. A gradient is a pathway along which energy flows. In the state of nature—that is, in the paradisal state as we imagine it—no work as such is required or gets done. Like the pet dog who lives in a comfortable home, sleeps a lot, begs for table scraps, and (if not neutered) engages in seasonal frenetic sexual activities, so a human being living purely in the state of nature would live by physical instinct and desire alone. But humans have created culture and have specialized in work, and this presupposes the ability to channel energy out of the natural gradients into other, seemingly artificial pathways. How does this happen?

Jung does not conceive of nature and culture as diametrically opposed to one another. Rather, he regards them both as belonging to human nature in a fundamental way. The human inventions of culture and specialization in work come about by means of the mind's creation of analogues to instinctual goals and activities. Such analogues function as symbols.[22] Ideas and images—mental contents—channel libido in new directions by diverting it from its natural gradient and objects. For example, an idea arises in the young child that is as appealing as the image of the breast. This idea, realized in play, draws more energy to itself than does the breast and allows the child to delay gratifying the urge to nurse and eventually to wean spontaneously. In later life, the analogue or symbol that replaces the breast may be a gourmet meal. The thought of enjoying *haute cuisine* offers the same type of soothing to the adult as the image of the full breast offers to the small child. An idea or a cultural object thus captures the energy that would otherwise have remained fixated on the breast of the mother. Both breast and restaurant are symbols for something that at that moment in psychological development can be expressed in no better way.

A *symbol* attracts a great deal of energy to itself and shapes the ways in which psychic energy is channeled and spent. Religions have traditionally attracted large amounts of human energy, and they rely for their power almost exclusively on symbols. Through their use of symbols they also become powerful politically and economically, but these powers are secondary to the symbolic one which undergirds them. Remove the symbolic power and the whole edifice collapses. When vibrant and alive, religious ideas and rituals have tremendous attractive power to pull human energy into certain activities and preoccupations. Why does the symbol have a steeper gradient than the natural object? How can an idea become more interesting and compelling to human beings than instinctively attractive objects like breasts or penises?

Jung knew well enough that this does not come about because of a decision taken by the ego. When "Bill W." (William G. Wilson), cofounder of Alcoholics Anonymous, wrote to Jung in 1961 and reported on Roland H's fate (a patient Jung had treated for alcoholism in the early 1930s), Jung responded by admitting that the therapist is essentially helpless in trying to overcome a patient's substance dependence.[23] Jung's message was—in my paraphrase of his letter—*You need a symbol, an analogue that will draw the energy that has gone into drinking. You must find an equivalent that is more interesting than getting drunk every night, that attracts your interest more than that bottle of vodka.* A powerful symbol is required to bring about such a major transformation in an alcoholic, and Jung spoke of the need for a conversion experience. Symbols emerge out of the archetypal base of the personality, the collective unconscious. They are not artificially invented by the ego but rather appear spontaneously from the unconscious especially during times of great need.

Symbols are the great organizers of libido. Jung's use of the term symbol is precise. A symbol is not a sign. Signs can be read and interpreted with no loss of meaning. A stop sign means "stop!" But a symbol is, in Jung's understanding, the best possible statement or expression for something that is either essentially unknowable or not yet knowable given the present state of consciousness. Interpretations of symbols are attempts to translate the symbol's meaning into a more understandable vocabulary and set of terms, but the symbol remains the best present expression of the meaning it communicates. Symbols open one up to mystery. And they also combine elements of spirit and instinctuality, of image and drive. For that reason, descriptions of exalted spiritual states and mystical experiences frequently refer to physical and instinctual gratifications like nourishment and sexuality. Mystics talk about the ecstasy of uniting with God as an orgasmic experience, and most likely it is. The experience of the symbol unites body and soul in a powerful, convincing feeling of wholeness. For Jung the symbol holds so much importance because of its ability to transform natural energy into cultural and spiritual forms. In this essay he does not discuss the timing of such symbolic emergences in the psyche. This is considered in other writings, importantly in the late work entitled "Synchronicity: An Acausal Connecting Principle."[24]

The difference between transformation and sublimation spells out a basic distinction between the theories of Jung and Freud. For Freud, civilized human beings are able to sublimate libidinal desires, but sublimation only produces substitutes for the true objects of such desire. Libido will attach to the substitutes, but these remain only second best. In reality, the libido wishes to return to early childhood, to mother and father fixations, to Oedipal fantasy fulfillment. Freud's analysis, therefore, was always reductive. Jung agreed that the libido originally seeks the mother's body because nurturance is essential for the baby's survival. Later, the libido is drawn into sexual channels and flows along those gradients: procreation is necessary for the survival of the species. But when the libido finds a spiritual analogue, an idea or image, it will go there because that is its goal, not because this is a substitute for sexual fulfillment. For Jung, this is a transformation of libido, and culture arises from such transformations. Culture is a fulfillment of desire, not an obstruction of it. Jung is convinced that the nature of the human being leads to culture formation, to the creation of symbols, to containment of energy so that its flow can be directed toward these spiritual and mental contents.

The Psyche's Boundaries
(Instincts, Archetypes, and the Collective Unconscious)

Before modern times mapmakers put a distinctive stamp on their works. You could identify a map by certain unique features that pointed to the hand of its creator. It was a work of art as well as a work of science. Up to this point, Jung's map of the soul does not look so different from other depth psychological accounts. With this chapter, however, we begin studying its truly unique features. It was Jung's exploration and account of what he called the *collective unconscious* that gave his work its most distinctive style.

To pick up where we left off in the preceding chapter on psychic energy, I will simply state that for Jung the archetype is a primary source of psychic energy and patterning. It constitutes the ultimate source of psychic symbols, which attract energy, structure it, and lead ultimately to the creation of civilization and culture. From hints in earlier chapters, it should be somewhat evident that the theory of archetypes is critical to Jung's overall conception of the psyche. In fact, it is the foundation.

A discussion of Jung's theory of archetypes, however, also means that we must take up his theory of instincts as well. Archetype and instinct are profoundly related, in Jung's view. For Jung, mind and body are so interrelated that they are nearly inseparable. If this is ignored, the discussion of archetypal images easily slips into an overly spiritualized and groundless psychology. To discuss the archetype from a psychological standpoint rather than from a philosophical or metaphysical one, one must ground it in life as lived in the human body, where it also becomes intertwined with personal history and psychological development. The theory of archetypes is what makes Jung's map of the soul Platonic, but the difference between Jung and Plato is that Jung studied the Ideas as psychological factors and not as eternal forms or abstractions.

As I said at the outset of this book, Jung was intent on exploring the psyche to its furthest boundaries. If he was not a systematic thinker, he was certainly an ambitious one, and his ambition pushed him to press on beyond the bounds of scientific knowledge in his time. Science is still catching up with many of his intuitions. Probing ever further into the dark unknown terrain of the mind, he made some of his most original contributions to psychology and psychoanalysis in his theory of a collective unconscious and its contents. It is sometimes asked whether what he described as psychic facts are discoveries or inventions. But this is the fate of the mapmaker when the continents he is outlining are brand new and still wholly unknown and unexplored. The early mapmaker is forced to draw on intuition and to risk guesswork. He also consults the maps of others and even studies ancient texts. These can be helpful, or they can be misleading. Jung was more than adequately aware of the pitfalls in this enterprise, and he was as cautious in formulating his speculations as he was adventurous in allowing himself to have them in the first place.[1]

For this chapter, I will refer mainly to Jung's late summation of theory, the classic paper "On the Nature of the Psyche." This essay does not depict the realm of the collective unconscious in the florid manner of grand images that Jung was so fond of in other works, particularly in his late works using the images and texts of alchemy. This is a sober and abstract theoretical account, rather difficult to read and dry to the taste of those who look to Jung for visionary inspiration. But this work supplies the theoretical bedrock on which those other formulations rest, and without understanding this basic theory the rest can look much like a collection of animals in a well-stocked zoo: a lot of exotic color but not much rationale.[2] The critics who read Jung in this way frankly do not understand the nature of his project. The rationale for his collections of abstruse and exotic facts is given in many places, but with special clarity in this theoretical paper.

This essay was written in 1945–46 and revised in 1954. I consider it arguably Jung's most comprehensive and synthetic theoretical work. A full understanding of this work actually requires extensive knowledge of all of Jung's previous writings. It presents little that is new in his thinking but rather pulls together many threads that have been dropped in numerous essays from the prior three decades. A brief review of the thinking that led up to this classic paper is in order and will provide the context for understanding its importance.

Jung's ambition from very early on was to participate in the creation of a general psychology that would map the psyche from its highest to its lowest dimensions, its closest to its farthest reaches, truly a map of the soul. This ambition can be traced back into the early years of his career. In a letter written in 1913 to editors Smith Ely Jelliffe and William Alanson White of the newly founded *Psychoanalytical Review* and published in the first issue of that journal, Jung offers a sketch of his bold vision for this new psychology. He applauds the editors on their plan to "unite in their journal the contributions of competent specialists in various fields."[3] The fields he cites as being relevant and useful to psychology are, amazingly, philology, history, archaeology, mythology, folklore studies, ethnology, philosophy, theology, pedagogy, and biology! If all of these contribute their specialized knowledge to the study of the human psyche, Jung writes, there will be a chance of reaching "the distant goal of a genetic psychology, which will clear our eyes for medical psychology, just as comparative anatomy has already done in regard to the structure and function of the human body."[4] Jung speaks in this letter also of a "comparative anatomy of the mind,"[5] which would be achieved by pooling expertise from many fields of research and study. His goal was to achieve a broad overview of the psyche and to grasp it as a whole, from which one could observe the various parts in their dynamic interplay.

As Jung penetrated more deeply into the sources of the unconscious material—primarily dreams and fantasies—presented by his patients and discovered in his own inner work on himself, he was led to theorize about some general structures of the human mind, structures that belong to everyone and not only to himself or to the individual patient before him. The deepest layer of the human psyche he named the "collective unconscious" and conceived of its contents as a combination of universally prevalent patterns and forces called "archetypes" and "instincts." In his view, there is nothing individual or unique about human beings at this level. Everyone has the same archetypes and instincts. For uniqueness one must look elsewhere in the personality. True individuality, he argued in *Psychological Types* and *Two Essays in Analytical Psychology,* is the product of a personal struggle for consciousness that he called the individuation process (see chapter 8). Individuation is the flower of a person's conscious engagement with the paradox of the psyche over an extended period of time. Instincts and archetypes, on the other hand, are nature's gift to each of us. They are given equally to one and all, and everyone shares them whether rich or poor, black or white, ancient or modern. This theme of universality is a basic feature of Jung's understanding of the human psyche. He gave it succinct expression late in life in the revision of a work entitled "The Father in the Destiny of the Individual":

> Man "possesses" many things which he has never acquired but has inherited from his ancestors. He is not born as a *tabula rasa,* he is merely born unconscious. But he brings with him systems that are organized and ready to function in a specifically human way, and these he owes to millions of years of human development. Just as the migratory and nest-building instincts of birds were never learnt or

acquired individually, man brings with him at birth the ground-plan of his nature, and not only of his individual nature but of his collective nature. These inherited systems correspond to the human situations that have existed since primeval times: youth and old age, birth and death, sons and daughters, father and mothers, mating, and so on. Only the individual consciousness experiences these things for the first time, but not the bodily system and the unconscious. For them they are only the habitual functioning of instincts that were preformed long ago.[6]

Archetypes (Psychic Universals)

The origin of Jung's notion of archetypes can be traced back in his written works to the period between 1909 and 1912 when, while still collaborating with Freud, he was investigating mythology and writing *Psychology of the Unconscious*. In that work he studied the fantasies of Miss Frank Miller, which had been made publicly available in a book published by his friend and colleague from Geneva, Gustav Flournoy. Jung wanted to explore the significance of these fantasies from his newly emerging point of view, which had been incubating since his early psychiatric study of his mediumistic cousin, Helene Preiswerk. His engagement with Frank Miller's fantasy materials became the occasion for Jung to begin distancing himself explicitly from Freud's libido theory and to start discussing general patterns in what he would later come to call the collective unconscious.

According to his autobiography, Jung got his first impression of impersonal layers of the unconscious from a dream he had during the voyage to America with Freud in 1909. He dreamed of a house (called "my house" in the context of the dream) that had many levels. In the dream he explores the storeys of the house from the main floor (the present age) down into the basement (the recent historical past) and beyond that down through several subcellars (the ancient historical past, like the Greek and Roman, and finally the prehistoric and Paleolithic past). This dream answered a question he had been asking during the trip, namely: "On what premises is Freudian psychology founded? To what category of human thought does it belong?"[7] The dream image, he writes, "became for me a guiding image" for how to conceive of psychic structure. "It was my first inkling of a collective a priori beneath the personal psyche."[8]

When he first examined the work of Flournoy, Jung knew little about Miss Miller or her personal life history. Perhaps this would be an advantage for theory, he mused, since now his thought could not be contaminated by personal associations and projections. Undistracted by the trees, he could look at the forest. He would be free to speculate about more general psychological patterns. And speculate he did, with considerable zest and abandon. As he looked at Miss Miller's fantasies, he imagined her reality from the few facts that were included in the account: an unmarried young woman traveling alone in Europe, attracted to an Italian sailor but unable to act upon her erotic interest, damming up unused sexual libido and falling into a profound regression. Using what he knew at the time about psychological dynamics—learned largely from Freud and fellow psychoanalysts—he also ventured to extend some of those understandings to the point of suggesting that libido, sexuality itself, has a dual nature. On the one hand, it seeks fulfillment in sexual involvement and pleasure; on the other hand, it inhibits such involvement and even seeks the opposite, death. He ventured to propose a death wish equal to the wish for life, the second becoming more prominent in the second half of life as one prepares to die. Innate to the human psyche was a tendency to sacrifice satisfaction, sexual or otherwise, and to pursue nonsexual tendencies and desires that could not be satisfied by any amount of sexual activity.

This was a strange course for Jung's thinking to take in reflecting on the psychological situation of this young woman. On the one hand, she was obviously seeking an erotic outlet in life and was not able to find one. Hence her regressions and attempts at sublimation: visions, poetry writing, daydreaming, all of which, Jung felt, showed evidence of premorbidity and could eventually lead to mental illness. On the other hand, perhaps Miss Miller's sexual inhibitions reflected a deeper conflict within her psyche, a conflict that one could see as generally human and indeed archetypal. There was the much larger issue of the whole course of human evolution and development, and Jung was theorizing that sexual libido had in the course of eons of human evolution been channeled into pathways of culture through metaphors and likenesses at first and then into deeper transformations. These could no longer be adequately defined in the least as sexual. He was arriving at a whole new theory of culture while tracing the libido fluctuations of Miss Miller. It is no wonder that many readers have found this book confusing.

As Jung explored human evolution, drawing many parallels between what was going on in a sort of morbid way with Miss Miller and what had happened hundreds and thousands and indeed hundreds of thousands of years in the past, he outlined the constellation of the hero myth and assigned to the hero the role of creating consciousness. The hero is a basic human pattern—characteristic of women equally as of men—that demands sacrificing the "mother," meaning a passive childish attitude, and assuming the responsibilities of life and meeting reality in a grown up way. The hero archetype demands leaving off with childish fantasy thinking and insists on engaging reality in an active way. If humans had not been able to take up this challenge, they would have been doomed eons ago. In order to meet reality consistently, though, a tremendous sacrifice of desire and wistful longing for the comforts of childhood is demanded. This was Miss Miller's dilemma: she was confronted with the task of growing up and meeting her adult roles in life, and she was shrinking from the challenge. She was not leaving fantasy thinking behind, and she was getting lost in a morbid unreal world that was relatively unrelated to her reality. She was in a massive regression to the "mother," and the question was: Would she get stuck there, like Theseus in Hades, and never return? Jung was not so sure, but he guessed she might fall into psychosis.

As he worked on these fantasies of Frank Miller, Jung brought together a host of related myths, fairy tales, and religious motifs from remote corners of the world to interpret her images. He was awestruck by these amazing parallels, and his mind groped for an explanation of why this woman had spontaneously produced images and themes resembling those of Egyptian mythology, of the aboriginal tribes of Australia, and of the native peoples of America. Why do such striking parallels occur to the human mind without much seeming effort? What does this mean? He connected these facts to his dream of the descending basements, and thus he began to realize that he was discovering evidence for the existence of a collective layer of the unconscious. This would mean that there is material in the unconscious that has not been put there by repression from consciousness. It is there to begin with.

The same pursuit of psychic universals, it must be noted, also intrigued Freud, but in quite a different way. Freud was looking for a single unconscious wish—a central complex—that would explain all psychic conflict, and he thought he had found it in the story of the primal horde. While Jung was writing *Psychology of the Unconscious*, Freud was working on *Totem and Taboo*. With clinical material in one hand and Frazer's *Golden Bough* in the other, Freud was pursuing a project similar to Jung's, and the race was on as to who would make the Great Discovery first. Whether Freud's or Jung's version is preferred, the common denominator is that the human mind has universal structures, just like the human body, and these can be discovered through an interpretive and comparative method.

In one sense, then, Freud, like Jung, produced a theory of archetypes. His notion of archaic residues acknowledged ancient patterns. While Freud's attitude toward this material was very different from Jung's discussions of mythology and its relation to the psyche, the two men were nevertheless following similar lines of thought and reaching for a similar conclusion.

The Unconscious

The parallels Jung found between images and myths of individuals and groups in unrelated historical periods and locations intensified his quest for an explanation. Is there a common point of origin for psychotic images, dream images, and personal fantasy productions on the one hand, and collective mythical and religious images and thoughts on the other? Jung was exploring commonalities in human thinking and imagining. In order to carry this research further, he had to get his patients to reveal their unconscious fantasies and thoughts.

In his paper "On the Nature of the Psyche," Jung tells how he activated fantasy activity in his patients: "I had often observed patients whose dreams pointed to a rich store of fantasy material. Equally, from the patients themselves, I got the impression that they were stuffed full of fantasies, without being able to tell me just where the inner pressure lay. I therefore took up a dream image or an association of the patient's, and, with this as a point of departure, set him the task of elaborating or developing his theme by giving free rein to his fantasy."[9] Freud's technique of free association had been similar, but Jung let imagination roam further and more freely. He encouraged his patients to elaborate fantasy material: "This, according to individual taste and talent, could be done in any number of ways, dramatic, dialectic, visual, acoustic, or in the form of dancing, painting, drawing, or modeling. The result of this technique was a vast number of complicated designs whose diversity puzzled me for years, until I was able to recognize that in the method I was witnessing the spontaneous manifestation of an unconscious process which was merely assisted by the technical ability of the patient, and to which I later gave the name 'individuation process.'"[10] This process of imaging unconscious contents brings them into conscious form.

> The chaotic assortment of images that at first confronted me reduced itself in the course of the work to certain well-defined themes and formal elements, which repeated themselves in identical or analogous form with the most varied individuals. I mention, as the most salient characteristics, chaotic multiplicity and order; duality, the opposition of light and dark, upper and lower, right and left; the union of opposites in a third; the quaternity (square, cross); rotation (circle, sphere); and finally the centring process and a radial arrangement that usually followed some quaternary system. . . . The centring process is, in my experience, the never-to-be-surpassed climax of the whole development, and is characterized as such by the fact that it brings with it the greatest possible therapeutic effect.[11]

Jung goes on to speak about "formative principles [that] are unconscious."[12] In addition to his consideration of the fantasy material produced by psychotics, Jung's experience with neurotic patients encouraged him to think that major formative elements exist within the unconscious. Since ego consciousness does not determine this process, the source of the forms that appear must lie somewhere else. Some forms might be determined by complexes, but others are more primordial and impersonal and cannot be accounted for by individual life experience.

Jung presented this paper in 1946 at the Eranos Conference at Ascona, Switzerland, where many of his major essays were given and which he attended from its inception in 1933 until 1960, the year before his death. Here people gathered annually from all over the world. Their interests lay particularly in psychology and religion, especially Eastern religions. Olga Froebe-Kapetyn, the founder whose longstanding serious interest in Eastern thought and all kinds of occultism had motivated the undertaking, brought together renowned experts to discuss various topics. This audience seemed truly to stimulate Jung and to draw out his best efforts. These people were members of a world class community of scientists and scholars, and they demanded papers of extremely high quality.

"On the Nature of the Psyche" is a mature summation of Jung's psychological theory. The historical sections of the paper deal with the unconscious in philosophy and academic psychology. Here Jung lays the groundwork for his own definitions of the unconscious, for his understanding of its relation to consciousness, and for intrapsychic dynamics. The notion of an unconscious is fundamental to all depth psychologies. This separates depth psychologies from other psychological models. As evidence for the existence of the unconscious, Jung cites the dissociability of the psyche. In certain altered states of consciousness, for example, one finds a subliminal self or subject, an inner figure who is not the ego but shows intentionality and will. The ego can enter into dialogue with this other subpersonality. Such a "Jekyll and Hyde" phenomenon indicates the presence of two distinct centers of consciousness within one personality. This also exists, Jung writes, in so-called normal personalities even if people are not aware of this fact.

But once one posits an unconscious psyche, how is one to define its limits? Can they be defined at all, or are they so indefinite as to be considered more or less limitless? As a scientist and thinker, Jung wanted some clear definitions and in this paper he proposes several of them. One of the most important is a theoretical concept called the *psychoid* aspect of the psyche, which forms a threshold:

> The sound frequencies perceptible to the human ear range from 20 to 20,000 vibrations per second; the wave-lengths of light visible to the eye range from 7700 to 3900 angstrom-units. This analogy makes it conceivable that there is a lower as well as an upper threshold for psychic events, and that consciousness, the perceptual system par excellence, may therefore be compared with the perceptible scale of sound or light, having like them a lower and upper limit. Maybe this comparison could be extended to the psyche in general, which would not be an impossibility if there were 'psychoid' processes at both ends of the psychic scale.[13]

Jung's view of the psyche posits that it moves along a scale whose outer limits gradually disappear into a psychoid (that is, psyche-like) area. Jung acknowledges that he is borrowing the adjective "psychoid" from Bleuler, who defined *das Psychoide* as "the sum total of all the purposive, mnemonic, and life-preserving functions of the body and central nervous system, with the exception of those cortical functions which we have always been accustomed to regard as psychic."[14] Bleuler thus proposed a distinction between (a) the psychic functions, which in Jung's terms include ego-consciousness and the unconscious (personal and collective), and (b) the other life-preserving functions of the body and the central nervous system, some of which appear to be quasi-psychic. The body itself is able to remember and to learn. For instance, once you learn to ride a bicycle, you do not need to recall this skill consciously. The body retains the memory of how to do it. The body is also purposive and oriented toward the preservation of life, struggling for survival in its own way, outside the range of the psyche. Jung works basically within this set of definitions regarding the psychic, the quasi-psychic, and the nonpsychic.

Jung uses Bleuler's term psychoid in a number of his writings, but with some reservations. He criticizes Bleuler for unduly linking psychoid to specific bodily organs and for encouraging a kind of pan-psychism that would find psyche in everything living. Psychoid for Jung is a term that describes processes that are psyche-like or quasi-psychic but not properly so. The term is used to distinguish psychic functions from vitalistic ones. Psychoid processes lie between somatic life-energy and sheer bodily processes on the one hand and true psychic processes on the other.

Instincts

At this point in his argument, Jung takes up the subject of human instinct. Instinct is rooted in the physical and enters the psyche as impulse, thought, memory, fantasy, and emotion. To be sure, the whole subject of instinct is a problem with regard to humans. Because humans have the ability to choose, to reflect, and to act or not to act on so-called instinctual impulses, as other animals do not, it is questionable how large a role instincts play in human behavior. Jung recognized that for humans the instinctual side of behavior is far less determinative than it is for animals. Nevertheless, people are to some degree influenced by physiological, as distinct from psychic, needs and processes. Using Janet's term, Jung calls this the *partie inferieur* of human existence. This part is controlled by hormones and shows a compulsive character that has led some to speak of "drives."[15] Insofar as hormones dictate what we do or feel, we are subject to drives and instinct. The *partie inferieur,* that is, the somatic level of the psyche, is strongly influenced by bodily processes.

Having recognized this somatic substrate, Jung then states:

> From these reflections it appears that the psyche is an emancipation of function from its instinctual form and so from the compulsiveness which, as sole determinant of the function, causes it to harden into a mechanism. The psychic condition or quality begins where the

function loses its outer and inner determinism and becomes capable of more extensive and freer application . . .[16]

As information moves from soma to psyche, it passes through the psychoid region, and as a result there is a considerable softening of biological determinism, which then gives way to a more "extensive and freer application . . . where it begins to show itself accessible to a will motivated from other sources."[17] The appearance of will is decisive for establishing a function as psychic. Hunger and sexuality, for instance, are somatically-based drives that involve the release of hormones. Both are instincts. One must eat, and the body craves sexual release. But will enters the picture, since choices can be made about what is eaten or how to satisfy one's sexual urges. Will can intervene to an extent, even if it cannot absolutely control a person's ultimate behavior in all respects.

If there is a limit on the psyche at the somatic end of the spectrum (the *partie inferieur*), there is also a limit at the *partie superieur* of consciousness: "with increasing freedom from sheer instinct the *partie superieur* [consciousness] will ultimately reach a point at which the intrinsic energy of the function ceases altogether to be oriented by instinct in the original sense, and attains a so-called 'spiritual' form."[18] Instinct loses control over the psyche at a certain point, but other factors enter to control and orient it. These factors Jung calls "spiritual," but the translation of the German *"geistlich"* presents a problem here. Another English adjective that could be used just as well is "mental." These controlling factors are mental—they are of the mind, in the sense of the Greek *nous*—and they are no longer organically based. They may operate like instincts, in the sense of calling the will into action, and they may even cause the body to secrete hormones. Jung wants to tie the whole system of soma, psyche, and spirit together while preserving analytic distinctions among the various aspects.

The ego is motivated in part by instincts, in part by mental forms and images. And the ego has some freedom of choice among its various options. It enjoys an amount of "disposable libido"[19] even if its motivations are grounded in instinct or governed by spirit. Jung, ever the biologist and medical psychologist, refused to distance himself very far from drives and instincts. Even the will, the very essence of what defines psyche, is motivated by biological drives: "the motivation of the will must in the first place be regarded as essentially biological."[20] The instincts lose their potency, however, at the mental end of the psychic spectrum: "at the . . . upper limit of the psyche, where the function breaks free from its original goal, the instincts lose their influence as movers of the will. Through having its form altered, the function is pressed into the service of other determinants or motivations which apparently have nothing further to do with the instincts."[21]

> What I am trying to make clear is the remarkable fact that the will cannot transgress the bounds of the psychic sphere: it cannot coerce the instinct, nor has it power over the spirit, in so far as we understand by this something more than the intellect. Spirit and instinct are by nature autonomous and both limit in equal measure the applied field of the will.[22]

The psychoid boundary defines the gray area between the potentially knowable and the totally unknowable—the potentially controllable and the wholly uncontrollable—aspects of human functioning. This is not a sharp boundary but rather an area of transformation. The psychoid thresholds show an effect that Jung calls "psychization": nonpsychic information becomes *psychized*, passing from the unknowable into the unknown (the unconscious psyche) and then moving toward the known (ego-consciousness). The human psychic apparatus, in short, shows a capacity to psychize material from the somatic and spiritual poles of nonpsychic reality.

If one observes psychic life concretely and clinically, it is never the case that instinctually-based drive data is totally free of mentally-based forms and images. The actual presentation is always a mixture. This is because instinct "bears in itself a pattern of its situation. Always it fulfills an image, and the image has fixed qualities."[23] Instincts function very precisely because they are guided by images and shaped by patterns, which also constitute the meaning of the instinct. At this point in his essay, Jung links archetypes, the basic mental patterns, with instincts. Instincts are guided and oriented by archetypal images. On the other hand, however, archetypes can behave like instincts:

> To the extent that the archetypes intervene in the shaping of con-scious contents by regulating, modifying, and motivating them, they act like the instincts. It is therefore very natural to suppose that these factors [the archetypes] are connected with the instincts, and to inquire whether the typical situational patterns which these collective form-principles apparently represent are not in the end identical with the instinctual patterns, namely, with the patterns of behavior.[24]

So closely connected are archetypal patterns and instinctual drives that one might be tempted to reduce one to the other, claiming one or the other holds priority. There was the Freudian option, but Jung rejected it as biological reductionism. Freud would hold that archetypes (though he did not use this term) are nothing but imaginal representations of the two basic instincts, Eros and Thanatos. This option would posit archetypes as images of instinct and as derivative from them. Jung concedes that this argument is formidable: "I must admit that up to the present I have not laid hold of any argument that would finally refute this possibility."[25] Since Jung could not prove unequivocally that archetypes and instincts are not identical, biological reductionism remained a possibility. However, he also knew that

> archetypes have, when they appear, a distinctly numinous character which can only be described as 'spiritual', if 'magical' is too strong a word. Consequently this phenomenon is of the utmost significance for the psychology of religion. In its effects it is anything but unam-biguous. It can be healing or destructive, but never indifferent, pro-vided of course that it has attained a certain degree of clarity. This aspect deserves the epithet 'spiritual' above all else. It not infrequently happens that the archetype appears in the form of a spirit in dreams or fantasy products, or even comports itself like a ghost. There is a mystical aura about its numinosity, and it has a corresponding effect upon the emotions. It mobilizes philosophical and religious convic-tions in the very people who deemed themselves miles above any such fit of weakness. Often it drives with unexampled passion and remorseless logic towards its goal and draws the subject under its spell, from which despite the most desperate resistance he is unable,

and finally no longer even willing, to break free, because the experience brings with it a depth and fullness of meaning that was
unthinkable before.[26]

Archetypal images and the ideas derived from them have an
extraordinary power to sway consciousness, every bit as forcefully
as the identifiable instincts. This tended to persuade Jung that
archetypes are not limited to instincts, that spirit is not reducible
to body, nor mind to brain.

When the ego comes upon an archetypal image, it may become
possessed by it, overwhelmed, and give up even wanting to resist,
for the experience feels so rich and meaningful. Identification
with archetypal images and energies constitutes Jung's definition
of inflation and even, eventually, psychosis. A charismatic leader,
for example, convinces people with powerful words and stimulates ideas for action, and suddenly those ideas become the most
important thing in life for the mesmerized followers and true
believers. Life itself may be sacrificed for images such as the flag
or the cross and for ideas like nationalism, patriotism, and loyalty
to one's religion or country. Crusades and countless other irrational or impractical endeavors have been engaged in because the
participants felt, "This makes my life meaningful! This is the most
important thing I've ever done." Images and ideas powerfully
motivate the ego and generate values and meanings. Cognitions
frequently override and dominate instincts.

In contrast to the impact of the instincts on the psyche—when
one feels driven by a physical need or necessity—the influence of
archetypes leads to being caught up in big ideas and visions. Both
affect the ego in a similar way dynamically, in that the ego is taken
over, possessed, and driven.

"In spite or perhaps because of its affinity with instinct, the
archetype represents the authentic element of spirit, but a spirit
which is not to be identified with the human intellect, since it is
the latter's *spiritus rector*."[27] The distinction between spirit and
intellect is easily confused, so Jung made an effort to state clearly
that he is not speaking of the thinking function, but rather of the
spiritus rector (guiding spirit), which guides the ego and its various functions. Gripped by an archetype, one's thinking function

may be used to rationalize the archetypal idea and to bring it toward realization. One might even become a theologian! When they are gripped by archetypal ideas, theologians will produce elaborate rationales to help integrate their archetypally based visions and ideas into a cultural context. But it is not the thinking function that grips them and motivates their efforts; rather it is the element of vision, archetypally rooted in nous, that directs the thinking function. Jung says baldly that the "essential content of all mythologies and all religions and all isms is archetypal."[28]

The Relationship between Archetypes and Instincts

While it is true that instincts and archetypes belong together "as correspondences,"[29] Jung clearly does not want to say that archetypes can be reduced to instincts or instincts to archetypes. They are intimately related as correspondences and they " subsist side by side as reflections in our own minds of the opposition that underlies all psychic energy."[30] The psyche exists in the space between pure body and transcendent mind, between matter and spirit, and "psychic processes seem to be balances of energy flowing between spirit and instinct."[31] The psyche is an inbetween phenomenon, and its processes "behave like a scale along which consciousness 'slides'. At one moment it finds itself in the vicinity of instinct, and falls under its influence; at another, it slides along to the other end where spirit predominates and even assimilates the instinctual processes most opposed to it."[32] There is a kind of eternal shuttle between *partie inferieur* and *partie superieur*, between the instinctual pole and the spiritual, archetypal pole of the psyche. Consciousness struggles "in a regular panic against being swallowed up in the primitivity and unconsciousness of sheer instinctuality"[33] on the one hand, but it also resists complete possession by spiritual forces (i.e., psychosis) on the other. When coordinated, however, the archetype provides form and meaning to the instinct, and instinct provides raw physical energy to archetypal images to assist them in realizing the "spiritual goal toward which the whole nature of man strives; it is the sea to which all rivers wend their way, the prize which the hero wrests from the fight with the dragon."[34]

Jung maps the psyche as a spectrum, with the archetype at the ultraviolet end and the instinct at the infrared end. "Because the archetype is a formative principle of instinctual power, its blue is contaminated with red; it appears to be violet, or again, we could interpret the simile as an apocatastasis of instinct raised to a higher frequency, just as we could easily derive instinct from a latent (i.e., transcendent) archetype that manifests itself on a longer wavelength."[35] In practice and actual experience, instincts and archetypes are always found in mixed and never in pure form. The archetypal and the instinctual ends of the psychic spectrum come together in the unconsciousness, where they struggle with one another, intermingle, and unite to form units of energy and motivation which then appear in consciousness as urges, strivings, ideas, and images. What we experience in the psyche has been first psychized and then packaged in the unconscious.

Imagine a line running through the psyche and connecting instinct and spirit at either end of it. This line is attached to archetype on one end and to instinct at the other. It passes information and data through the psychoid realm into the collective and then into the personal unconscious. From there these contents make their way into consciousness. Instinctual perceptions and archetypal representations are the data of actual psychic experience, not the instincts and archetypes in themselves. Neither of the ends of the spectrum can be experienced directly, for neither is psychic. At the ends, the psyche fades into matter and spirit. And what are experienced as archetypal images "are very varied structures which all point back to one essentially 'irrepresentable' basic form."[36] All the archetypal information patterns come from a single source, an entity beyond human grasp for which Jung reserves the term *self*. This basic form "is characterized by certain formal elements and by certain fundamental meanings, although these can be grasped only approximately."[37] It is Jung's God term. (The self will be discussed in detail in chapter 7.) The archetypal images that link the self and ego-consciousness form a middle realm, which Jung calls *anima* and *animus*, the realm of soul (treated in chapter 6). In Jung's view, polytheistic religions stem from and represent the realm of the anima and animus, while monotheistic religions base themselves on and point to the self archetype.

On Jung's map, the psyche is a region that is located in the space between pure matter and pure spirit, between the human body and the transcendent mind, between instinct and archetype. He shows it as stretched between two ends of a spectrum that has openings at either end permitting an entrance of information into the psyche. At the ends of the psyche are the psychoid areas that produce quasi-psychic effects like psychosomatic symptoms and parapsychological happenings. As information passes through the psychoid area, it becomes psychized and transformed into psyche. In the psyche, matter and spirit meet. First these packages of information pass into the collective unconscious where they become somewhat contaminated by other contents already in the unconscious, and eventually they may enter consciousness in the form of intuitions, visions, dreams, perceptions of instinctual drives, images, emotions, and ideas. The ego must deal with emerging unconscious contents by making judgments about their value and sometimes decisions about whether or not to act on them. The burden of choice is placed on ego-consciousness to deal ethically with these invasions from inner space.

The Revealed
and the Concealed in
Relations with Others
(Persona and Shadow)

It was an early observation of Jung's—later developed into theoretical propositions—that the psyche consists of many parts and
centers of consciousness. In this inner universe, there is not simply one planet, but an entire solar system and more. One can speak
of people as having *a* personality, but in fact this is made up of a
cluster of subpersonalities.

Jung elaborated these. There is the ego complex; then there are
the multitude of lesser personal complexes, of which the mother
complex and the father complex are the most important and most
powerful; and finally one finds the many archetypal images and
constellations. In a sense, we are made of many potentially divergent attitudes and orientations, and these can easily fall into opposition with one another and create conflicts that lead to neurotic
personality styles. In this chapter, I will describe a pair of these
divergent subpersonalities, the *shadow* and the *persona*. They are
complementary structures and exist in every developed human

psyche. Both of these are named after concrete objects in sensate experience. The shadow is the image of ourselves that slides along behind us as we walk toward the light. The persona, its opposite, is named after the Roman term for an actor's mask. It is the face we wear to meet the social world around us.

At the beginning of life, the personality is a simple undifferentiated unity. It is unformed and more potential than real, and it is whole. As development takes place, this wholeness becomes differentiated, and it separates into parts. Ego-consciousness comes into being, and as it grows it leaves behind much of the whole self in what is now the "unconscious." The unconscious, in turn, becomes structured as material clusters around imagoes, internalizations, and traumatic experiences to form the subpersonalities, the complexes. The complexes (as I discussed in chapter 2) are autonomous, and exhibit consciousness of their own. They also bind a certain amount of psychic energy and have a will of their own.

The Ego's Shadow

One of the unconscious psychic factors that the ego cannot control is the shadow. In fact, the ego is usually quite unaware that it even casts a shadow. Jung used the term shadow to denote a psychological reality that is relatively easy to grasp on an imagistic level but more difficult to grapple with on the practical and theoretical levels. He wants to highlight the flagrant unconsciousness that most people exhibit. Rather than referring to the shadow as a thing, however, it is better to think of psychological traits or qualities that are "in the shadow" (i.e., hidden, behind one's back, in the dark) or "shadowy." Whatever parts of the personality that would ordinarily belong to the ego if they were integrated, but have been suppressed because of cognitive or emotional dissonance, fall into the shadow. The specific contents of the shadow may change, depending upon the ego's attitudes and its degree of defensiveness. Generally, the shadow has an immoral or at least a disreputable quality, containing features of a person's nature that are contrary to the customs and moral conventions of society. The

shadow is the unconscious side of the ego's operations of intending, willing, and defending. It is the backside of the ego, so to
speak.

Every ego has a shadow. This is unavoidable. In adapting to
and coping with the world, the ego, quite unwittingly, employs the
shadow to carry out unsavory operations that it could not perform
without falling into a moral conflict. Without the ego's knowledge,
these protective and self-serving activities are carried out in the
dark. The shadow operates much like a nation's secret espionage
system—without the explicit knowledge of the head of state, who
is therefore allowed to deny culpability. Although introspection
can to some extent bring these shadowy ego operations to consciousness, the ego's own defenses against shadow awareness are
usually so effective that little can penetrate them. Asking close
friends or a longterm spouse to reveal their honest perceptions is
usually more useful as a method of gathering information about
the ego's shadow operations than introspection.

If the ego's willing, choosing, and intending are tracked deeply
enough, one comes to realms of darkness and coldness where it
becomes apparent that the ego has the capacity, in its shadow, to
be extremely selfish, willful, unfeeling, and controlling. Here a
person is purely egoistic and intent on fulfilling personal desires
for power and pleasure at any cost. This heart of darkness within
the ego is the very definition of human evil[1] as it is played out in
myth and story. The figure Iago in Shakespeare's *Othello* is a classic example. In the shadow reside all the familiar cardinal sins.
Jung identified Freud's notion of the *id* with the shadow.

If shadow traits to some extent become conscious and integrated, a person is very different from the average individual.
Most people do not know that they are quite as self-centered and
egotistical as they are, and they want to appear unselfish and in
control of their appetites and pleasures. People tend rather to hide
such traits from others and themselves behind a facade that
shows them to be considerate, thoughtful, empathic, reflective,
and genial. The exceptions to this social norm are those who have
formed a "negative identity"—the black sheep who are proud of
their greed and aggressiveness and flaunt such traits in public,

while in their hidden shadow side they are sensitive and sentimental. Other exceptions are those who have nothing to lose, the
out-and-out criminals and sociopaths. Some notorious individuals, like Hitler or Stalin for instance, gain so much power that
they can afford to indulge their evil passions to the fullest degree
imaginable. Most people, however, think of themselves as decent
and conduct themselves according to the rules of propriety in
their social circles and only reveal shadowy elements by accident,
in dreams, or when pushed to extremes. For them the shadow side
of the ego still operates, but through the unconscious, manipulat-
ing the environment and the psyche so that certain intentions and
needs get satisfied in a socially acceptable manner. What the ego
wants in the shadow is not necessarily bad in and of itself, however, and often the shadow, once faced, is not as evil as imagined.

The shadow is not experienced directly by the ego. Being
unconscious, it is projected onto others. When one is tremen-
dously irritated by a really egotistical person, for instance, that
reaction is usually a signal that an unconscious shadow element
is being projected. Naturally the other person has to present a
"hook" for the shadow projection, and so there is always a mixture
between perception and projection in such strong emotional reactions. The psychologically naive or the defensively resistant person will focus on and argue for the perception and will ignore the
projective part. This defensive strategy, of course, forecloses the
possibility of using the experience to gain awareness of shadow
features and for possible integration of them. Instead, the defensive ego insists on feeling self-righteous and casts itself in the role
of innocent victim or simple observer. The other person is the evil
monster, while the ego feels like an innocent lamb. Of such
dynamics are scapegoats made.

The Making of the Shadow

The specific contents and qualities that go into making up this
internal structure, the shadow, are selected by the process of ego
development. What ego-consciousness rejects becomes shadow;
what it positively accepts and identifies with and absorbs into

itself becomes a part of itself and of the persona. The shadow is characterized by the traits and qualities that are incompatible with the conscious ego and the persona. The shadow and the persona are both ego-alien "persons" that inhabit the psyche along with the conscious personality that we know ourselves to be. There is the official and "public person" that Jung called the *persona,* and this is more or less identified with ego-consciousness and forms the psycho-social identity of the individual. And yet it is also, like the shadow, ego-alien, although the ego is more at ease with it because it is compatible with social norms and mores. The shadow personality is hidden away from sight and comes out only on special occasions. The world is more or less unaware of this person. The persona is much more evident. It plays an official role, daily, of adaptation to the social world. Shadow and persona are like two brothers (for a man) or sisters (for a woman); one is out in public, and the other is hidden away and reclusive. They are a study in contrasts. If one is blond, the other is dark; if one is rational, the other is emotional. Narcissus and Goldmund, Dr. Jekyll and Mr. Hyde, Cain and Abel, Eve and Lilith, Aphrodite and Hera—these figures are such pairs. The one complements—or more often opposes—the other. Persona and shadow are usually more or less exact opposites of one another, and yet they are as close as twins.

The persona is the person that we become as a result of acculturation, education, and adaptation to our physical and social environments. As I mentioned, Jung borrowed this term from the Roman stage where *persona* referred to the actor's mask. By putting on a mask, the actor assumed a specific role and an identity within the drama, and his voice was projected out through the mouthpiece cut into the mask's face. Taken psychologically, the persona is a functional complex whose job is both to conceal and to reveal an individual's conscious thoughts and feelings to others. As a complex, the persona possesses considerable autonomy and is not under the full control of the ego. Once in role, the actor rattles off his or her lines willy-nilly and often without much consciousness. "How are you?" someone asks on a rainy morning, and quick as a wink, without a moment's hesitation, you say, "Just fine, how about you?" The persona makes casual social interaction go more easily, and it smoothes the rough spots that might otherwise cause awkwardness or social distress.

The shadow, a complementary functional complex, is a sort of counter-persona. The shadow can be thought of as a subpersonality who wants what the persona will not allow. Mephistopheles in Goethe's *Faust* is a classic example of a shadow figure. Faust is a bored intellectual who has seen it all, has read all the important books and has learned everything he wants to know, and now he has run out of gas and the will to live. He is depressed and contemplating suicide when a little poodle suddenly runs across his path and then changes into Mephistopheles. Mephistopheles entices Faust to leave his study and to go out into the world with him, to experience his other side, his sensuality. He introduces Faust to his inferior functions, sensation and feeling, and to the thrills and excitement of his hitherto unlived sexual life. This is a side of life that his persona as professor and intellectual had not permitted. Under the guidance of Mephistopheles, Faust goes through what Jung called enantiodromia, a reverse of the personality into its opposite character type. He embraces the shadow and indeed for a time becomes identified with its energies and qualities.

To an ego that has been identified with the persona and its assumed values and qualities, the shadow stinks of rottenness and evil. Mephistopheles does embody evil—pure, intentional, willful destructiveness. But the encounter with the shadow also has a transformative effect on Faust. He finds new energy, his boredom vanishes, and he sets out on adventures that will in the end give him a more complete experience of life. The problem of integrating the shadow is a moral and psychological problem of the most thorny sort. If a person completely shuns the shadow, life is proper but it is terribly incomplete. By opening up to shadow experience, however, a person becomes tainted with immorality but attains a greater degree of wholeness. This is truly a devil's bargain. It is Faust's dilemma, and it is a core problem of human existence. In Faust's case, his soul is saved in the end, but only by the grace of God.

The Persona

In his official writings Jung does not go into much detail about the shadow, but he does give an interesting and detailed account of the persona. From this we can draw as well some information about the shadow and its constellation within a personality. I will look now somewhat more closely at what Jung writes about the persona, its position in the psyche and its formation.

He defines this term in the major work *Psychological Types*, published in 1921. This volume concludes with a long chapter titled "Definitions," in which Jung tries to be as clear as possible about the terminology he has adapted from psychoanalysis and taken from psychology in general as well as about the terms he has created for his own analytical psychology. As far as psychology and psychoanalysis are concerned, the term *persona* is Jung's own special intellectual property. Section 48, one of the longest in this chapter, is devoted to the term *soul*, and this is where the persona is discussed. Here Jung reflects on two complementary structures, the persona and the anima. I will discuss the latter in the next chapter.

Today the term persona has been somewhat accepted into the vocabulary of psychology and contemporary culture. It is used frequently in popular parlance, in newspapers, and in literary theory. It means the person-as-presented, not the person-as-real. The persona is a psychological and social construct adopted for a specific purpose. Jung chose it for his psychological theory because it has to do with playing roles in society. He was interested in how people come to play particular roles, adopt a conventional collective attitude, and represent social and cultural stereotypes rather than assuming and living their own uniqueness. Certainly this is a well-known human trait. It is a kind of mimicry. Jung gave it a name and worked it into his theory of the psyche.

Jung begins his definition of the persona by making the point that many psychiatric and psychological studies have shown that the human personality is not simple but complex, that it can be shown to split and to fragment under certain conditions, and that there are many subpersonalities within the normal human psyche. However, "it is at once evident that such a plurality of personalities can never appear in a normal individual."[2] In other words, while we are not all "multiple personalities" in a clinical sense, everyone does manifest "traces of character splitting."[3] The normal individual is simply a less exaggerated version of what is found in pathology. "One has only to observe a man rather closely, under varying conditions, to see that a change from one milieu to another brings about a striking alteration of personality . . . 'angel abroad, devil at home'."[4] In public such an individual is all smiles, backslapping, gladhanding, extroverted, easygoing, happy-go-lucky, joking; at home, on the other hand, he is sour and grumpy, doesn't talk to his kids, sulks and hides behind the newspaper, and can be verbally or otherwise abusive. Character is situational. The story of Jekyll and Hyde represents an extreme form of this. Another novel with the same theme is *The Picture of Dorian Gray*, where the main character keeps a picture of himself in the attic. As he grows older, the portrait ages, revealing his true nature and character; yet he continues to go out in public without wrinkles—youthful, sophisticated, and cheerful.

Jung goes on to discuss the fascinating subject of human sensitivity to milieus, to social environments. People are usually sensitive to other people's expectations. Jung points out that particular milieus such as families, schools, and workplaces require one to assume specific attitudes. By "attitude" Jung means "an a priori orientation to a definite thing, no matter whether this be represented in consciousness or not."[5] An attitude can be latent and unconscious, but it is constantly operating to orient a person to a situation or a milieu. Further, an attitude is "a combination of psychic factors or contents which will . . . determine action in this or that definite direction."[6] An attitude is a feature of character, therefore. The longer an attitude persists and the more frequently it is called upon to meet the demands of a milieu, the more habitual it becomes. As behaviorism would express it, the more frequently a behavior or attitude is reinforced by the environment, the stronger and the more entrenched it becomes. People can be trained to develop specific attitudes to certain milieus and thus to respond in particular ways, reacting to signals or cues as they have been trained to do. Once an attitude has been fully developed, all that is required to activate behavior is the appropriate cue or trigger. Jung observed this in 1920, about the time that behaviorism was gaining ground in North America, led by John Broadus Watson, whose first major publication appeared in 1913.

In contrast to people living and working in rural or natural areas, which are relatively unified environments, many educated urban dwellers move in two totally different milieus: the domestic circle and the public world. This was more true of men than of women in the Europe of Jung's day. Men of Jung's time and culture worked in one environment and lived domestically in another, and they had to respond to two distinctly different milieus, each of which provided a different set of cues. "These two totally different environments demand two totally different attitudes, which, depending on the degree of the ego's identification with the attitude of the moment, produce a duplication of character."[7]

A friend of mine has a midlevel managerial job in a government agency, and so he must set the tone for employees in his group regarding values and behavioral patterns in the public sector. The agency is a milieu, and he finds out from other sources what the correct values are and then informs the workers under him that, for example, they must be sensitive to such issues as nondiscrimination, sexism, and affirmative action. My friend told me that he plays that role easily and well in the workplace, but when he watches TV in the privacy of his own home he has very different reactions. There he is ultraconservative. In the workplace he is a liberal and enlightened modern man. His ego is not, however, strongly identified with the attitude of that milieu. He has a functional persona: one that he puts on and takes off easily without identifying with it. My friend is very clear in his own mind that he does not identify with that workplace persona.

Frequently, however, the ego does identify with the persona. The psychological term *identification* points to the ego's ability to absorb and unite with external objects, attitudes, and persons.

This is a more or less unconscious process. One simply finds one-self unintentionally imitating another person. Perhaps one does not even notice it oneself, but other people see the mimicry. In principle, one can say that the ego is quite separate from the per-sona, but in actual life this is often not the case, because the ego tends to identify with the roles it plays in life. "The domestic char-acter is, as a rule, molded by emotional demands and an easy-going acquiescence for the sake of comfort and convenience; whence it frequently happens that men who in public life are extremely energetic, spirited, obstinate, willful and ruthless appear good-natured, mild, compliant, even weak, when at home and in the bosom of the family. Which is the true character, the real personality? This question is often impossible to answer."[8]

Even so, there is always more to the ego than persona identifi-cation. The persona will at most form a close wrapping around the side of the ego that faces out into the social world. But people will usually still recognize a difference between role and true inner identity. The ego's core is archetypal as well as individual and personal. This is the still, small point of reflection, the center of the "I." The archetypal side of the ego's core is pure "I am," a manifestation of the self. It is simply "I-am-ness" (see chapter 1).

On the personal side, however, the ego is permeable to influence from external forces. Such influence makes its way into the ego and pushes aside this pure "I-ness" as the ego identifies with the new content. This is the ego "learning." We learn our names. After that we become our names, we identify with the sounds of them. When the ego is identified with the persona, it feels identical to it. Then I *am* my name; I *am* the son of my father and mother, the brother of my sister. Once this identification is made, I am no longer simply "I am that I am," but instead, I am Murray Stein, born on such-and-such a date, with this particular personal history. This is who I am now. I identify with memories, with a construction of my history, with some of my qualities. In this way the pure "I-ness"—the arche-typal piece—can get obscured and go into hiding or disappear from the conscious altogether. Then one is truly dependent upon the per-sona for one's entire identity and sense of reality, not to mention one's sense of self-worth and belonging.

Of course this can also fluctuate. At times one can be in the pure "I-am" state, not identifying with anything in particular; at other times one is firmly identified with some content or quality and heavily invested in a persona image. T.S. Eliot said of cats that they have three names: one that everybody knows, one that only a few know, and one that only the cat knows! The first and second refer to the persona, the third refers to the archetypal core of the ego.

The Two Sources of the Persona

Jung found two sources of the persona: "In accordance with social conditions and requirements, the social character is oriented on the one hand by the expectations and demands of society, and on the other by the social aims and aspirations of the individual."[9] The first, the expectations and demands of the milieu, includes such requirements as being a certain kind of person, behaving appropriately according to the social mores of the group, and often believing in certain propositions about the nature of reality (such as consenting to religious teachings). The second source includes the individual's social ambitions.

In order for society to be able to influence one's attitudes and behavior, one must want to belong to society. The ego must be motivated to accept the persona features and the roles that society requires and offers, or else they will simply be avoided. There will be no identification at all. An agreement must be struck between the individual and society in order for persona formation to take hold. Otherwise the individual lives an isolated life on the margins of culture, forever a sort of uneasy adolescent in an adult world. This is different from the heroic rebel who goes his own way and ignores social norms. That is another kind of persona, and one that is offered by all societies and groups. There are many roles to play.

Generally speaking, the more prestigious the role, the stronger is the tendency to identify with it. People do not usually identify with lower-class persona roles like garbage collector or janitor, or even middleclass roles like manager or superintendent. If they do, they often do so humorously. These jobs have their own value and dignity but they do not imply roles to wear proudly in society, and the temptation to identify strongly with them is minimal. Role identification is generally motivated by ambition and social aspiration. For example, a person who is elected to the United States Senate acquires a role with high collective value and enormous prestige. With it come fame, honor, and high social visibility, and the person who is a senator tends to fuse with this role, even to the extent of wishing to be treated by close friends with conspicuous respect. It has been reported that after John F. Kennedy's election as president of the United States even his close family members called him Mr. President.

In Ingmar Bergman's autobiographical film *Fanny and Alexander,* a little boy is sent to live with a horrible, abusive bishop who is emotionally remote and cold and deeply identified with a religious persona. In one scene of the film, the bishop is shown dreaming. In the dream, he is struggling to tear off a mask, which he cannot detach, and he ends up pulling his face off along with the mask. The bishop's ego is utterly fused with the bishop persona because that role has guaranteed his personal aspirations in life. A bishop is without doubt a highranking person in society. Similarly physicians, military men, and royalty are granted personas that attract strong identification. And yet the bishop, in his nightmare, tries to remove the mask from his face. Why?

The relation between ego and persona is not simple because of the contradictory aims of these two functional complexes. The ego moves in a fundamental way toward separation and individuation, toward consolidating a position first of all outside of the unconscious, and then also somewhat outside of the family milieu. There is in the ego a strong movement toward autonomy, toward an "I-ness" that can function independently. At the same time, another part of the ego, which is where the persona takes root, is moving in the opposite direction, toward relating and adapting to the object world. These are two contrary tendencies within the ego—a need for separation and independence on the one hand, and a need for relationship and belonging on the other. The ego's radical desire for separation/individuation is often rooted in the shadow because it is so threatening both to group life and to the individual's well-being. Objectively, we all need other people in order to survive physically and psychologically. The ego's movement toward relationship and adaptation to the present milieu, which seeks to insure survival, provides the opportunity for the persona to take hold. And this then becomes a person's self-presentation to the world.

Persona Development

This conflict in the ego between individuation/separation and social conformity generates a good deal of the ego's basic anxiety. How can one be free, unique, and individual while also being accepted and liked by others and accommodating to their needs and wishes. Clearly a source of fundamental conflict exists between ego and persona development. By early adulthood, one hopes that sufficient development has taken place in both ego and persona so that the ego's dual needs for independence and relationship are satisfied, while at the same time the persona has made a suitable enough adaptation so that the ego can live in the real world. Famous geniuses like Wagner, Beethoven, and Picasso seem to be exceptions to this rule in that their gifts grant them license to be themselves as individuals to an extraordinary degree. They are forgiven their excesses because of what they offer the world in compensation.

The ego does not deliberately choose to identify with a particular persona. People find themselves in milieus in which they have to survive, and most do their best to make their way ahead. Birth order is an important factor, also gender. A little girl or boy observes what other kids are doing and imitates them. Little girls try out their mothers' attitudes while trying on their mothers' clothes. Little boys also try on their mothers' clothes sometimes, and their parents worry about it. Clothes represent the persona. Little boys more frequently imitate their fathers or brothers, wearing caps when they do, and swagger and spit if that's what the others are doing. Gender is certainly one way in which we sort ourselves out early on, and these features are taken up in the persona. A youngster realizes that he or she is treated in a certain way if the behavior is right, and responds in a gender-appropriate manner. This may come quite naturally to the individual child or not. Sometimes the persona fits, sometimes it does not. Eventually an attitude is formed that is at least adequate, if not enhancing, in terms of gender-related attractiveness. (The deeper issues related to gender and gender identification will be discussed in the following chapter.)

Persona development has two potential pitfalls. One is over-identification with the persona. The individual becomes unduly concerned with pleasing and adapting to the social world and comes to believe that this constructed image is all there is to the personality. The other problem lies in not paying enough attention to the external object world and being too exclusively involved with the inner world (a condition that Jung will describe as anima or animus possession). Such a person attends to impulses, wishes, desires, and fantasies, and is so taken up with that world and identified with it that not enough attention is paid to other people. Consequently, such a person tends to be inconsiderate, blind, and unrelated to others, and gives up these characteristics only when forced to do so by the harshest blows of fate.

Persona development is typically a major problem in adolescence and early adulthood, when there is so much activity in the inner world, so many impulses, fantasies, dreams, desires, ideologies and idealisms on the one side and so much peer pressure toward conformity on the other. Relatedness to the larger social world may look very primitive and collective, unbalanced by a kind of horde mentality, an identification with the peer group and its collective values. Such identification with the peer group assists the adolescent in breaking free from parents, a necessary step toward maturity. At the same time, the teenager is blindly inconsiderate, indeed, almost unaware, of the object world and lives in a fantasy of invincibility. Adults tend to apply terms like inflation and grandiosity to describe this combination of hypertrophy of the inner world and maladaptation to outer reality. On the other hand, some adolescents pay too much attention to adult values and expectations. Dressed in their button-down shirts, carrying briefcases, and, at fifteen, talking about becoming corporate attorneys, they are so adapted to expectations of family and culture that not much personal identity is developing. They are on the way to becoming mere stereotypes of cultural forms, victims of premature persona adaptation.

Both introverts and extroverts develop a persona, for both attitude types must relate to the world of objects. For extroverts, however, the development of the persona is a simpler process than it is for introverts. Extroverted libido goes to the object and stays there, and extroverts record and relate to objects without much fuss or complication. For introverts, attention and psychic energy go out to objects but then return to the subject, and this creates a more complicated relation to objects. An object is not only something outside the psyche but is also, for the introvert, profoundly inside the psyche. Attachment is more difficult. Extroverts, therefore, have an easier time finding a suitable persona. They are more at ease with the object world because it doesn't threaten them so intimately. The introvert's persona is more ambiguous, diffident or uncertain, and varies from one context to another.

For everyone, though, the persona must relate to objects and protect the subject. This is its dual function. While introverts can be very outgoing with a few people, in a large group they shrink and disappear and the persona often feels inadequate, particularly with strangers and in situations in which the introvert does not occupy a defined role. Cocktail parties are a torture, but acting a role on stage may be a pure joy and pleasure. Many famous actors and actresses are quite deeply introverted. In private they may be shy, but given a public role they feel protected and secure and can easily pass as the most extroverted types imaginable.

The persona, when used creatively within the context of a strong psychological development, functions to express as well as to hide aspects of the personality. An adequate persona is broad enough not only to express the socially appropriate aspects of the personality but also to be genuine and plausible. The individual can, without much damage, identify with a persona to the extent that it is an true expression of personality. Of course this may change with age, and new personas appear as individuals enter new stages of life. Social extroverts may become more introverted, for example, as they pass into their 50's and 60's. Later in life one also realizes there is a difference between feeling that the persona is true, honest, and genuine on the one hand and fully and unconsciously identifying with it on the other.

Essentially, the persona, which is the psychic skin between ego and world, is not only a product of interaction with objects, but includes as well the individual's projections onto those objects. We adapt to what we perceive other people are and what they want. This may be considerably different from how others see them or how they see themselves. Wrapped into the fabric of the persona are projections that originate in the complexes, for instance in the parental complexes, and return to the subject via the introjective process and enter into the persona. This is why early childhood has such a profound effect upon adult personas. Even after parents are long since outgrown and left behind, they continue to affect the persona because they are projected into the world from the parental complexes and are continually adapted to by the individual's persona. We are good little boys and girls long after we need to be. Carrying the persona over from one context to another presents problems because, in a continuing effort to adapt, the original context is projected onto new, quite different situations. This was Freud's observation concerning "transference." The old context of childhood is transferred into the new context of the doctor-patient relationship. Until one realizes how milieus are different, one perseveres in old habitual behaviors, responding to the new milieu as though it were the old familiar one.

The Persona's Transformations

The archetypal core of the ego does not change over time, but the persona can be and is modified many times in the course of a lifetime, depending on the ego's perception of the changed environment and its ability to interact with it. A major change occurs in the passage from childhood into adolescence; another in the passage from adolescence into adulthood; another in the course of the mid-life transition from early adulthood into middle age; yet another in the transition into old age. The competent ego meets each of these adaptational challenges with appropriate alterations in self-concept and persona self-presentation. People think differently of themselves, dress differently, cut their hair differently, buy different kinds of cars and houses depending on their age, marital status, economic and social class, and peer-group preferences. All of this is reflected in persona changes.

The various roles one assumes in the course of a lifetime have, of course, a collective and to some extent archetypal basis. The persona has, like every functional complex, an archetypal core. There are predictable, typical roles to be filled in all human groups. For example, there is the oldest child who is the Little Adult, and the mischievous Trickster Kid who is still playing practical jokes in middle and old age, and the alluring Femme Fatale who flirts and seduces her way through life beginning in earliest childhood. Families assign roles in typical ways to their children and their adult members. Birth order of children often plays a large role in the personas they will adopt. The first child is a responsible little grownup, the middle child is a mediator, and the youngest child is the creative baby. The black sheep role is found everywhere and in all times, as is the scapegoat. People are assigned such roles by unconscious dynamics within families and groups, and when they accept them in childhood they often carry some version of the role with them throughout life.

What is it that causes personas to stick to people with tenacity? In part it is identification and sheer familiarity. A persona becomes identified with one's personality. It offers a psychosocial identity. But shame is also a fundamental motivator. The persona protects one from shame, and the avoidance of shame is probably the strongest motive for developing and holding on to a persona. Ruth Benedict's writings on shame and guilt cultures showed that western nations are characteristically guilt cultures and eastern countries are by contrast shame cultures. Shame cultures emphasize persona more than do guilt cultures, in the sense that if one loses *face* one might as well die. Loss of face is the ultimate crisis. The situation is quite different in guilt cultures where guilt can be assuaged or redressed: the guilty person can pay the price and be restored to community.

Guilt involves a discrete action, whereas shame wipes out one's whole sense of self-worth. Shame is a more primitive, and potentially a more destructive kind of emotion. We tend to feel either guilty about or profoundly ashamed of the things we do that are at odds with the adopted persona. This is the realization of shadow in the personality. Shadow induces shame, a sense of unworthiness, a feeling of uncleanness, of being soiled and unwanted. To be well-trained is to be proud; to soil oneself is shameful. Nature has been conquered by the toilet-trained ego. Such experiences of shame include anything that does not fit into the way we were trained: to be a good person, the right kind of person; to fit in, to be accepted. In a puritanical culture like ours, particular kinds of sexual fantasies and behaviors that are not appropriate to a "good person's" persona easily lead to feelings of shame. Another shadow feature is aggression. Feeling aggressive, hateful, or envious are shaming emotions.

These normal human reactions tend to be hidden away; we are embarrassed by them, in the same way that we are ashamed of certain physical or character flaws that we see in ourselves. The persona is the face we put on to meet the other faces, to be like them and to be liked by them. We do not want to be too different, for our points of difference, where the persona ends and the shadow begins, make us ashamed.

Integrating Persona and Shadow

The shadow and persona are a classic pair of opposites, standing in the psyche as polarities of the ego. Since the overall task of psychological development ("individuation," discussed in chapter 8) is integration, and wholeness is the over-arching and supreme value, we need to ask here in a preliminary way at least: What does it mean to integrate persona and shadow? In the context of this chapter's topic, integration hinges on self-acceptance, on fully accepting those parts of oneself that do not belong in the persona image, which is itself usually an image of an ideal or at least of a cultural norm. The personal aspects of which one is ashamed are often felt to be radically evil. While some things truly are evil and destructive, frequently shadow material is not evil. It is only felt to be so because of the shame attached to it due to its nonconformity with the persona.

What is it like when somebody has achieved a measure of integration between persona and shadow? Jung quotes a letter from a former patient, written some time after he saw her for analysis:

> Out of evil, much good has come to me. By keeping quiet, repressing nothing, remaining attentive, and by accepting reality—taking things as they are, and not as I wanted them to be—by doing all this, unusual knowledge has come to me, and unusual powers as well, such as I could never have imagined before. I always thought that when we accepted things they overpowered us in some way or other. This turns out not to be true at all, and it is only by accepting them that one can assume an attitude towards them. So now I intend to play the game of life, being receptive to whatever comes to me, good and bad, sun and shadow forever alternating, and in this way also accepting my own nature with its positive and negative sides. Thus everything becomes more alive to me. What a fool I was! How I tried to force everything to go according to the way I felt it ought to![10]

This woman has stepped back both from the persona and from splitting persona and shadow into opposites, and she is now simply observing, reflecting on and accepting her psyche as it comes to her, then sorting, seeing what it was about, and making some choices. She has created a psychological distance between the ego complex and the persona, as well as between the ego and the shadow. She is no longer possessed on either end of the spectrum.

Jung holds that opposites are united in the psyche through the intervention of a "third thing." A conflict between opposites—persona and shadow, for example—can be regarded as an individuation crisis, an opportunity to grow through integration. Coming into conflict are collective values on the persona side, and shadow aspects of the ego that belong to the individual's native instinctual makeup (Freud's *id*) and also some that are derivative from the archetypes and the unconscious complexes. Since shadow content is not acceptable to the persona, the conflict may be fierce. Jung held that if the two poles are held in tension, a solution will appear if the ego can let go of both and create an inner vacuum in which the unconscious can offer a creative solution in the form of a new symbol. This symbol will present an option for movement ahead that will include something of both—not simply a compromise, but an amalgamation that calls forth a new attitude on the part of the ego and a new kind of relation to the world. This process can be observed as people develop both in therapy and through life experience—as they outgrow their former conflicts, assume new personas, and integrate formerly unacceptable parts of the self.

People do change through therapy and in the course of life development. The persona, as a tool of adaptation, has a great potential for change. It can become increasingly flexible, given that the ego is willing to modify old patterns. Stories such as *Dr. Jekyll and Mr. Hyde* describe a complete split between persona and shadow. In these stories there is no integration, only fluctuation back and forth between the opposites. Shadow roles and impulses are acted out, without the appearance of a transcendent function to bring about an integration of those opposites. One wonders about people in real life who cannot integrate such opposites. In some cases, the dark side may be so extreme and so highly charged with energy that its integration with a socially acceptable persona of any kind is impossible. Today the only solution to this problem is psychotropic medicine, which can put a severe damper on the unconscious and inhibit the shadow's power sources. In other cases, the ego is too unstable and weak to moderate impulsivity enough to allow for the constellation of the transcendent function.

6

The Way to the
Deep Interior
(Anima and Animus)

In his autobiography Jung tells a story about the discovery of the anima.[1] He writes that during his years of intense inner work after breaking with Freud in 1913 there was a period when he questioned himself about the nature and value of what he was doing. Is this science? he asked himself. Or is it art? He was recording his dreams, interpreting them, sometimes painting them, and trying to understand the meaning of his spontaneous fantasies. At a certain moment he heard a female "voice" say, "It is art." Surprised, he entered into a dialogue with her and gradually recognized that she resembled a patient of his. She was thus a sort of internalized figure, but she also spoke for some of his own unconscious thoughts and values. In his own ego and persona Jung was self-identified as a scientist, not an artist. But this voice spoke for another point of view. While retaining his conscious ego position, he began a dialogue with this figure and a study of her. There was more to her than simply the internalized image of his patient. Gradually, through dialogue, she took shape and assumed a fuller personality. "I felt a little awed by her. It was like the feeling of an invisible presence in the room,"[2] he relates.

125

For Jung this was an important inner experience of the *anima*, and it has become a key reference point for the anima's manifestation in the collective memory of analytical psychology. Since Jung many other people who have engaged in active imagination have discovered similar inner figures. Conventionally, for men the anima is a feminine figure; for women the equivalent inner figure—called the *animus*—is masculine. The anima and animus are subjective personalities that represent a deeper level of the unconscious than the shadow. For better or worse, they reveal the features of the soul and lead into the realm of the collective unconscious.

Throughout this chapter I will refer to this inner structure as the anima/us. It is, like the shadow, a personality within the psyche that does not match the self-presentation and self-identity reflected by the persona. It is different from the shadow, however, in that it does not belong to the ego in the same way: it is more "other" than the shadow is. If the distinction between persona and shadow is "good versus bad"—plus and minus, positive and negative aspects of the ego—the distinction between ego and anima/us is marked by the masculine-feminine polarity. It is not the difference between Cain and Abel but between Solomon and the Queen of Sheba.

Defining Anima and Animus

Of all the aspects of Jung's theory, the topic of this chapter has become in many ways the most controversial, for it raises profound gender issues and suggests essential differences in the psychology of men and women. Whereas this subject may have seemed calm and settled in Jung's time, today it stirs a hornet's nest. To some contemporaries it seems that Jung was a man before his time who anticipated and indeed advocated a type of protofeminism. To others he appears to be a spokesman for stereotypic traditional views on the differences between men and women. In fact, I think he was a little of both.

In his later works Jung refers to the anima and animus as archetypal figures of the psyche. Thus they lie essentially beyond the influence of the forces that mold and shape the consciousness of individuals such as family, society, culture, and tradition. Archetypes are not derived from culture; rather cultural forms (in Jung's theory) are derived from archetypes. This definition of the anima/us as archetype therefore places its deepest essence outside of the psyche altogether, in the realm of impersonal spiritual forms and powers. Anima and animus are basic life forms, and they shape human individuals and societies, in addition to other influences that impact them. The archetype is, as we saw in chapter 4, a *Ding an sich* (Kant: "a thing in itself"), and therefore it lies beyond the range of human perception. We can only perceive it indirectly by noting its manifestations.

The anima/us, strictly speaking, is a scientific hypothesis about "something" that exists but cannot be observed directly, like an unknown star whose position and size are known only from measurements of gravitational pulls in its vicinity. And yet, since the manifestations of anima and animus, as Jung noted and described them, do in fact often resemble well-known cultural images embodied by traditional men and women, the question has been raised: Was Jung a victim of his cultural blinders who inadvertently became the exponent of cultural stereotypes? In other words, are the "archetypes" in fact social constructions? *Or,* was Jung investigating deeper structures that perhaps are embedded in these cultural patterns but transcend them and are indeed universal forms of human psychological traits and behavior? I will not answer this question definitively in this chapter, but I hope to advance the case that the issue is more complicated and Jung's thinking more complex than many of his critics have granted. In the meantime, I will try to present his thought as clearly as possible.

We will enter this territory carefully, trying to grasp Jung's meanings for these elusive terms step by step. If the places on the map of psyche which we have examined up to this point seem relatively clear and well-defined, the territory of anima and animus seems at times like a deep and tangled wilderness. Perhaps this is as it should be, for here we are entering the deeper layers of the unconscious, the collective unconscious, the territory of the archetypal images, where boundaries are blurred.

Before approaching the issue of gender in relation to these terms, I should point out that an account can be given of anima and animus that does not draw gender into it at all. Gender can be seen as a secondary feature of the anima/us, just as an object's essence is not determined by blue or pink. There is an abstract, structural way of understanding the anima/us. Because it is possible to speak of this feature of the psyche as abstract structure, I will use, throughout this chapter, the notation "anima/us." This indicates a psychic structure that is common to men and women. The differentiated endings of -a and -us will be used when I mean to refer to the gendered features of this inner object. Abstractly, the anima/us is a psychic structure that (a) is complementary to the persona and (b) links the ego to the deepest layer of the psyche, namely to the image and experience of the self.

As discussed in the previous chapter, the persona is the habitual attitude that an ego adopts to meet the world. It is a public personality and facilitates adaptation to the demands of physical and (primarily) social reality. It is a "functional complex," to use Jung's term from his definition in the 1921 text *Psychological Types*. It operates like the skin on the body, providing a protective barrier between the ego and the outside. The anima/us is similarly a functional complex, but one that is concerned with adaptation to the inner world. "The natural function of the animus (as well as of in the anima) is to remain in place between individual consciousness and the collective unconscious; exactly as the persona is a sort of stratum between the ego-consciousness and the objects of the external world. The animus and the anima should function as a bridge, or a door, leading to the images of the collective unconscious, as the persona should be a sort of bridge into the world."[3] In other words, the anima/us allows the ego to enter into and to experience the depths of the psyche.

In 1921, now freed from his dependence on Freud and ready to launch his own views on depth psychology, Jung published *Psychological Types*, in which he summarized his own new theory to date. In this volume many new terms appeared and were used to define his revisionist views on the nature and structure of the psyche. So much was this the case, that he felt (as I indicated in chapter 5) a need to include a whole chapter of definitions at the conclusion of this work. These are detailed definitions and can be read as a kind of early textbook in analytical psychology. Here he gives extensive coverage to the concepts of anima and animus in the entries on "soul" and "soul-image." These definitions, while somewhat mechanical and simplistic, do help to provide boundaries and to give shape to his terms, at least in the way he was using them at that time.

In approaching the definition of the anima/us, he contrasts it with the persona: "The persona is exclusively concerned with the relation to objects,"[4] while the anima/us concerns the ego's relation to the subject. "By the 'subject' I mean first of all those vague, dim stirrings, feelings, thoughts, and sensations which flow in on us not from any demonstrable continuity of conscious experience of the object, but well up like a disturbing, inhibiting, or at times helpful influence from the dark inner depths."[5] The "subject" here is primarily the world of the unconscious, not the ego. This is the subjective side of the psyche, its ground, its inner space. It contains "inner objects," so to speak, sometimes called by Jung "imagoes" or simply "images" or "contents." Because the term "subject," at least in this specific context, refers to the unconscious, it follows quite logically that "just as there is a relation to the outer object, an outer attitude [i.e., the persona], there is a relation to the inner object, an inner attitude."[6]

Jung concedes that it "is readily understandable that this inner attitude, by reason of its extremely intimate and inaccessible nature, is far more difficult to discern than the outer attitude, which is immediately perceived by everyone."[7] One can easily enough observe a person's treatment of others, but it requires more subtlety to see how people treat themselves. What is their attitude toward the inner world? Is it receptive and warm (as the persona may be), or is it harsh and hypercritical? Many generous people are their own worst enemies within—their own meanest judges and harshest critics—but this is concealed behind a charming and hospitable persona. Or a person may be extremely judgmental of others while treating his own inner life with sentimental self-indulgence. One must know people well before learning how they actually treat themselves inwardly. Do they take themselves seriously? Do they treat themselves like children? The ways they actually feel about their own deeper inner selves characterize their anima or animus attitude.

Jung says further in this passage: "one man will not allow himself to be disturbed in the slightest by his inner processes . . . another man is just as completely at their mercy . . . a vaguely unpleasant sensation puts the idea into his head that he is suffering from a secret disease, a dream fills him with gloomy forebodings . . . One man takes them as physiological, another attributes them to the behaviour of his neighbours, another finds in them a religious revelation."[8] "Thus, Jung concludes, the inner attitude . . . is correlated with just as definite a functional complex as the outer attitude. People who, it would seem, entirely overlook their inner psychic processes no more lack a typical inner attitude than the people who constantly overlook the outer object and the reality of facts lack a typical outer one."[9]

The above summarizes Jung's structural definition of the anima/us as he presented it in 1921 in *Psychological Types*. The anima/us is an attitude that governs one's relationship to the inner world of the unconscious—imagination, subjective impressions, ideas, moods and emotions. So far this says nothing whatever about content of this structure nor about gender. The usual shorthand definition is that the anima is the inner feminine for a man and the animus is the inner masculine for a woman. But one can also simply speak of them as functional structures that serve a specific purpose in relation to the ego. As psychic structure, the anima/us is the instrument by which men and women enter into and adjust to the deeper parts of their psychological natures. As the persona faces out into the social world and assists with necessary external adaptations, so the anima/us faces inward to the inner world of the psyche and helps a person to adapt to the demands and requirements of intuitive thoughts, feelings, images, and emotions that confront the ego.

For instance, a man who is frequently moody is said to have an "anima problem." "He is in the anima today," one might say to a friend. His anima, instead of helping to manage emotions, releases a mood that seeps like a gas into ego consciousness and carries with it, in suspension so to speak, a lot of raw and undifferentiated affect. This has been known to interfere with ego functioning, to say the least. This man's ego becomes identified with the anima personality, which is as a rule hypersensitive and soggy with emotionality. His anima is not highly developed, and instead of helping him to cope with an overwhelming mood it draws him deeper into it. A man given to frequent and intense moodiness has too close a relation with this—usually inferior—part of his personality. Of course if he is a poet like Rilke, who had an anima problem of the first order, he can use this relation creatively. But he may be only uncommonly emotional and overreactive to slights and minor annoyances and injuries and therefore psychologically dysfunctional. His relationships typically are fraught with conflict because he has emotional reactions that are too powerful for him to manage. The anima overwhelms him rather than helps him.

Similarly, a woman with an "animus problem" is also overcome by her unconscious, typically by emotionally charged thoughts and opinions which control her more than she controls them. This is not very different from the anima-possessed man, only the accent tends to be more intellectual on the woman's side. These autonomous ideas and opinions end up disturbing her adaptation to the world because they are delivered with the emotional energy of a bully. Often they wreak havoc on her relationships, because the people near her must build self-protective shields around themselves when they are with her. They feel on the defensive and uncomfortable in her presence. Hard as she may want to be receptive and intimate, she cannot because her ego is subject to these invasions of disruptive energies that transform her into anything but the kinder, gentler person she would like to be. Instead, she is abrasive and gripped by unconscious strivings for power and control. This is what Jung called animus possession. The animus is a powerful personality that is not congruent with the ego or the desired persona. It is "other."

Men in the grip of the anima tend to withdraw into hurt feelings; women in the grip of the animus tend to attack. This is a conventional distinction between the genders, and of course it is subject to revision in the light of recent cultural developments. In both cases, however, whatever the content of the "possession" happens to be, the inner world of the unconscious is not sufficiently held in check, and emotional and irrational neediness disturbs and distorts normal relations with other people and with life in general. Anima/us possession throws the gates of the unconscious wide open and lets in practically everything that has enough energy to come through. Moods and whims sweep in and carry one away. Impulse control is minimal. There is no containment of thought or affect. This is an ego problem, too, of course— symptomatic of an undeveloped ego that cannot hold and contain the contents that normally float into consciousness but need to be reflected upon and digested before being carried into verbal or physical action. But there is also the problem of too little development in the anima/us structure. This lack of development is like an undeveloped muscle. It is too flabby and inadequate to do its job when called upon. Men will then typically look for a woman to help them manage their emotions, and women will typically find a man who can receive their inspired thoughts and do something with them. Thus other people enter the game of ego-anima/us relations.

For the sake of discussion, let me describe an *ideal* psychological development (highly theoretical and improbable as this may be). The conscious and unconscious parts of the psychic system work together in a balanced and harmonious interplay, and this takes place in part between the anima/us and the persona. Here the ego is not flooded by material from without or within but is rather facilitated and protected by these structures. And life energy—libido—flows in a progressive movement into adaptation to the tasks and demands of life. This is a picture of healthy, highly functioning personality with access to inner resources and skilled at outer adjustment. The attitude toward the outer world is balanced, and it is complemented by an attitude toward the world within. Neither is out of joint or inadequately developed. The persona is able to adapt to the demands of life and to manage stable relations with the surrounding social and natural worlds.

Internally there is well managed and steady access to a wellspring of energy and creative inspiration. Outer and inner adaptations are adequate to the demands of life.

Why isn't life more like this? Actually, many people experience something like this from time to time in their lives. These are the good periods of work and love. But these are often relatively shortlived interludes in a much more conflict-ridden picture. One large reason for this is that we develop unevenly. And very little attention is paid in our contemporary culture to true inner development—to what Jung called "individual culture" as opposed to collective (persona-based) culture. Inside, most of us are extremely primitive. It is only when the persona is stripped away and the anima/us opens the gates to the deeper layers of the unconscious—when, as at midlife, for example, the ego is torn by conflict between persona and anima/us—that the need for inner development becomes an acute issue and is taken seriously. While this may look like an outbreak of neurosis, it may well be the call for further individuation, and the challenge to take a deeper journey into the interior on the road toward individual development.

Gender and Anima and Animus

Turning now to the views on anima and animus that imply gender directly, it is first of all noteworthy that these are terms taken from the Latin. Like most cultivated Europeans of his day, Jung was fluent in the classical languages and he found it quite natural and convenient to use these sources to name psychic figures and structures. Anima means "soul" in Latin, and animus means "spirit." (In German these appear as *Seele* and *Geist*.) From one point of view, there is not actually much difference in meaning between these two Latin terms. If one thinks of the *soul (anima)* as leaving the body at death, as the Greeks and Romans supposed, it is equivalent to saying that the *spirit (animus)* has departed. Spirit is often depicted as breath or air, and to catch a person's last breath as it leaves the body is to catch the person's soul. Thus the terms spirit and soul are nearly interchangeable. Also, both words refer to the inner world of persons, to the soulful and the spiritual.

The questions to ask about one's own anima and animus are: What kind of soul do I have? What kind of spirit?

Of course Jung is not speaking of the religious meaning of soul when he uses the term anima. He does not mean the immortal part of a human being, as traditional religious writers use this term. He is capturing the term for psychology, and by it he means to denote the hidden inner side of a man's personality. Similarly, with the term animus he is not referring to something metaphysical and transcendent—the Holy Spirit, for instance—but rather to the hidden inner side of a woman's personality.

The endings of the words connote a gender difference. The ending of anim-a is feminine and the ending of anim-us is masculine. (*Seele* and *Geist* are similarly feminine and masculine respectively in the German language.) So by assigning these terms, the one to men and the other to women, Jung was setting up his theory to show fundamental (that is, archetypal) differences between the sexes. While he would often say that all humans beings share the same archetypes, in this instance he is saying that men have one and women another. Had Jung not wanted to do this he could easily have used the same term for both. Or he could have invented a neutral term, such as "anime." He did not, however, and this is significant. How and why are men different from women in this essential inner way?

Jung argues that both genders have both masculine and feminine components and qualities. In some passages he links this to the fact that each has both masculine and feminine genetic material. Their empirical differences are only a matter of degree. In this emphasis he is perhaps a protofeminist. Jung seems to avoid dividing the human race into two clearly different gender groups with little in common. In his theory, both men and women are both masculine and feminine. However, these qualities are distributed differently. And this difference is archetypal, not societal or cultural. It is not a difference, in other words, that can be erased by changes in social policy. In this respect he runs afoul of at least those contemporary feminists who want to insist on little or no essential psychological difference between men and women. Jung says that men are masculine on the outside and feminine on the inside, and that women are the other way around. Women are relational and receptive in their ego and persona, and they are hard and penetrating on the other side of their personality; men are tough and aggressive on the outside and soft and relational within. Take away the personas of male and female adults, and the perception of gender will be reversed. Women will be harder and more controlling than men, and men will be more nurturing and relational than women.

Statistically at least, if not for each individual, Jung's definition appears to be the rule. If politics are guided by perceptions at the persona level, which is about as much as people will reveal to pollsters, the campaigns of savvy public officials are geared to the view that to win the votes of women they must show compassion, sentiment, and a desire for unity and tolerance; if they are after the male vote they must demonstrate logic, competitiveness, toughness, and moral judgment.[10] On the other hand, according to Jung, the inner worlds of men and women—their hidden personalities, their unconscious other selves—would be the exact opposite of this. In other words, human beings are more complex than public appearance and polls make out. When women look within, they come upon (and reveal to those intimately involved with them) logic, competitiveness, toughness, and moral judgment aplenty. Likewise men show compassion, sentiment, and a desire for unity and tolerance. In part, it is this complexity of human beings that Jung is trying to sort out with his theory of anima and animus.

In his 1921 definition of anima and animus, Jung offers some generalizations from his own observation and experience. These give a glimpse of what he would focus on and emphasize in many of his other later writings. "As to the character of the anima, my experience confirms the rule that it is, by and large, complementary to the character of the persona. The anima usually contains all those common human qualities which the conscious attitude lacks."[11] He had not yet at this point put his notion of shadow in place. This distinction between shadow and anima/us will be sorted out later, and the shadow will take up many of the contents that are complementary to the persona but are excluded from conscious identity because they are incompatible with the persona image. In this passage, Jung is thinking about the type of counter-persona that the shadow will later describe, rather than about complementary attitudes toward outer and inner objects. "The anima usually contains all those common human qualities which the conscious attitude lacks. The tyrant tormented by bad dreams, gloomy forebodings, and inner fears is a typical figure . . . his anima contains all those fallible human qualities his persona lacks. If the persona is intellectual, the anima will quite certainly be sentimental."[12] While these features would later be assigned to the shadow, it is this line of thought that leads to the gender issue: "The complementary character of the anima also affects the sexual character, as I have proved to myself beyond a doubt. A very feminine woman has a masculine soul, and a very masculine man has a feminine soul."[13] Here it is only because the anima/animus structure is seen as complimentary to the persona that the gender features become included in its image. If a man's persona contains the qualities and features commonly associated with masculinity in a particular culture, then the features of personality that do not conform with that image will be suppressed and gathered together in the complementary unconscious structure, the anima. The anima then contains the features that are typically identified as feminine in that culture. So a man very masculine in the persona will have be equally feminine in the anima.

But what about women who are not very feminine and men who are not very masculine in their personas? Does a not-very-feminine woman have a nonmasculine animus, and a not-very-masculine man have a nonfeminine anima? Jung would be obliged to follow this line of thought, given his premises. Some individuals may not be very much internally polarized between masculine and feminine features. The more androgynous style of recent decades has clearly moved away from the classic gender polarization of macho males and passive females. Women dress and behave in more masculine ways than they did in earlier generations, and many men are similarly more feminine in their personas than their forefathers were. How does this affect the features of the anima and animus? As the predominant collective images for correct male and female dress and behavior change, the inner images of anima and animus would also shift accordingly. According to the rule, whatever is left out of the conscious adaptation to the regnant culture of the individual person is relegated to the unconscious and will collect around the structure that Jung named anima/us. For an extremely effeminate man the inner attitude (anima) will be masculine in quality because this is what has been left out of the persona adaptation.

What do these gender qualities actually mean, then, when it comes to defining the nature and quality of the inner attitude, the anima and animus? Masculine has been almost universally defined by such adjectives as active, hard, penetrating, logical, assertive, dominant; feminine has been widely defined as receptive, soft, giving, nourishing, relational, emotional, empathic. Whether housed in a male or female body, these categories of attributes seem to remain stable. The debate is whether these categories should be associated with gender. Some women are more masculine than feminine in their personas, some men more feminine than masculine, but this does not change their genders as biological females and males. The Chinese terms Yin and Yang have been proposed as more suitable and neutral terms for these groups of attributes, and they might be used in exchange for the terms masculine and feminine. Either way we are speaking of the same qualities. Taking off from there, Jung would say that the inner attitude shows the qualities that are left out in the persona: if a person is Yang in the persona, he or she will by Yin in the anima/us structure. But the inner attitude, because it is in the unconscious, is less under the control of the ego and is less refined and differentiated than the persona is. So it is an inferior Yang that appears in a Yin-dominated persona individual, and an inferior Yin that crops up in unguarded moments of a Yang-dominated consciousness.

Thus a very feminine woman has a masculine soul, but not a very refined one. In her relationship to the world she holds a distinctive and marked feminine attitude, which we recognize and describe as receptive, warm, nurturing, and embracing. Within that person there is a very different inner attitude: hard, critical, aggressive, domineering. The inner face of that very feminine-looking woman reveals a personality made of steel. Similarly the very masculine appearing man, who is hard-driving, tough-minded, detached, and aggressive contains an inner personality that is sentimental, touchy, easily wounded, and vulnerable. The macho man loves his mother, loves his daughter, loves his horse, but refrains from admitting it (even to himself), and in public he will shun those feelings although in private he may give way occasionally and blubber into his beer. "This contrast is due to the fact that a man is not in all things wholly masculine, but also has certain feminine traits. The more masculine his outer attitude is, the more his feminine traits are obliterated: instead, they appear in his unconscious. This explains why it is just those very virile men who are most subject to characteristic weaknesses; their attitude to the unconscious has a womanish weakness and impressionability. Conversely, it is often just the most feminine women who, in their inner lives, display an intractability, an obstinacy, and a willfulness that are to be found with comparable intensity only in a man's outer attitude. These are masculine traits which, excluded from the womanly outer attitude, have become qualities in her soul."[14] It is obvious that Jung is not speaking here of the inner masculine and feminine in their highest and most developed forms but rather as caricatures, inferior versions of masculinity and femininity that are based on undeveloped parts of the individual's personality.

The Development of the Anima/us

It is precisely the above lack of development and inferiority, however, that gives the anima and animus such potential for further development in the psyche. Because the persona is based on collective values and features—whatever happens to be "in" in the way of male and female behavior and attitudes at a given moment in culture—the potential for becoming unique as an individual resides not in the persona but elsewhere in the psyche. As long as a person's ego-consciousness is identified with the persona and feels at one with it, there is no room for qualities of personality and expression of individuality that would depart from the collective images. The impulse to be an individual is suppressed (or repressed altogether) for the sake of adaptation, in order to "fit in." What these individual qualities may be in a particular case cannot be determined by examining the persona. They may be somewhat included in the persona presentation or they may be almost completely excluded. "This is a fundamental rule which my experience has borne out over and over again . . . as regards individual qualities, nothing can be deduced about them [from the persona] . . . We can only be certain that when a man is identical with his persona, his individual qualities will be associated with the anima."[15]

This is the man in the gray flannel suit, who rides the train to work every morning and is so closely identified with his collective role that he has no personality outside of its framework. His inherent uniqueness will show up in the anima: he will be (perhaps secretly) attracted by extremely unconventional women because they carry the anima projection for him, they portray his soul, they capture his spirit of adventure and daring. Precisely the same rule holds true for women: when they are collective and conventional in their persona presentations, they harbor a secret inner lover (often unconscious to them) who is anything but the portrait of their conventional mate. When he appears he will mesmerize them and lead them into abandon. This fundamental rule of the psyche can be observed operating in life, and it is portrayed in countless novels, operas, and films. The outcome of an actual encounter with someone who is a carrier of the anima or animus projection "frequently gives rise in dreams to the symbol of psychic pregnancy, a symbol that goes back to the primordial image of the hero's birth. The child that is to be born signifies the individuality, which, though present, is not yet conscious."[16] The real psychic purpose of the conventional man's affair with his very unconventional anima woman is to produce a symbolic child, which represents a union of the opposites in his personality and is therefore a symbol of the self.

It is this encounter of the ego with the anima or animus that
Jung thought was so rich with potential for psychological development. The meeting with the anima/us represents a connection
to the unconscious even deeper than that of the shadow. In the
case of the shadow, it is a meeting with the disdained and rejected
pieces of the total psyche, the inferior and unwanted qualities. In
the meeting with the anima/us, it is a contact with levels of the
psyche which has the potential to lead into the deepest and highest (at any rate the furthest) reaches that the ego can attain.

In order to pursue this intuition, however, Jung had to change
course and begin to redefine the nature of the anima/us. The
shadow does not usually lead one much past the parts of the psyche rejected from the persona, unless it takes one to an encounter
with absolute evil. The anima/us structure, on the other hand, has
the potential to bridge to the self, a much further reach. The
anima/us cannot then be simply the converse of the persona, a
sort of negative reflection of the collective attitudes of the times.
It must be more deeply anchored in the collective unconscious
and in the structures of archetype and archetypal image. Its roots
must extend further out and down into the depths than those of
the shadow. In 1921 Jung was just on the verge of tracking these
trails into the hinterland of the collective unconscious. He gives a
hint of what is to come: "in the same way as the persona, the
instrument of adaptation to the environment, is strongly influenced by environmental conditions, the anima is shaped by the
unconscious and its qualities."[17] Here the concept of the anima
changes a small but highly significant bit. Instead of simply being
the complement of the persona, and therefore critically shaped
and colored by what is in the persona, the anima is now seen as
shaped by the unconscious and *its* qualities. Later, when Jung
comes to conceive of the animus and anima as archetypal images
which receive their forms from the spiritual end of the psychic
spectrum (see chapter 4), he will conclude that the anima/us is
shaped by the archetype more than by the collective consensus of
the time. The anima and animus will become enduring forms of
psyche, powers that shape the psyche as much as they are shaped
by it, dynamic forces that can break the forms of culture and

impose their own agendas upon a surprised and sometimes unwilling ego.

"Every man carries within him the eternal image of woman; not the image of this or that particular woman, but a definitive feminine image,"[18] Jung writes in 1925 in an essay on marriage. This has come to be the more or less standard definition of the anima in analytical psychology. Here Jung is pointing to the archetypal nature of the anima/us, and he leaves aside the way in which this inner attitude is complementary to the persona. He goes on to say that this is "an hereditary factor of primordial origin" and offers an image of woman *as she appears to man* and not as she is in herself. Similarly, the animus is a woman's internal image of the male personality. The images, thoughts, and assumptions generated by these internal structures are behind all the confusions and obfuscations between men and women. They misunderstand one another because they are often relating to *images* of the other sex rather than to actual people. It is evident how these inner structures can distort reality and cause misperceptions between otherwise fairly rational and well-meaning individuals. The male and female images housed in the unconscious of each gender respectively are primordial and relatively unchanged by historical and cultural circumstance. They are close to permanently stable images that repeat their portraits in individual human psyches from generation to generation. What confused Plato and Socrates about women is the same as the anima image that creates pitfalls for men today. And the expectations and longings that filled the heart of Mary Magdalene continue to infiltrate the consciousness of modern women in spite of the vast cultural and social distances that separate them. The anima/us is the great creator of illusion that provides chuckles for the jaded and heartbreak for the naive.

"The projection-making factor is the anima, or rather the unconscious as represented by the anima,"[19] Jung writes from the vantage point of old age in 1950 in *Aion,* where he attempts to offer once again a definition of this elusive inner factor. Jung had always held that projections are created by the unconscious and not by the ego. We are not responsible for our projections, only for not becoming conscious of them, taking them back, or analyzing them. They occur spontaneously and create a view of the world and of reality that is based on unconscious images and structures rather than on tested perceptions of reality. Jung now locates the origin of all projections in the anima/us, thereby highlighting the dynamic and active nature of this psychic factor.

We are of course projecting constantly, and our views of life, of other people, and of the way the world is constructed are made up quite importantly of unconscious contents that are projected into the environment and clung to as absolute verities. The anima/us, Jung says in this passage, is like Maya, the Indian Goddess who creates illusory worlds, and the ego ends up inhabiting a world that is largely based on projections. Jung had learned this not primarily from study of Eastern religions but from his own firsthand experience as a psychiatrist and analyst. It is amazing how distorted some people's views really are. And it is equally remarkable that all of us believe in our own views absolutely even when we find serious flaws in them. It is rare that we question a set of basic assumptions.

Raising Consciousness with Anima/us

The anima/us image, based on the archetypal structures underlying the psyche, assumes particular shape and form by being filtered through the psychic system and perceived by ego consciousness. If the image of the shadow instills fear and dread, the image of the anima/us usually brings excitement and stimulates desire for union. It engenders attraction. Where there is anima/us, we want to go, we want to be a part of it, we want to join it, if we are not too timid or afraid of adventure. The charismatic charge that electrifies an audience when a great orator casts his spell enlists the anima/us and constellates its presence. The audience wants to believe, and individuals will follow the clarion call to action. A perception of reality is created and conviction follows upon the strong emotional command of the anima/us. The anima/us is therefore transformative.

For purposes of psychological development and increase of consciousness, however, the essential ego action is to engage the anima/us in a dialectical process and not to follow the call immediately to action. This process of dialogue and confrontation is called by Jung an *Auseinandersetzung*. This is a German word that means literally "taking something to pieces" and refers to the process that takes place when two people strongly engage one another in dialogue or negotiation, neither one fleeing the conflict. As they stand head to head and have it out physically or verbally, the differences between them that were at first gross and barely articulate become more differentiated. Lines are drawn, distinctions made, clarity eventually achieved. What began as a highly emotional confrontation turns into a conscious relationship between two very different personalities. Perhaps an agreement is reached, a contract drawn up and signed.

So it is with the engagement between ego and anima/us. This is the work of raising consciousness, of becoming aware of projections, of challenging our most romantic and carefully guarded illusions. To have an *Auseinandersetzung* with the anima/us is to dismember the illusory world of unconscious fantasy. It is also to allow oneself to experience most profoundly the heights and depths of one's own mental universe, the unconscious assumptions that keep us salivating for more when we are already overfed, that keep us lusting although we should have long since been satisfied, that drive us to repeat endlessly the emotionally engorged patterns in the iron chain of stimulus-response sequences. Dungeons and dragons, myths and fairytales, romantic excess and sarcastic recriminations are all a part of the world woven in our psychic interiors by the anima/us. At most we may feign to give it up while clinging all the more tenaciously to our most precious self-deceptions and illusions. "What we can discover about them [anima and animus] from the conscious side is so slight as to be almost imperceptible. It is only when we throw light into the dark depths of the psyche and explore the strange and tortuous paths of human fate that it gradually becomes clear to us how immense is the influence wielded by these two factors that complement our conscious life."[20] This is perhaps a reply to Freud who held that character was fate. In Jung's view, the anima/us is fate. We are guided to our fates by the images of archetypal powers far beyond our conscious will or knowledge.

In the *Aion* text, which is arguably the master text on anima/us in Jung's writings, Jung also acknowledges the centrality of relationship in the process of becoming conscious of the hidden territory within our psyches. "I should like to emphasize," he writes, "that the . . . shadow can be realized only through a relation to a partner, and anima and animus only through a relation to a partner of the opposite sex, because only in such a relation do their projections become operative."[21] As I said earlier, we might need to revise this point in light of contemporary developments in gender identity, where the anima/us images are sometimes carried by members of the same sex. Nevertheless, the point is that it is in emotional relationships that these developments of consciousness become possible. Becoming conscious is not a project carried out in isolation, although it does require a good deal of introspection to bring it to its full flowering. But experience must precede insight. The shadow is experienced in projection upon someone who captures those qualities of the personal unconscious. Similarly the anima/us is captured in projection by a person who bears its traits and features to some quite important extent, a person who can evoke the response of the unconscious from this sector. When this happens, Jung continues, the psychic constellation is such that three figures become relevant: "The recognition of the anima gives rise, in a man, to a triad, one third of which is transcendent: the masculine subject, the opposing feminine subject, and the transcendent anima. With a woman the situation is reversed."[22] This assumes a considerable degree of consciousness because generally the projection-carrier and the projection are fused, anima/us and other subjects becoming one. Here Jung assumes a degree of separation, however, such that there is (1) a conscious ego along with its personal subjectivity, (2) another person, the partner, with her/his conscious ego and personal subjectivity, and (3) the archetypal image of the anima/us. This triad is completed, Jung writes, by a fourth figure, the Wise Old Man in the male instance and the Chthonic Mother in the female. The anima/us and the wisdom figures are transcendent, in the sense of belonging essentially to the unconscious and originating in the realm of spirit, while the ego and the partner are the conscious persons involved in the emotional relationship that has stimulated this constellation. In the presence of this quaternity, we find the numinous experience of the self, as a relationship. Provided that enough consciousness prevails to see the differences between human and archetypal features in this situation of love and attraction, there is the opportunity here for a full experience of the self (see chapter 7).

The complicating feature is that this experience of the anima/us-in-projection happens to people at many stages of psychological maturity. If it is only a matter of fascination and falling in love, it can take place in childhood between parents and children; then it happens again (classically and intensely) in adolescence; and fortunately it continues to happen as people move into adulthood. It even continues into old age (Goethe is reported to have whispered a prayer of thanks in his seventies that he was still able to fall in love with a young woman). The anima/us is eternally active in psychological life, and its absence defines the nature of depression. Beyond the sexuality of the body, this is the psyche's sexuality. It begins before the physical organism is ready for sexual experience and continues to be vibrantly active beyond the physical body's ability to perform the rigors of the sexual act. Yet to get the full psychological benefit of the anima/us experience, a person must have arrived at an unusually advanced level of consciousness. The ability to differentiate between projection and projection-carrier, between fantasy and reality, is rare indeed. So the realization of what Jung is speaking of—the quaternity involved in this constellation and the realization of the transcendent features in the experience—is reserved for the few individuals with the kind of subtle psychological discernment that pertains to Kundalini masters and others like them. For the rest, the anima/us is Maya, the creator of illusions, the mystifier, the trickster, the ever-receding mirage of the eternal beloved. To see through the anima/us game of illusions without recognizing the transcendent figures at work leads to cynicism and despair: The anima is truly *la belle dame sans merci*.

Sexuality and Relationships

For good reason many people steer clear of the shoals of the anima/us experience. The native defenses of the ego hold this temptation at a distance. Little boys run away from little girls who are too powerful and attractive, knowing intuitively they are not able to meet the challenge. Grown men are sometimes wise enough to do the same, for the anima is a wrecker of conventional marriages and careers. Women too will resist the call of the Dionysian animus drawing them toward ecstasy and promises of fulfillment by abandoning themselves to love, for here also lie the dangers of dismemberment and madness. It is not without reason that many have prayed to be delivered from temptations beyond their ability to remain standing. One of Jung's favorite illustrations of the power of the anima was Rider Haggard's *She*, a second-rate novel that depicts an immortal *femme fatale* in the wilds of Africa whose commands must be obeyed. ("She who must be obeyed" is not simply a humorous appellation for Rumpole's bossy wife; the phrase comes from Haggard's novel.) She is an eternally dying and resurrecting goddess who leads men into the flames of passion and finally to their destruction. But Jung also felt that if one was able to endure the fires of emotion and passion, one could be transformed. The experience of the archetype, of the collective unconscious and its powers, can lead to a new state of consciousness in which the reality of the psyche becomes as convincing to the ego as the reality of the material world is to the senses. The anima/us, once experienced as transcendent and recognized as Maya, becomes the bridge to a wholly new apprehension of the world. The anima/us experience is the Royal Way (the *via regia*) to the self.

Jung's anima/us theory seems in part to be a highly imaginative variation on Freud's old theme of sexuality as the central source of libido. But in human sexuality Jung sees a good deal more than animals rutting in heat and trying to relieve themselves of tension or to pursue pleasure. Psychic attractors are involved, and when these are distinguished from the accompanying biological activity, the image emerges. This image is a psychic fact whose source lies at the archetypal end of the psychic spectrum. It is wedded to the sexual instinct, and this combination gives the anima/us its driving physical power.

Human sexuality is guided by the archetypal image, but the image is not reducible to the drive. We are attracted to certain people. Why does one choose this person for a soulmate and not another? This is governed by the images that are projected. Typically, "the animus likes to project itself upon 'intellectuals' and all kinds of 'heroes', including tenors, artists, sporting celebrities, etc. The anima has a predilection for everything that is unconscious, dark, equivocal, and unrelated [viz., at a loose end] in woman, and also for her vanity, frigidity, helplessness, and so forth."[23] Why do such difficult women attract men so frequently and with such ease? Why is it that strong women often do not attract men? Jung suggests that this predilection for weak and helpless women is based on an anima projection, the anima being undifferentiated and inferior in the unconscious of a strongly male-identified person. Age-old wisdom tells women that to attract a man, "Be helpless!" The anima represents the undeveloped side of a man, where he is unconsciously helpless and at loose ends, dark and equivocal. He is attracted by that. Similarly, strong women will be attracted often to weak men, sometimes fatefully, and then become filled with fantasies of saving them from alcoholism or some other decrepitude. Again, they are seeking a lost part of themselves, the animus, who appears as an inferior male in projection. Or, if she is a weak and helpless woman, her unconscious may compensate with images of male competence, and she will find herself hopelessly attracted to an heroic animus projection carrier.

Once persons get together and spend some time in each other's company, the ensuing relationship begins showing some other typical anima-animus characteristics. In an intimate relationship, it is not only the egos of the partners that enter into the mixture of psyches; it is also the unconscious parts, and importantly the anima and animus. They have been there all along, supplying the attractors to both members of the couple, but now they may appear surprisingly different from what they looked like in the courtship stage of the relationship. Here is Jung-the-psychologi-cal-realist describing the situation: "no man can converse with an animus for five minutes without becoming the victim of his own anima. Anyone who still had enough sense of humour to listen objectively to the ensuing dialogue would be staggered by the vast number of commonplaces, misapplied truisms, clichés from newspapers and novels, shop-soiled platitudes of every description interspersed with vulgar abuse and brain-splitting lack of logic. It is a dialogue which, irrespective of its participants, is repeated millions and millions of times in all languages of the world and always remains essentially the same."[24] On the male side the anima becomes touchy, overly sensitive, and emotional; on the female side the animus become abusive, power-ridden, and opinionated. This is not a pretty picture and surely offers a stark contrast to the more romantic version of the *mysterium coniunctionis* ("mystical union") of song and story. The one partner becomes possessed by the animus—an undifferentiated collection of opinions motivated by a power drive—and the other retreats into a mood that is undifferentiated and driven by the need for love. One is dogmatic, the other becomes withdrawn or emotional and starts throwing things around. It is a typical anima versus animus cat-and-dog fight.

If the emotionality and vituperation, the heat and fireworks, of this conflict dies down a bit, there is a possibility that things will have been said that are important for the couple. Once the egos are restored to their normal positions, they may even realize that some transcendent event has taken place. What was said was probably not very personal. It was more general, collective, perhaps even archetypal and universal. Perhaps there is a germ of wisdom hidden in the dark mass of material that has erupted from each partner. Perhaps some clarifications and insights can result from the storm that has now passed. This would be the work of consciousness, rising above the level of emotionality and arriving at insight and empathy. At the very least, one will have had a glimpse into the depths of oneself and of the other, into the emotional far reaches that are normally hidden behind the socialized and adapted persona.

It would of course make sense to look at Jung's own life to amplify further the meaning the anima figure held for him. That is beyond the scope of this study. I have used some passages from his autobiography, and biographical works are in print and others are underway that give fuller depictions of his profound relationships with women. Jung once said that all psychological theory is also personal confession, and this is especially true of these areas that speak of the inner figures and personalities of the psyche such as the shadow, the anima/us, and the self. These concepts and abstract theories were based on concrete psychological experiences, much of it interpersonal and not only solitary and private. With respect to the anima, she was for Jung both a living inner reality, a true inner figure of the first rank, and she was also powerfully experienced by him in projection and in relationship. Beginning early in life with his nursemaid and extending through his romantic courtship and marriage to Emma Rauschenbach and his deep and enduring relationship with Toni Wolff, the anima was a constant companion in Jung's inner and outer life. To him, she seemed to be the guide of his fate. And the most profound experience of the self, a concept which I will describe in the following chapter, occurred for Jung in the conjunction between man and woman, when the anima and animus were the guiding figures in their union.

7

The Psyche's
Transcendent Center
and Wholeness
(The Self)

I was tempted to begin this book with a chapter on the self, because it is the most fundamental feature of Jung's entire vision. It is the key to his psychological theory, and in some respects it is the piece that most sets him apart from all other figures in depth psychology and psychoanalysis. It is instructive to note that psychoanalytic theory has moved significantly in Jung's direction over the past half century, and yet few if any other psychoanalytic theorists have ventured as far as his conception of the self in their theorizing. While many other writers today use the term *self* in their clinical studies and theoretical statements, none has in mind the same domain that Jung was trying to encompass with his concept. To begin with Jung's theory of the self would have been misleading, however, historically and conceptually. It is not only the most fundamental feature of his theory, it is also the capstone. It therefore needs preparation in order to grasp its full range and importance.

For Jung the self is transcendent, which means that it is not defined by or contained within the psychic realm but rather lies beyond it and, in an important sense, defines it. It is this point about the self's transcendence that makes Jung's theory different from those of other self-theorists like Kohut. For Jung, the self is paradoxically *not* oneself. It is more than one's subjectivity, and its essence lies beyond the subjective realm. The self forms the ground for the subject's commonality with the world, with the structures of Being. In the self, subject and object, ego and other are joined in a common field of structure and energy. This is the point I hope will become most salient from what follows in this chapter.

The typical English usage of the word "self" makes it difficult to appreciate what Jung is getting at in his theory. As used in everyday parlance, self is equivalent to ego. When we say that someone is selfish, we mean that they are egotistical or narcissistic. But in a Jungian vocabulary, self has the opposite meaning. To say that someone is self-centered is to say that they are precisely not egotistical and narcissistic, but rather philosophical, having a wide perspective, and not personally reactive or easily thrown off balance. When the ego is well connected to the self, a person stands in relationship with a transcendent center and is precisely not narcissistically invested in nearsighted goals and short-term gains. In such persons there is an ego-free quality, as though they were consulting a deeper and wider reality than merely the practical, rational, and personal considerations typical of ego consciousness.

Jung's Experience of the Self

Before entering into a discussion of *Aion*, the central text of Jung's self theory, I think it will be useful to the reader to have an impression of Jung's original experiences that led him to postulate the existence of the self. His later theorizing sprang from his experience.

Jung's own account of his first major experience of the self places it in the period between 1916 and 1918. During this difficult time in his life he made the major discovery that at bottom the psyche rests on a fundamental structure and that this structure is able to withstand the shocks of abandonment and betrayal which threaten to undo a person's mental stability and emotional balance. This was the discovery of a deep, largely unconscious pattern of psychological unity and wholeness.

For Jung the experience of the self—that most impersonal of all archetypes—had a highly dramatic quality. It came out of his inner struggles and turmoil and capped a period of his life that often had him wondering if he was losing his way in a psychic wilderness. There were no maps for him to consult as he groped through a jungle of tangled emotions, ideas, memories, and images. In his autobiography, he calls this the period of "Confrontation with the Unconscious."[1] At the time of his momentous discovery, Jung was already well-launched into his midlife crisis. About forty-one years old, he had broken with Freud some five years earlier and had after that suffered emotional disorientation and professional uncertainty, from which he was now gradually recovering. He refers to the first half of his midlife period (1913–1916) as the time when he discovered the inner world, the anima, the plurality of unconscious images and fantasies. Throughout these years of inner exploration, Jung recorded his dreams, fantasies, and other important experiences in an elaborately detailed and illustrated document which has come to be called the "Red Book." While struggling to sort out the images and emotions that had burst upon him from the unconscious, he had also been trying to understand how they fit together and what they meant. He had used practices such as yoga breathing to maintain his emotional equilibrium. When his emotions threatened to destroy his psychic equilibrium and sanity, he used meditation, play therapy, active imagination, and drawing to calm down. A therapist to himself, he worked out techniques (which he later would use with patients) to keep his own ego-consciousness stable in the midst of this flood of material from the unconscious.

Now, as he continued to observe, listen, and record his inner experiences, his openness increased to the archetypal end of the psychic continuum and to the spirit world into which it merges.

After spending several years at the "anima level," he began to enter into a territory that revealed the archetype of the self, the most fundamental architect of psychic wholeness and order. This discovery of the self is recounted in his autobiography and took place over the period of several years.

First there was the peculiar incident of the ringing door bell. Jung tells of how one Sunday afternoon in 1916, as he was sitting in his living room on Seestrasse in Küsnacht, he sensed a heavy emotional atmosphere in the house. The members of his household seemed tense and irritable. He did not understand why, but the air seemed charged with the presence of unseen figures. Suddenly the doorbell rang. He went to answer it, but no one was there. Yet the knocker was clearly moving. He swears he saw it move. By itself! When the maid asked who had rung the bell, Jung said he did not know since there was no one at the door. It rang again. This time the maid also saw the knocker move. He was not hallucinating. And then Jung heard the following words suggest themselves:

> The dead came back from Jerusalem, where they found not what they sought. They prayed me let them in and besought my word, and thus I began my teaching . . . [2]

He decided to write these words down. More came:

> Harken: I begin with nothingness. Nothingness is the same as fullness. In infinity full is no better than empty. Nothingness is both empty and full. As well might ye say anything else of nothingness, as for instance white is it, or black, or again, it is not, or it is. This nothingness or fullness we name the PLEROMA.[3]

Over the next few days Jung took down, as if by dictation, a Gnostic text entitled "Seven Sermons to the Dead." This teaching, delivered in the words and under the identity of the ancient Gnostic master, Basilides, is a message that came to Jung from the archetypal realm of the psyche.[4]

Of course one knows that Jung was very interested in Gnosticism prior to this visitation and that he had read many fragments of ancient Gnostic texts, so there were undoubtedly many connections to this visionary experience in his living room and library. Yet this was also a highly imaginative and creative new work, albeit in the form of a grandiose religious text, and it came spontaneously from the depths of Jung's own psyche. He was not simply quoting from memory—even cryptomnesia does not account for it, since it cannot be found elsewhere in the classic texts of Gnosis. Nor was he trying deliberately to write in the style of the Gnostics. This writing was not intentional. In retrospect it can be seen that this text, which was completed in about three days, contains the seeds of many ideas that Jung would work out in the following decades in more rational intellectual and scientific terms.

This was one of many unusual psychic experiences during these years of confrontation with unconscious. At a more mundane level, Jung carried on with his life and his professional practice. This period coincided almost exactly with World War I, during which Switzerland, a neutral country, was isolated from Europe and the wider world. Travel was impossible. Like all Swiss adult men, Jung was in the Army—he was a medical officer—and he was assigned the role of commandant at the prisoner of war camp in Chateau d'Oex in the French-speaking part of the country. It must have been a more or less tedious administrative job, and he began routinely to spend some time each morning drawing circles and elaborating them as he felt inclined to do so. After this exercise he would feel refreshed and ready for the day ahead. This activity centered him, he says in his autobiography.[5]

Some of these drawings turned into very elaborate paintings. Jung later compared them to what Tibetan Buddhists call mandalas, images that represent the cosmos, the spiritual universe of the Buddhist practitioner. (Some twenty years later on his trip to India Jung would note with great interest how people paint these traditional images on the walls of their homes or in temples in order to stay connected to cosmic spiritual powers or to fend off evil forces and influences. Mandalas have both a protective and a prayerful function.) Jung came to realize that he was reproducing a universal underlying archetypal pattern that has to do with putting things in order. This experience led him eventually to the conclusion that if a spontaneously unfolding psychic process is followed to its own logical end and is permitted to express itself fully, the goal of this process will be fulfilled, namely to manifest universal images of order and a unity. The mandala is a universal symbol that expresses the intuition of ordered wholeness. To name the archetypal factor that is operative in the psyche producing this goal and this pattern, Jung chose the term *self*, following the Indian Upanishads in their designation of the higher personality, the *atman*. This experience of drawing and elaborating mandalas would stay with Jung as the central experience of the self: emerging slowly, experientially, spontaneously into consciousness.

Finally, Jung recorded a dream in 1928 that represented for him the completion of his realization of the self. (Although the intensity of his midlife crisis was over by 1920, the lingering aftermath continued until 1928 when Jung was fifty-two years old.) Throughout his forties Jung lived in a kind of psychological liminality, or limbo, at first intensely and deeply and then less so. At the end he had a dream in which he found himself in the English city of Liverpool. He was walking through the streets with a group of Swiss friends on a rainy night, and soon they came upon an intersection that was shaped like a wheel. Several streets radiated from this hub, and in the middle of the intersection there was a square. While everything was dark in the surrounding area, this center island was brightly lit. On it there grew a single tree, a Magnolia full of reddish blossoms. His companions did not seem able to see the beautiful tree, but Jung was overcome with the beauty of it. Later he interpreted this dream to mean that he had been given a vision of the center, the self, an image of unearthly beauty that is located in the "pool of life" (Liverpool). From this dream experience, he writes, "emerged a first inkling of my personal myth."[6] In this key passage, Jung declares the self to be the center of his personal myth. He later conceived of it as the prime archetype (the One) from which all the other archetypes and archetypal images ultimately derive. The self is the magnetic center of Jung's psychological universe. Its presence pulls the ego's compass needle to true north.

Jung's Definition of the Self

Turning now from Jung's own personal experience of the self to his theory, a few remarks will pave the way for the discussion of the key text on this subject, *Aion*. Jung's writings on the self are scattered throughout his *Collected Works* in the volumes and essays that were published after 1925 (the year of Jung's 50th birthday), and of these the most focused on this subject is *Aion*. This work was published in 1951 and is, according to the editors of the volume, "a long monograph on the archetype of the self." Its subtitle, "Researches into the Phenomenology of the Self," makes the same point. The book's title is taken from the ancient religion of Mithraism, where Aion is the name of a god who rules over the astrological calender and thus over time itself. The title therefore suggests a factor that transcends the time/space continuum that governs ego-consciousness.

The first four chapters of *Aion* function as a brief general introduction to Jung's psychology, covering the concepts of ego, shadow, and animus/anima, and a first pass at the theory of the self. From there he enters into discussions of many symbolic representations of the self, primarily in the Biblical traditions and the relevant "heresies" such as Gnosticism and alchemy. The work concludes with a grand theoretical summation in the final chapter entitled "The Structure and Dynamics of the Self." Jung's argument, often difficult to follow as he threads his way through astrology, Gnosticism, alchemy, theology, and various traditional symbol systems, claims that this transcendent factor of the psyche—which we now call the self—has been studied and experienced by many people in earlier times, and their accounts of it in symbolic terms can be useful for grasping its nature and energy.

The introductory chapter on the self begins as follows: "the self . . . is completely outside the personal sphere, and appears, if at all, only as a religious mythologem, and its symbols range from the highest to the lowest . . . anyone who wants to achieve the difficult feat of realizing something not only intellectually, but also according to its feeling-value, must for better or worse come to grips with the anima/animus problem in order to open the way for a high union, a *coniunctio oppositorum*. This is an indispensable prerequisite for wholeness."[7] At this point in the text, Jung introduces "wholeness," a term that is equivalent to the self. Wholeness results, practically speaking, when the self is realized in consciousness. In fact, this is not completely achievable, since the polarities and opposites resident in the self are forever generating more and new material to integrate. Nevertheless, practicing wholeness on a regular basis is the way of the self, Jung's version of living in Tao. "Although 'wholeness' seems at first sight to be nothing but an abstract idea (like anima and animus), it is nevertheless empirical in so far as it is anticipated by the psyche in the form of spontaneous or autonomous symbols. These are the quaternity or mandala symbols, which occur not only in the dreams of modern people who have never heard of them, but are widely disseminated in the historical records of many peoples and many epochs."[8]

Symbols of the self determine the focus of *Aion*. As Jung sees it, they are ubiquitous and autochthonic (that is, innate and spontaneous), and they are delivered to the psyche through the archetypal psychoid region from the archetype per se. The self, a transcendent nonpsychological entity, acts on the psychic system to produce symbols of wholeness, often as quaternity or mandala images (squares and circles). "Their significance as symbols of unity and totality is amply confirmed by history as well as by empirical psychology. What at first looks like an abstract idea stands in reality for something that exists and can be experienced, that demonstrates its a priori presence spontaneously. Wholeness is thus an objective factor that confronts the subject independently of him."[9]

In this passage, Jung goes on to describe a hierarchy of agencies within the psyche. As the anima or animus has "a higher position in the hierarchy than the shadow, so wholeness lays claim to a position and a value superior to those of the syzygy."[10] At the most immediate level is the shadow, and over this the anima/animus—the syzygy—stands as a superior authority and power. Presiding over the entire psychic government is the self, the ultimate authority and highest value: "unity and totality stand at the highest point on the scale of objective values because their symbols can no longer be distinguished from the *imago Dei.*"[11] Jung contends that every one of us bears the God-image—the stamp of the self—within ourselves. We carry the mark of the archetype: *typos* means a stamp impressed on a coin, and *arche* means the original or master copy. Each human individual bears an impression of the archetype of the self. This is innate and given.

Since each of us is stamped with the *imago Dei* by virtue of being human, we are also in touch with "unity and totality [which] stand at the highest point on the scale of objective values." When needed, this intuitive knowledge can come to our assistance: "experience shows that individual mandalas are symbols of order, and that they occur in patients principally during times of psychic disorientation or re-orientation."[12] When people spontaneously draw or dream about mandalas, this suggests to the therapist that there is a psychological crisis in consciousness. The appearance of self symbols means that the psyche needs to be unified. This was Jung's own experience. During his most disoriented time, he spontaneously began drawing mandalas. Compensatory symbols of wholeness are generated by the self when the psychic system is in danger of fragmenting. This is the point at which the archetype of the self intervenes in an effort to unify it.

The emergence of unity symbols and of integrative movements in the psychic system generally are marks of the action of the self archetype. The self's task seems to be to hold the psychic system together and to keep it in balance. Its goal is unity. This unity is not static but dynamic, as we shall see in the next chapter on individuation. The psychic system is unified by becoming more balanced, interrelated, and integrated. The self's influence on the psyche as a whole is mirrored by the influence of the ego upon consciousness. Like the self, the ego too has a centering, ordering, unifying function, and its goal is to balance and integrate functions insofar as this is possible, given the existence of the complexes and defenses. In chapter 1, I discussed the ego as the center of consciousness and the locus of will. It has the ability to say "I" and "I am," or "I think" or "I will." At another stage, it becomes a self-conscious psychic entity and able to say not only "I am" but "I know that I am." It may be the case, although one cannot be

certain, that the self also knows that it is. Does the archetype possess self-awareness? Does it know that it is? Jung discovered what
he thought to be a kind of consciousness in the archetypes. When
archetypal images invade the ego, for example, and take possession of it, they have a voice, an identity, a point of view, a set of
values. But is there self-awareness within the archetypal unit
itself? One myth strongly points to such awareness. When Moses
confronted God at the burning bush and asked, "Who are you?"
the archetypal voice replied, "I am that I am." Whatever this may
mean theologically, it seems to demonstrate self-reflexive consciousness in the archetype.

Jung believed that a privileged relation exists between the ego
and the self. It may be that the self has the highest form of self-
awareness and shares this with the ego, which in turns shows this
property most strongly within the more familiar regions of the
psychic world. Because of this intimate connection between ego
and self, it might be argued that the self is in fact an image of the
ego, a kind of super-ego or ideal of the ego. Jung, however, wanted
to insist that he had discovered something psychoid—psyche-like
but not strictly only psychic—that exists in a realm beyond the
psyche itself, something that affects the psychic system through
its images, mental contents, and mythological ideas, and through
revelatory experiences such as that of Moses at the burning bush
or receiving the Law on Mount Sinai, but is not a product of the
ego or of social constructions.

Symbols of the Self

Although the entire book is about the self, *Aion* has two chapters
specifically on this subject. The first of these, chapter 4, which we
have just considered, is introductory. The book's final chapter, on
the other hand, is perhaps Jung's most sophisticated and complete
statement on the self. It assumes the intervening discussion of
symbols from Gnosticism, astrology, and alchemy, which have
threaded through manifestations of culture in the West over the
past two millennia.

This chapter begins by referring to the self as the archetype
underlying ego-consciousness. Ego-consciousness is the point of

individual will, awareness, and self-assertion. Its function is to look out for the individual and to keep him or her alive. The ego— as I described in chapter 1—is a complex that is organized around a dual center, a trauma and an archetype (the self). To talk about the self, Jung now lists a host of possible images for it.[13] Some of them are images that manifest in dreams or fantasies, and others appear in relationships and interactions with the world. Geometrical structures, such as the circle, the square, and the star, are ubiquitous and frequent. These may appear in dreams without drawing special attention to themselves: people sitting around a round table, four objects arranged in a square space, a city plan, a home. Numbers, particularly the number four and multiples of four, indicate quaternity structures. (Jung was not so fond of the number three, which he regards as only a partial expression of the self: three "should be understood as a defective quaternity or as a stepping stone towards it."[14] He is more positive about threes and trinities in other passages, but mainly he views them as only a theoretical approximation to wholeness that leaves out the concreteness and groundedness which wholeness requires.)

Other self images are gemstones, like diamonds and sapphires, stones that represent high and rare value. Yet further self representations include castles, churches, vessels and containers, and of course the wheel, which has a center and spokes radiating outward ending in a circular rim. Human figures that are superior to the ego personality, such as parents, uncles, kings, queens, princes and princesses, are also possible self representations. There are also animal images that symbolize the self: the elephant, the horse, the bull, the bear, the fish, and the snake. These are totem animals that represent one's clan or people. The collective is greater than the ego personality.

The self may also be represented by organic images, such as trees and flowers, and by inorganic images such as mountains and lakes. Jung also mentions the phallus as a self symbol. "Where there is an undervaluation of sexuality the self is symbolized as a phallus. Undervaluation can consist in an ordinary repression or in overt devaluation. In certain differentiated persons a purely biological interpretation and evaluation of sexuality can also have this effect."[15] Jung blames Freud's excessively rationalistic attitude for his overemphasis on sexuality. This led Jung to adopt a mystical attitude toward this instinct.

The self contains opposites and "has a paradoxical, antinomial [amoral] character. It is male and female, old man and child, powerful and helpless, large and small. [He might also have added, good and evil.] It is quite possible that the seeming paradox is nothing but a reflection of the enantiodromian changes of the conscious attitude which can have a favourable or an unfavourable effect on the whole."[16] In other words, the form in which the self is represented is influenced by the conscious attitude of the person regarding it. Changes in the conscious attitude could bring about shifts in the features of the self symbol.

As he moves toward his summary statement, Jung begins to draw diagrams of the self by which he hopes to clarify his vision. The diagrams in paragraphs 390 and 391 of *Aion* are attempts to summarize a vast amount of material. It is somewhat unusual for Jung to diagram his thought, but he is reaching for a level of complexity and intelligibility that may be beyond human grasp. The first diagram shows what might be called a cross-sectional view of levels in the self.

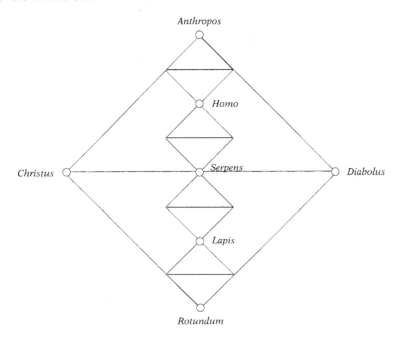

Each level is built of a quaternity, and each of them represents complexity and wholeness at that level. The image of the four quaternities, which are stacked in an order that ascends from material to spiritual poles on a continuum, expresses totality and wholeness.

What appear as quaternities from one viewpoint are, from another angle, three-dimensional six-pointed figures attached to each other end to end.

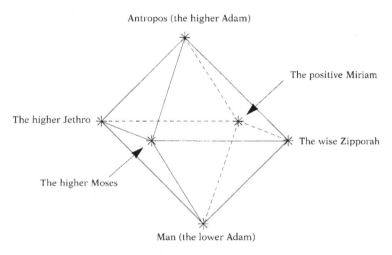

A. The Anthropos Quaternio

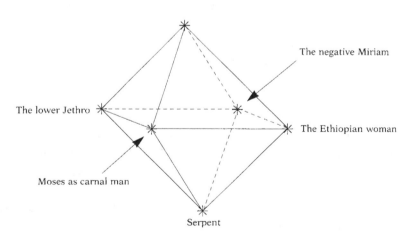

B. The Shadow Quaternio

Each of these three-dimensional double pyramids shares a common point with the one above and below itself. As arranged in a stack of four, there is a line that divides them in half—the Christus—Diabolos line—above which are the Homo and Anthropos quaternities and below which fall the Lapis and Rotundum quaternities. The circle at the Homo position locates the position of ego-consciousness. Directly above it rises the Anthropos quaternity, an expression of ideal wholeness at the spiritual level. This is symbolized by the Gnostic Anthropos or Higher Adam, an ideal figure. Jung states that the present historical age, consisting of the last two thousand years, began with an emphasis on this spiritual quaternity. Man was regarded as a spiritual being in the image of Christian ideal spiritual image projected onto a historical figure, Jesus of Nazareth. The metamorphosis of Jesus into the Christ was the result of people projecting onto this figure their own spiritual higher (Anthropos) selves.

Below the Homo circle (ego-consciousness) lies a quaternity that represents the shadow of the one above it. It rests on the circle of the Serpent. This "lower self" mirrors the "higher self" above it, but darkly. Shadow figures occupy each of the four points of the quaternity (the lower Jethro versus the higher Jethro, etc.). Jung calls this the Shadow quaternity. It corresponds point for point to the Anthropos quaternity above it and represents a less idealized expression of the same wholeness. From the Shadow the trajectory continues downward: from spirit to instinct and on down into matter itself. The Serpent point signifies the base of the Shadow and connects it to the material world.

The shadow is the inferior personality, the lowest levels of which are indistinguishable from the instinctuality of animals. This connects our ideal spiritual wholeness to our biological animal nature. A person who is not connected in consciousness to this quaternity lives in the head, in a realm of intellectual and spiritual ideals that has little relation to everyday life or to the biological stratum of existence. A person identified with and living primarily out of the Shadow quaternity, on the other hand, is more or less limited to consciousness at the level of animal existence: the survival of the individual (nourishment) and of the species (sexuality), a state of spiritual and moral underdevelopment.

The serpent symbolizes the self in its strongest and most bla-tant paradoxicality. On the one hand, it represents everything that is "snaky" in human nature: cold-blooded instincts of survival, ter-ritoriality, base physicality. On the other hand, it symbolizes the wisdom of the body and the instincts—somatic awareness, gut intuitions and instinctual knowledge. The serpent has tradition-ally been a paradoxical symbol, referring both to wisdom and to evil (or the temptation to do evil). The serpent therefore symbol-izes the most extreme tension of opposites within the self.

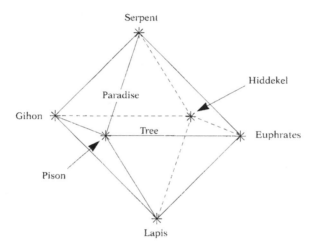

C. The Paradise Quaternio

Continuing downward, the Paradise Quaternio represents a descent into the level of organic material processes. Human beings share this level not only with animals but with plants. This refers to the physical fact that organic life is organized around the nature of the carbon atom and its properties. Organic chemistry is the scientific discipline that studies this level of human exis-tence systematically. And below that lies the Lapis quaternity, which is the absolute physical base of being. At this level, the chemical elements and atomic particles must forge some kind of unity and organization, interacting in such a way as to produce a stable creature that can maintain physical equilibrium sufficient for life at the organic and psychic and spiritual levels.

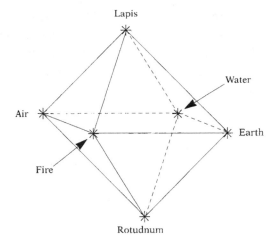

D. Lapis Quaternio

This level, which underlies the psyche and the organic body, passes into the inorganic realm, indeed all the way down to the molecular level. By the time the structure of the self arrives at the level of the rotundum, it has reached the level of pure energy itself, which passes through the atomic level into and past the sub-atomic level. The rotundum, Jung says, is an abstract transcendental idea: the idea of energy.

The psyche proper is left behind at the Christus–Diabolus line, that is at the Serpent Quaternio. That line is equivalent to the psychoid boundary where psyche merges into matter. Although the serpent is somewhat psychic, or quasi-psychic, being cold-blooded it represents an energy that is also very distant from ego-consciousness and from the personal will. It shows movement and a type of consciousness, but one very far from human ego-consciousness. The serpent represents the autonomic nervous system. There is wisdom in the body, but its consciousness consists only of flickers of awareness that might be read and interpreted by the ego. On the other hand, the body may well be responsible for some dreams. The serpent's ambiguity as a symbol derives either from the ego's ambivalence towards it—because we are attached to the higher anthropos level, to our ideals, and therefore in conflict with our body's instincts—or from its capacity to arouse the fear of losing contact with the higher levels of consciousness, which would be destructive. The serpent level is a consciousness-creator, and in this it represents the psychization process.

Penetrating through the inorganic level leads to the realm of pure energy, which modern physics has also discovered. This comes about by continuing to move ever further into matter until one finally arrives at a point that dissolves into pure energy. But energy is so intangible. In fact, it is an idea, an abstraction, a concept used to describe something that cannot be observed directly, though it can be measured by its effects. Psychic energy, as we saw in chapter 3, is for Jung the lifeforce, the vitality we bring to our projects, the interest we take in life and in others. It is a power to reckon with, as anyone who has ever suffered from its absence in a clinical depression knows only to well. It can move mountains, but it is nebulous and unfathomable, too. So the descent through the layers of psyche from the highest levels of idea and ideal and image through the concreteness of the ego's existence and the body's reality into the chemical and molecular composition of our physical being leads finally to pure energy and back into the realm of ideas, which is the world of *nous,* of mind, of spirit. Thus the quaternities touch at the poles of their greatest opposition, at the extremes of spirit and matter. Jung drew this as dynamic circulation:

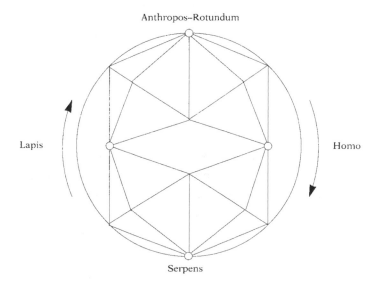

The arrows move in a circle, and eventually Anthropos and Rotundum come together again at the top.

The Self as Central Mystery of the Psyche

It is obvious from Jung's writings that unity and totality were his highest values and that the self formed his personal myth. But it is a myth that he attempted to ground in evidence and theory. More correctly, the theory of the self—the concept that there is a transcendent center that governs the psyche from outside of itself and circumscribes its entirety—was a means that Jung used to account for basic psychological phenomena such as the spontaneous appearance of circles or mandalas, the self-regulating functioning of the psyche in what he called "compensation," the progressive development of consciousness through the life span in what he called "individuation," and the existence of numerous polarities evident in psychological life that form coherent structures and generate energy. Jung has been criticized by some conservative theologians for transforming the self into a God-concept and then worshipping at the shrine which he himself created. He would likely counter such an accusation by arguing that, as an empirical scientist, he was simply observing facts and trying to account for their existence and for their relation to one another. To him the concept of the self offered the best explanation he could provide for one of the central mysteries of the psyche—its seemingly miraculous creativity, its centering dynamics, and its deep structures of order and coherence.

The psychic system as a whole consists of many parts. Thoughts and archetypal images stand at one end of the spectrum, representations of the drives and instincts at the other end, and in between are a vast amount of personal material such as memories forgotten and recalled and all the complexes. The factor that orders this whole system and ties it all together is an invisible agent called the self. This is what creates the balances among the various other factors and ties them together into one functioning unit. The self is the center, and it unifies the pieces. But it does so at a considerable distance, like the sun influencing the orbits of the planets. Its essence lies beyond the boundaries of the psyche. It is psychoid, and it extends into regions beyond human experience and knowing. In that sense, Jung would say the self is infinite. At least we cannot say from empirical evidence where its edges may lie. This is as far as Jung would go, as he notes in his autobiography, but it is surely a good distance.

8

Emergence of the Self
(Individuation)

The features of Jung's map of the soul are now in place, and with that in the foreground one is now prepared to consider the psychological journey taken in this territory over the course of a person's lifetime. I have touched on this theme of psychological development many times already, but now with the whole theory in mind it is possible to convey the full range of what Jung called the *individuation process*. People develop in many ways throughout their lifetimes, and they undergo multiple changes at many levels. The total experience of wholeness over an entire lifetime—the emergence of the self in psychological structure and in consciousness—is conceptualized by Jung and called individuation.

Jung's concept of individuation is based partially on the common observation that people do grow and develop in the course of the seventy or eighty years they normally live now in Western societies. *Physically*, people are born as infants, pass after several years into childhood, then enter adolescence and early adulthood. The apex of physical development generally occurs in the period of late adolescence and early adulthood, and physical growth is more or less completely achieved by the age of twenty. The healthy body is now vibrant and fully capable of biological reproduction and the heroic feats of effort and endurance required for coping with the physical world. Physically one is complete at this point, although muscles can be built up further and athletic skills sharpened and honed. After the mid-thirties, the decline and decay of bodily function becomes an increasingly important factor. One has to conserve and protect one's body and become careful about stressing it too much lest it be damaged beyond repair. As midlife and middle age set in, the physical changes and developments that occur are often unwelcome and may cause considerable anxiety. Wrinkles, sagging stomachs and breasts, aches and pains in the joints—all of these are daily reminders of mortality. Adulthood and middle age are inevitably followed by old age, which can last a long time or only a short while. It is considered to begin in the seventies. In the next century it will no doubt become commonplace for people to live to a hundred or even to a hundred and twenty. Physical decline accelerates during this late period. The physical body grows, matures, ages, and declines in the course of the full lifespan. Physical growth and decay are governed importantly by genetic programs, which in Jung's theory of the psyche are interfaced with archetypal patterns. Each stage of life is undergirded and supported by a set of archetypal images that shape psychological attitudes, behavior, and motivations. The infant, for example, enters the world prepared to play its role in constellating suitable mothering attitudes and behaviors in its caretaker by cooing, smiling, sucking, and generally making itself lovable. At the same time (if all goes well) the mother is prepared to assume the role of nurturing and feeding her infant. The mother-infant pair describe an archetypal pattern of human fantasy and interpersonal interaction that is primordial and has important survival value. For each stage of life there are such constellations of instinct and archetype, which result in patterns of behavior and feeling and mentation.

The Psychological Lifespan

Jung was the first of what have come to be called *psychological* lifespan theorists. As opposed to those who suppose that the most important features of psychological and character development occur in infancy and early childhood and nothing of major import follows after that, Jung saw development as ongoing and the opportunities for further psychological development as an option for people at any age, including middle and old age. This is not to say that he minimized early development, and certainly he paid great attention to inherited features and tendencies of the personality, but the full expression and manifestation of the personality takes an entire lifetime to unfold. The self emerges bit by bit through the many stages of development described by Jung and other theorists such as Erik Erikson.

For Jung, psychological development follows the path of physical development to a point. It can be divided into the first half of life and the second. In a short but seminal article called "The Stages of Life," he describes this developmental trajectory by using the image of the sun rising in the morning, reaching its apex at noon, and descending in the afternoon to set finally in the evening.[1] This corresponds more or less to the pattern of the physical, but Jung adds that there are important differences, particularly with respect to the second half of life. In the beginning, consciousness arises like the dawn as the infant ego emerges from the waters of unconsciousness, and its growth and expansion and increasing complexity and power coincide with the growth and development of physical body that houses it. As the body grows and the brain matures and learning capacities develop and expand, the ego also develops its strength and capacities. A first step is to distinguish the individual body from objects in the surrounding world. This runs parallel to separating from the unconscious matrix within. The world becomes more real and concrete and is no longer simply the recipient of gross projections. Distinctions begin to be made and observed. Persons begin to move rapidly toward a capacity to function as separate entities. They begin to act as individuals, with the ability to control themselves and their environments to a reasonable degree, and to contain affect and the flow of thought as required by social standards of behavior. The ego learns, quite naturally and spontaneously, to manipulate the environment for individual survival in the ambient culture and to achieve personal benefits. It develops a persona. The healthy child's and young person's ego busily learns to set up its own world by becoming self-reliant and self-supporting in the terms offered by circumstance of birth. Adaptation, which is based on archetypal images such as the mother-infant unit and the later hero pattern of separation and conquest, takes place in relation to whatever the circumstances may be. Eventually, if all goes well, people are able to free themselves from dependency on their families of origin; they are able to reproduce biologically and to raise their children in a nurturing environment created by themselves; and they can play a role in the adult world of the society in which they exist. Inwardly they form an ego structure and a persona which are based upon archetypal potentials and typological tendencies. The major developmental project in the first half of life is ego and persona development to the point of individual viability, cultural adaptation, and adult responsibility for raising children.

How this is achieved and how it looks concretely depends to a large extent on the family, the social stratum, the culture and historical period into which a person is born. These factors will influence and shape many of the details in the differences between development in males and females, in the rich and the poor, in Eastern and Western individuals. These same factors also somewhat dictate the details of timing regarding the assumption of roles and responsibilities. What is universal, however, and therefore archetypal, is that every culture expects and demands of the young person the achievement of ego development and adaptation. In all cultures, the image of the hero and heroine are held up as ideals. The hero is an ideal image of someone who achieves ego development as men are supposed to emulate and admire; the heroine is an image that supplies this pattern for women. In some societies, ego development and persona development are completed for all practical purposes by the time adolescence is fully attained, in others (like modern societies, with seemingly interminable educational requirements) it may not be completed until middle age is immanent.

Individuation

Jung used the term individuation to talk about psychological development, which he defines as becoming a unified but also unique personality, an individual, an undivided and integrated person. Individuation includes more than the project achieved ideally in the first half of life, namely ego and persona development. When that is done, another task begins to emerge, for the ideal development of ego and persona have left a great deal of psychological material out of the conscious picture. The shadow has not been integrated, the anima and animus remain unconscious, and although it has been instrumental behind the scenes, the self has been hardly glimpsed directly. But now the question becomes, How can a person achieve psychological unity in the larger sense of the term, which entails uniting conscious and unconscious aspects of the personality? It is possible to fail in the task of individuation. One can remain divided, unintegrated, inwardly multiple into deep old age and still be considered to have lived a socially and collectively successful, albeit superficial, life. Deep inner unity on a conscious level is in fact a rare achievement, although it is undoubtedly supported by a very strong innate impulse: Jung speaks of an individuation drive, not primarily as a biological imperative but rather as a psychological one. I will explain its mechanism in a moment.

Here I want to insert a cautionary note for readers who wish to compare Jung to other psychological theorists. One should be careful not to confuse Jung's concept of individuation with notions that go under this term in other psychological theories. This is similar to the problem of comparing Jung's concept of the self with that of other writers. In Margaret Mahler's work, for instance, there is a strong emphasis on a process that she termed "separation/individuation." The child separates from its mother beginning at about age two by saying "no." That movement, built into the natural development of the psychological individual, takes place spontaneously and facilitates ego development. It is archetypally based and can be related to the early appearance and the first approximation of the archetypal pattern of the hero. For

Jung this would be one aspect of lifelong individuation, but certainly it is not the whole story. The purpose of this movement toward separation is to create a psychological situation that can later proceed toward further steps of consciousness and finally to integration and unification of the personality as a whole. For Mahler, separation is not an end in itself, but only a way station. Individuation for Jung *is* an end in itself.

The psychological mechanism by which individuation takes place, whether we are considering it in the first or the second half of life, is what Jung called *compensation*. The fundamental relation between conscious and unconscious is compensatory. The growth of the ego out of the unconscious—driven by a powerful instinct to become separated from the surrounding world in order to adapt more effectively to the ambient environment—results in a separation between ego-consciousness and the unconscious matrix from which it comes. The tendency of the ego is to become onesided, to become excessively self-reliant. This is, as we have seen, based on the archetypal pattern of the hero. When this happens, the unconscious begins to compensate for this onesidedness. Compensations happen classically in dreams. The function of compensation is to introduce balance into the psychic system. These compensations are tuned precisely to the present moment, and their timing is governed strictly by what consciousness is doing or not doing, by the onesided attitudes and developments of ego-consciousness. *Over time*, however, these many small daily compensations add up to patterns, and these patterns lay down the groundwork for the spiral of development toward wholeness that Jung terms individuation. Jung finds this happening especially clearly in long series of dreams: "these apparently separate acts of compensation arrange themselves into a kind of plan. They seem to hang together and in the deepest sense to be subordinated to a common goal . . . I have called this unconscious process spontaneously expressing itself in the symbolism of a long dream-series the individuation process."[2] One can also apply this same rule to psychological development generally. The unconscious compensates ego-consciousness over the whole life span and in many ways—by slips of the tongue, forgetfulness, or miraculous revelations; by arranging accidents, disasters, love affairs, and windfalls; by generating inspirational ideas and hairbrained notions that lead to disaster. In the lifelong unfolding that Jung calls individuation, the driving force is the self, and the mechanism by which it emerges in the conscious life of the individual is compensation. This is equally true in the first half of life and in the second.

The second half of life involves a different kind of movement from what transpires in the first, however. In this second phase of individuation, the pattern's accent is not the separation of the ego from its background and from its identifications with the milieu, but rather the unification of the whole personality. Jung would sometimes speak of the "return to the mothers," which is a metaphorical way of saying that when ego development climaxes at midlife there is no further meaning in continuing to pursue the same old goals. In fact, some of the goals already achieved are now called into question as ultimate values, and this leads to reassessment of what has been achieved and reassessment on where further meaning lies.[3] There is more to life than making one's way in the world with a solid and well-structured ego and persona. "Been there, done that" sums up the mood of the midlifer. Now what? Meaning lies elsewhere, and psychic energy changes its course. The task now becomes to unify the ego with the unconscious, which contains the person's unlived life and unrealized potential. This development in the second half of life is the classic Jungian meaning of individuation—becoming what you already are potentially, but now more deeply and more consciously. This requires the enabling power of symbols which lift up and make available contents of the unconscious that have been obscured from view. The ego is unable to carry out this larger unification of the personality by its own efforts. It needs an angel to assist.

Jung himself did not spend much time considering the issues of the first half of life after his break with Freud. He was mainly interested in people such as the fifty-three-year-old woman described in "A Study in the Process of Individuation."[4] Most of his own patients were adults of this type. Not seriously mentally ill, not in need of hospital or medical treatment, no longer in the early stages of their lives, these people came to Jung for wisdom and guidance in pursuing further inner development. This is not to say that some were not neurotic and in need of psychological help too, but they were not typical psychiatric patients. In fact, Jung preferred working with people whose ego-building and child-bearing years were past and whose first half of life developments had already taken place. Now was the opportunity to pursue the second great phase of the individuation process, the more explicit emergence of the self into consciousness. The methods Jung used to help them with this complex project have come to be called Jungian analysis.

Psychological change and development in adulthood and old age are in some ways more subtle than development in the first half of life. One has to observe people very carefully and at deep levels to perceive it. And sometimes there is not much to observe because the development has been so minimal. For instance, my best childhood friend's father, at eighty-nine, had aged noticeably in the thirty years since I had last seen him. Clearly he was nearing the end of his life. Yet, although his body had altered greatly, his persona, his sense of humor, his personality had not seemingly changed very much, and on this account he was as familiar and recognizable as ever. When I met him again after all these years, I knew him immediately. To me, his personality, as I could see it and experience it, was utterly intact and the same. While his energy may have been less than it once was, he could still muster enough to carry on a lively conversation about the newest models of his favorite automobiles. He remained more or less the same person he always was, even though his body was shrunken and weaker.

Had there been any development in his psyche in the course of his adulthood after the age of 50? Had his attitudes changed? How well did I know him? I knew him as a child and then no more, so I had only a child's view of him. I knew his persona, but that is all. To all appearances, his persona had remained intact. But as we know, there is a good more to the psyche than the persona. And yet, if the persona does not change, is there deeper change either?

Is it so subtle we can't see it without deep interpretive, probing interviews? Perhaps his consciousness had developed dramatically beyond where it was when I knew him so long ago, but I could not see it. Jung resisted the notion that the psychological trajectory is identical to the physical, which shows mostly only decline in old age. Are there psychological compensations that outweigh the physical decay and show a different pattern?

The Five Stages of Consciousness

To get a handle on this question of development of consciousness in the second half of life, we can apply some general measuring sticks. Jung described five stages of development of consciousness,[5] which I will summarize and expand a bit. We can use these to measure and assess development of consciousness in children and also in adults in their later years.

The first stage is characterized by *participation mystique*, a term borrowed from the French anthropologist, Lévy-Bruhl. Participation mystique refers to an identification between an individual's consciousness and the surrounding world, without awareness that one is in this state; consciousness and the object with which one is identified are mysteriously the same thing. There is an absence of awareness of a difference between oneself and one's perceptions on the one hand and the object in question on the other. To some extent, people stay in this state of participation mystique all their lives. For example, many people identify in this way with their cars. They experience all kinds of self feelings about their cars. When the car develops a problem, its owner feels sick, comes down with a cold, gets a stomach ache. We are unconsciously united with the world around us. This is what Jung called participation mystique.

Most people are connected to their families, at the beginning of life at least, by participation mystique, which is based on identification, introjection, and projection. These terms describe the same thing: an intermingling of inner and outer contents. The infant is at first literally not able to distinguish where it leaves off and where mother begins. The infant's world is highly unified. In this sense the first stage of consciousness anticipates the final stage: ultimate unification of the parts into a whole. At the beginning, however, it is unconscious wholeness, whereas at the end the sense of wholeness is conscious.

In the second stage of consciousness, projections become more localized. After the hit-or-miss projections in the first stage, some self/other distinctions begin to appear in consciousness. The infant becomes aware of certain places where its own physical being collides with outside objects, and it begins to watch out for things and to recognize differences between self and other and among the objects in the world around it. Slowly this differentiation between self and other and between inner and outer increases and sharpens. When good subject/object differentiation exists and when self and other are distinct and clearly different, projection and participation mystique change. This does not mean that projection has been overcome, but only that it has become more localized, focusing on a few objects rather than on the whole wide world. Some objects in the world are clearly now more important and interesting than others because they carry projections and are the recipients of libidinal investment. Mother, favorite toys, bright moving objects, pets, father, other people become special and singled out and distinct. So as conscious development proceeds, differentiation takes place and projection becomes fixed on specific figures. And since projections fall on the unknown, the world offers plenty of opportunity to continue the process of projecting throughout one's entire lifetime.

Parents are early major carriers of projection, and children unconsciously project omnipotence and omniscience onto them. These are what Jung called archetypal projections. The parents become gods, invested with powers that people have attributed to the divine. "Daddy can do anything! He's the strongest guy in the whole world!" "Mother knows everything and can perform miracles. She also loves me unconditionally!" The shocking realization that one's parents do not know everything and are anything but godlike usually occurs during the teenage years, and then for a time parents don't know anything at all (another kind of projection). We also project onto siblings; this lies at the root of sibling rivalry and the kind of competitive and sometimes vicious dynamics that go on in families. Teachers and school itself also receive many projections. In fact, numerous figures in our environment become carriers of projection in the second stage of consciousness. This gives people and institutions the power to form and shape our consciousness powerfully, filling it with their knowledge and opinions and gradually replacing our own personal experience with collective opinions, views, and values. This is the process of acculturation and adaptation that takes place in childhood and adolescence.

Falling in love and getting married are typically based on massive anima and animus projections, and this leads directly into childbearing and rearing during which the children become carriers of divine child projections. Like the first stage, the second is one that no one leaves behind completely. As long as one is able to be enchanted, to feel the stir of adventure and romance, to risk all for a mighty conviction, one continues to operate out of projection onto concrete objects in the world. And for many the development of consciousness stops here. Such individuals continue to project positive and negative features of the psyche massively into the world around and to respond to the psyche's images and powers as though they were located in external objects and persons.

If conscious development does continue—which can begin when a new phase of cognitive development leads to the ability to reach a level of abstraction that is relatively free of concretism—one becomes aware that specific projection carriers are not identical with the projections they carry. The persons who have carried the projections can step out from behind the projections, and as a result they often become de-idealized. At this stage, the world loses much of its naive enchantment. The projected psychic contents become abstract, and they now manifest as symbols and ideologies. Omniscience and omnipotence are no longer granted to human beings, but such qualities are projected onto abstract entities such as God, Fate, and Truth. Philosophy and theology become possible. Supreme values take on the numinous power once attributed to parents and teachers. The Law or the Revelation or the Teachings become invested with archetypal projections, and the concrete everyday world becomes relatively free of projections and can be interacted with as neutral. To the extent that this stage of consciousness is attained, a person becomes less vulnerable to fears of evil enemies and forces. One need not fear the reprisals of human enemies because God is in control. Or it is assumed that one can manipulate and take control of the world rationally because it obeys the laws of nature and is free of spirits and demons who might not like a highway here or a dwelling place there. One does not seem to keep running into oneself, feeling so directly the pain of what one is doing to the object.

The spontaneous empathic response to suffering among creatures in the world and to the destruction of the natural world is decreased to a considerable extent when the self/object dichotomy has reached this point. To many this does not seem to be an advance but rather a decline in consciousness. But it must be recognized that the emotional reactions of empathy manifested in the earlier developmental stages are largely based on projection and have little to do with an objective evaluation of what is happening to the object. When projections are removed from concrete objects in the world, visionary political leaders and charismatic ideologues create abstractions in the form of ideas, values, or ideologies by the projections fed into concepts that state what is of highest value and the greatest good in their perception. On the basis of these values, one can develop a set of imperatives and "oughts" that stand in place of the natural, spontaneous emotional relationships that less conscious people enjoy with the world. In place of unconscious empathy based on participation mystique or projection, one has rules that dictate duty. One does the right thing ecologically, for instance, not out of feeling but out of duty, not because one gets sick with pain for the destruction of the natural world but because of a moral imperative to sort the garbage and burn less fuel.

In this third stage of consciousness—which is I believe what my friend's father reached, for he was a religious man in the traditional sense—there are still projections of unconscious material. But these projections are invested not so much in persons and things but in principles and symbols and teachings. Of course, these projections are still considered "real" in an almost concrete sense. God really does exist somewhere, He or She is a distinct personality, and so on. As long as one believes that an actual God will punish or reward one in the afterlife, this indicates a Stage 3 level of consciousness. The projection has simply become transferred from the human parent to a more abstract, mythological figure.

The fourth stage represents the radical extinction of projections, even in the form of theological and ideological abstractions. This extinction leads to the creation of an "empty center," which Jung identifies with modernity. This is the "modern man in search of his soul."[6] The sense of soul—of grand meaning and purpose in life, immortality, divine origin, a "God within"—is replaced by utilitarian and pragmatic values. "Does it work?" becomes the primary question. Humans come to see themselves as cogs in a huge socio-economic machine, and their expectations for meaning are scaled down to bite size chunks. One settles for moments of pleasure and the satisfactions of manageable desires. Or one becomes depressed! Gods no longer inhabit the heavens, and demons are converted into psychological symptoms and brain chemical imbalances. The world is stripped of projected psychic contents. No more heroes, no more evil villains—humans become realistic. Principles are only relatively valid, and values are seen as derived from cultural norms and expectations. Everything cultural appears to be manufactured and without inherent meaning. Nature and history are regarded as the product of chance and the random play of impersonal forces. Here we arrive at the attitude and feeling-tone of the modern person: secular, atheistic, perhaps slightly humanistic. A modern person's values seem hedged about with reservations, conditions, "maybe's," "not sure's." The modern stance is relativistic.

In this fourth stage of consciousness, it *seems* as if psychic projections have disappeared altogether. Jung points out, however, that this is undoubtedly a false assumption. In actuality the ego itself has become invested with the contents previously projected out onto others and objects and abstractions. Thus the ego is radically inflated in the modern person and assumes a secret God-Almighty position. The ego, rather than Laws or Teachings, is now the recipient of projections, good and bad. The ego becomes the sole arbiter of right and wrong, true and false, beautiful and ugly. There is no authority outside of the ego that exceeds it. Meaning must be created by the ego; it cannot be discovered elsewhere. God is not "out there" any more, it's me! While the modern person appears to be reasonable and grounded, actually he is mad. But this is hidden, a sort of secret kept even from oneself.

Jung believed this fourth stage to be an extremely dangerous state of affairs for the obvious reason that an inflated ego is unable to adapt very well to the environment and so is liable to make catastrophic errors in judgment. While this is an advance of consciousness in a personal and even a cultural sense, it is dangerous because of the potential for megalomania. Anything goes! If I want to do it and figure I can get away with it, it must be okay. Not at all immune to the seductive persuasions of the shadow, the ego is easily led to indulge in the shadow's lust for power and its wishes to gain total control of the world. This was Nietzsche's Superman, and this hubris is reflected in the various social and political catastrophes of the twentieth century. Already prefigured in Dostoevski's protagonist Raskolnikov in *Crime and Punishment,* we now witness a human being who will kill an old woman simply to see how it feels. The Stage 4 person is no longer controlled by societal conventions related either to people or values. Consequently the ego can consider unlimited possibilities of action. This does not mean that all modern people are sociopathic, but the doors for such a development are wide open. And the worst cases might be those that look most reasonable—the "best and the brightest" who think they can calculate an answer to all questions of policy and morality.

Jung said jokingly that on the street one meets people at all stages of development—Neanderthals, medieval people, moderns, people at all conceivable levels of conscious development. Living in the twentieth century does not automatically confer the status of modernity on one's development of consciousness. Not everybody approaches Stage 4. In fact, many people cannot bear its demands. Others consider it evil. The fundamentalisms of the world insist on clinging to Stages 2 and 3 out of fear of the corrosive effects of Stage 4 and of the despair and the emptiness it engenders. But it is a real psychological achievement when projections have been removed to this extent and individuals take personal responsibility for their destinies. The trap is that the psyche becomes hidden in the ego's shadow.

These first four stages in the development of consciousness have to do with ego development and the first half of life. The person who has achieved the self-critical and reflective ego characteristic of Stage 4 without falling into megalomaniac inflation has done extremely well in developing consciousness, and is highly evolved in Jung's assessment. But further development in the second half of life is reserved by Jung for a fifth stage, a postmodern stage, which has to do with approaching the re-unification of conscious and unconscious. In this stage, there is conscious recognition of ego limitation and awareness of the powers of the unconscious, and a form of union becomes possible between conscious and unconscious through what Jung called the transcendent function and the unifying symbol. The psyche becomes unified but, unlike Stage 1, the parts remain differentiated and contained within consciousness. And unlike Stage 4, the ego is not identified with the archetypes: the archetypal images remain "other," they are not hidden in the ego's shadow. They are now seen as "in there," unlike in Stage 3 where they are "out there" in metaphysical space somewhere, concretely, and they are not projected onto anything external.

The expression "postmodern" is mine, not Jung's. His fifth stage of consciousness is not "postmodern" in the sense of the word as used in the arts and in literary criticism but in the sense of a stage that transcends and supersedes the "modern." It goes beyond the modern ego that has seen through everything and does not believe in the reality of the psyche. The modern stance is a "nothing but" attitude. It is convinced that projections have been eliminated and that they were nothing but a lot of smoke and mirrors signifying nothing. The postmodern attitude recognizes that there is psychic reality in projections, but not in the concrete or material sense. If we heard so much noise in the woods, maybe something was out there after all. Not what we thought, but something real nevertheless. Can we observe it? Can we intuit it? Can we conceive of it? The psyche itself then becomes the object of scrutiny and reflection. How to capture it in our observations? How to relate to it when we do? These are the postmodern issues and questions. And so Jung's attempts at formulating a suitable epistemology in *Psychological Types* (a "critical psychology," as he called it) was an effort to lay the groundwork for approaching the psyche as an entity in its own right. His techniques of active imagination and dream interpretation lend themselves to interacting with the psyche directly and forming a conscious relationship with it. In this way, he was forging the tools to relate to life in a postmodern, conscious way and to take up a respectful position toward the same contents that primitive and traditional peoples find in their myths and theologies, that infants and young children project into their parents and toys and games, and that the deeply insane and psychotic mental patients see in their hallucinations and visions. The contents are common to all of us, and they make up the deepest and most primitive layers of the psyche, the collective unconscious. To approach the archetypal images and to relate to them consciously and creatively becomes the centerpiece of individuation and makes up the task of the fifth stage of consciousness. This stage of consciousness produces another movement in the individuation process. The ego and the unconscious become joined through a symbol.

Officially Jung stopped at Stage 5, although in several places he indicates that he contemplated further advances beyond it. There are suggestions in his writings for what could be considered a sixth and perhaps even a seventh stage. For example, in his Kundalini Yoga Seminar,[7] given in 1932, Jung clearly recognizes the attainment of states of consciousness in the East that far surpass what is known in the West. While he is dubious about the prospects for Westerners to achieve similar stages of consciousness in the foreseeable future, he nevertheless does grant the theoretical possibility of doing so and even describes some of the features such stages would have. The type of consciousness revealed in Kundalini could be considered a potential Stage 7.

Backing up a bit, there is a type of consciousness that is more accessible to the West and would occupy a place between Stage 5 and this putative Stage 7. Later in his own life when he explored the structure and function of the archetypes in the context of synchronicity, Jung suggested that perhaps these apparently inner structures correspond to structures of being in the nonpsychic world. I discuss this in more detail in chapter 9, but for now it is sufficient to suggest that a possible sixth stage of consciousness would be one that takes into account the wider ecological relation between psyche and world. For Westerners, who are fundamentally conditioned by a materialistic attitude, this is a possible developmental option. Stage 6, then, could be seen as a state of consciousness that recognizes the unity of psyche and the material world. Jung moved cautiously in exploring such territories, however, because here he was clearly passing from psychology as we have known it in the West into physics, cosmology and metaphysics, areas in which he did not feel intellectually qualified and competent. Nevertheless his thinking led him step by step in that direction, and we have to grant that he showed the courage to follow his intuitions. His conversations with modern physicists like Wolfgang Pauli, with whom he published a book,[8] were an attempt to work out some of those correlations and correspondences between the psyche and the physical world.

The five stages of development of consciousness described above are mentioned briefly by Jung in two paragraphs in the essay, "The Spirit Mercurius."[9] I have expanded upon that by using several other sources in his work. The theme of individuation appears throughout his written works from 1910 onwards. It is a constant preoccupation that deepens as he pursues his investigations of the structure and dynamics of the psyche. It is still on his mind in the late essay "A Psychological View of Conscience,"[10] which was published in 1958 some three years before his death at the age of 86. Almost everything he wrote touches in one way or another upon the theme of individuation. There are two classic texts on this topic, however, and in the remainder of this chapter I will focus on them. They are "Conscious, Unconscious, and Individuation"[11] and "A Study in the Process of Individuation."[12]

In the paper, "Consciousness, Unconsciousness, and Individuation," Jung offers a succinct summary of what he means by the term individuation. He begins by saying it is the process by which a person becomes a psychological individual, which is to say, a separate undivided conscious unity, a distinct whole. I have explained some of the implications of this above, as a process of first unifying ego-consciousness and then the whole psychic system of conscious and unconscious, in order to approach what Jung would ultimately call wholeness. Wholeness is the master term that describes the goal of the individuation process, and it is the expression within psychological life of the self archetype.

The way into the unconscious, Jung points out, lies initially through emotion and affect. An active complex makes itself known through disrupting the ego with affect. This is a compensation from the unconscious and offers potential for growth. Eventually, he goes on, these affective disturbances can be traced to primordial roots in instinct, but they can also lead to images that anticipate the future. Jung posits a finalistic point of view, a movement toward a goal. In order to approach wholeness, the conscious/unconscious systems must be brought into relationship with one another: "The psyche consists of two incongruous halves which together form a whole."[13] He then presents a practical method that people can use to work on uniting the disparate halves of the psyche.

He is addressing what I described above as Western people in Stage 4 who "believe in ego-consciousness and in what we call reality. The realities of a northern climate are somehow so convincing that we feel very much better off when we do not forget them. For us it makes sense to concern ourselves with reality. Our European ego-consciousness is therefore inclined to swallow up the unconscious, and if this should not prove feasible we try to suppress it. But if we understand anything of the unconscious, we know that it cannot be swallowed. We also know that it is dangerous to suppress it, because the unconscious is life and this life turns against us if suppressed, as happens in neurosis."[14] Neurosis is based on an internal conflict that guarantees one-sidedness: The unconscious is repressed, and a person ends up in an energic impasse. With energy being used for such a narrow range of activities and for defenses against the sealed-off unconscious, much of life's possibilities for wholeness and satisfaction are denied. Often a person becomes extremely isolated, and life becomes sterile and may reach a standstill. "Conscious and unconscious do not make a whole when one of them is suppressed and injured by the other. If they must contend, let it at least be a fair fight with equal rights on both sides. Both are aspects of life. Consciousness should defend its reason and protect itself, and the chaotic life of the unconscious should be given the chance of having its way too—as much of it as we can stand. This means open conflict and open collaboration at once. That, evidently, is the way human life should be. It is the old game of hammer and anvil: between them the patient iron is forged into an indestructible whole, an 'individual'."[15]

Forging an indestructible whole between hammer and anvil! This vivid image speaks of the nature of the individuation process as Jung understood it. Not fundamentally a quiet process of incubation and growth, it is instead a vigorous conflict between opposites. What one gains by taking up the task of facing the conflict between persona and shadow, for instance, or between ego and anima, is "mettle," the knowledge gained through experience of the encounter (*Auseinandersetzung*, as Jung named it in German) between conscious and unconscious. "This, roughly, is what I mean by the individuation process. As the name shows, it is a process or course of development arising out of the conflict between the two fundamental psychic facts [conscious and unconscious]."[16]

A Case Study in Individuation

In the second essay, "A Study in the Process of Individuation," Jung provides more concrete detail about the individuation process, at least in its earlier stages during the second half of life. In this study, he describes a woman patient who is fifty-five years old and comes to work with him after moving back to Europe from abroad. She is a "father's daughter," highly cultured and educated. She is unmarried, "but [she] lived with the unconscious equivalent of a human partner, namely the animus . . . in that characteristic liaison often met with in women with an academic education."[17] He is speaking here about a modern woman. This was obviously a fascinating and instructive case for him. She was not a traditional mother and housewife who needed to develop her intellect and spiritual side (animus development) in the second half of life, which was the way he had usually thought of women's individuation. Rather, this was a women with a very strong intellectual development and a career. But she was male-identified, and she was now on a quest to discover something about her Scandinavian mother and her motherland. She wanted to get in touch with the feminine side of her personality, which to her was unconscious.

Actually many women of this type would continue to come to Jung for treatment in the following years. This patient is similar to many women today who, having put education ahead of starting a family and having children, pursue a career, perhaps to the point where childbearing becomes a receding mirage. In 1928, however, this was still a rather unusual woman.

The patient started drawing pictures and painting. She was not a trained artist, which was an advantage for analysis because this allowed the unconscious to express itself in a more direct and spontaneous way. This patient commented that her eyes wanted to do one thing, but her head wanted her to do another, and she let the eyes have their way, indicating that the emerging new center of consciousness had a will of its own. It wanted it this way, not that way, and she could allow that to happen. *Geschenlassen* ("letting it happen") is the way to capture the unconscious at work. Jung did not actively interpret the psychological meaning of her drawings and painting but rather participated in the process by encouraging the woman to "let it happen" as her unconscious wanted. Often he did not even understand what the pictures wanted to say beyond their manifest content. He simply encouraged her to stay with it. Gradually a story could be seen unfolding, a development took place, and this showed its purpose in due time.

Picture 1[18] shows the patient's initial situation: it depicts the condition of being psychologically and developmentally stuck. A woman's body is embedded in rock and is obviously struggling to become free. This is the condition of the patient as she begins analysis. Picture 2 shows a bolt of lightning striking the rock and separating a round stone from the others. This stone represents the woman's core (the self). Jung comments that this picture represents the release of the self from the unconscious: "The lightening has released the spherical form from the rock and so caused a kind of liberation."[19] The patient associated the lightning with her analyst. The transference has begun to have its profound effect upon her personality. In the drama, Jung is represented by lightning, which is also the masculine element of her own personality that strikes and fertilizes. Jung notes the sexual overtones of this imagery.

Later in the text, Jung speaks of himself as a projection-carrier for the patient's inferior function, intuition: "The 'inferior' function . . . [has] the significance of a releasing or 'redeeming' function. We know from experience that the inferior function always compensates, complements, and balances the 'superior' function. My psychic peculiarity would make me a suitable projection carrier in this respect."[20] As the carrier for her projections, Jung's words and presence became compensatory to the patient's consciousness and also greatly exaggerated in their power and effectiveness. She would see him as a genius of intuition, one who knows and understands everything. This is the kind of thing a strong transference typically says to a patient. It is Jung's intuition, then, that hits the patient like a lightning bolt and has such a profound effect on her. Because it is also the patient's inferior function, "it hits consciousness unexpectedly, like lightning, and occasionally with devastating consequences. It thrusts the ego aside, and makes room for a supraordinate factor, the totality of a person."[21]

This picture therefore represents the ego being pushed aside. and the self making its first appearance. The rock that is broken loose does not represent her ego but rather the self. The lightning frees her potential for wholeness, which until now had been locked away in the unconscious. "This self was always present, but sleeping."[22] This woman's remarkable ego development had left the self behind, and she had gotten stuck in persona adaptations and in an identification with the father complex and the animus, the "rocks" of her painting. From these identifications she needed to be freed. The possibility for contacting and becoming more connected to the self, which lies at the heart of the individuation process, must be released from the unconscious, and in this case it happens through the action of therapeutic lightning. For good reason Jung said that transference is critical for success in therapy.

Before his comments on the third picture, a crucial one in the series, Jung says in passing that "the third picture . . . brings a motif that points unmistakably to alchemy and actually gave me the definitive incentive to make a thorough study of the works of the old adepts."[23] This is a remarkable statement in light of the fact that Jung spent a good deal of the rest of his life studying alchemy in great depth and intensity. Picture 3 depicts "an hour of birth—not of the dreamer but of the self."[24] The image is of a dark blue sphere floating freely in space, a "planet in the making."[25] This is the appearance of what the patient called her "true personality," and she felt at the moment of making this picture that she had reached the culminating point of her life, a moment of great liberation.[26] Jung associates this with the birth of the self[27] and indicates that the patient is here at the point of conscious realization of the self when "the liberation has become a fact that is integrated into consciousness."[28]

In Picture 4 there is a significant change in the sphere. Now there is some differentiation: it is divided into "an outer membrane and an inner nucleus."[29] The snake that was floating above the sphere in the earlier picture is now penetrating the sphere and impregnating it. The fourth picture deals with fecundation and employs more or less explicit sexual imagery. She has put her male identification aside and is opening her being to new possibilities for life. As the patient and Jung interpret this picture, it comes to hold an impersonal meaning as well: the ego must experience "letting go" in order to expand the horizon to include positive and negative aspects of the whole personality (shadow integration). The union of snake and sphere represent a union of the psychic opposites in the patient's psyche. Jung avoids the concrete sexual transference interpretations that could so easily be made here because they would lead into sexual reductionism and would fail to advance the individuation process. The suffering the patient was undergoing here was precisely letting go of the personalistic interpretations, namely of her sexual wishes for Jung the man, and realizing instead that she was not falling in love with her analyst, with whom she had become so psychologically intimate, but that an archetypal level of the process of individuation had been activated and this was at work beyond their personal relationship. It was the self in operation, emerging through this imagery.

The picture series now takes up in much greater depth and detail the problem of the shadow and the integration of good and evil. In Picture 5 evil is rejected, and the serpent is placed outside the sphere. Picture 6 shows an attempt to unite the opposites outside and inside, a movement towards conscious realization. Picture 7 indicates some depression and some further consciousness as a result. Picture 8, which is very important, illustrates a movement toward the earth, the mother, the feminine. This was what this woman came to Europe for; she was trying to make firm contact with the feminine side of her being. Picture 9 again shows her struggle with uniting the opposites, good and evil. In Picture 10, the opposites are balanced, but the image of cancer appears for the first time. (This women, in fact, died of cancer sixteen years later.) Picture 11 suggests that the rising importance of the outside world was beginning to cloud the value of the mandala. From here on the theme of the mandala is repeated in many variants, each one attempting further integration and expression of the self. The series concludes with Picture 19 initially, but then the woman continues for ten more years after treatment and eventually ends with Picture 24, a beautiful white lotus image with a yellow center, placed inside a golden circle that hangs against a solid black background. A single gold star sits above the lotus. The lotus itself rests on a bed of green leaves, and below the leaves are what appear to be two golden serpents. It is a gorgeous image of the self, manifest and fully realized. Jung declines to comment on the images beyond Picture 19, but they speak for themselves of a further deepening and consolidating of the selfhood uncovered and experienced during and after the period of analysis.

Jung's concluding statement about the case is that this woman was, during her analysis, in the early stages of a powerful individuation process. During the time he saw her in analysis, she experienced the never-to-be-forgotten emergence of the self into consciousness, and in subsequent weeks and months she struggled to unite the opposites within her psychic matrix. She was able to disidentify with the animus and to reunite with the feminine core of herself. Here ego became relativized vis-a-vis the self, and she was able to experience the impersonal archetypal psyche. These are classic features of what he would call the process of individuation in the second half of life.

The Movements of the Self

Just a final word on the subject of individuation. Jung's view of the self is both structural and dynamic. In the previous chapter, I focused mostly on its structural features. But when one considers the process of individuation, the feature that comes to the fore is its dynamic quality. Jung thinks of the self as undergoing continual transformation during the course of a lifetime. Each of the archetypal images that appear in the developmental sequence from birth to old age—the divine infant, the hero, the puer and puella, the king and queen, the crone and the wise old man—are aspects or expressions of this single archetype. Over the course of development, the self impacts the psyche and creates changes in the individual at all levels: physical, psychological, and spiritual. The individuation process is driven by the self and carried out through the mechanism of compensation. While the ego does not generate it or control it, it may participate in this process by becoming aware of it.

At the end of his late work *Aion*, Jung presents a diagram to illustrate the dynamic movements of the self. The diagram looks like a sort of carbon atom.

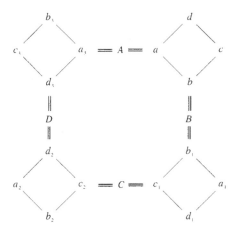

This represents a formula for the transformation of a single entity, the self, within the context of the continuum of an individual's psychological life. In this diagram, Jung is attempting to portray a movement within the self from pure potential to actualization: "The process depicted by our formula changes the originally unconscious totality into a conscious one."[30] Since it describes a continual process of transformation of one and the same substance, it is a process of transformation and renewal as well as a movement towards consciousness.

The movement starts in Quaternio A, which represents the archetypal level, the spirit end of the psychic spectrum. Here it manifests as an ideal image. As it circulates through the A quaternio, the B quaternio, the C quaternio, the D quaternio, and then returns to A to repeat again, a psychic content, an archetypal image, enters the psychic system at the archetypal end of the spectrum and an integration process ensues on each of the other three levels. First, the image rotates through the four points of the archetypal quaternio, and the idea becomes clearer. Then the idea shifts to level B, entering through the doorway of small b, by a process similar to shifting an energy level in an atom. This is a shift to another level of consciousness. Now the idea exists at the shadow level, and here it enters into reality and everyday life where objects cast shadows. The idea acquires substantiality, and the idea of unity, totality, and wholeness now must be lived out in life. The idea works its way through this psychic level, and it must now be realized concretely in space and time, and this introduces limitations and problems. Jung says that every human act can be regarded either positively or negatively[31] and when moving from thought to action one is entering a world of shadow potential. Every action leads to a reaction. It has an external impact, and so when someone actually begins individuating, making changes that other people start complaining about, this person is moving within the shadow quaternio. The idea is materializing, taking effect in real-life behavior, and reaching down into the instinctual level. Archetypes and instincts are becoming connected at this level, and as the idea moves into the Shadow Quaternio, it takes on more and more instinctual and embodied attributes.

When the idea descends into level C, it reaches the level of physis, which is extremely deep in the material substrate of the body, and the body itself begins to change. The organizing principle that begins with the image and entering the psyche becomes behavior, then touches on and constellates instinct, now begins to effect the body in such a way that it actually rearranges molecules. This deep physical level lies beyond the psychoid barrier of the psyche. This is one motive force behind evolution itself. Structure follows form.

With level D, the energy level itself is reached. Here lies the origin of the crystallization energy into matter. It is the submolecular and subatomic level of energy and the forms that shape it. To touch this level is to imply profound change indeed, change at the level of energy itself and its organization.

> The formula presents a symbol of the self, for the self is not just a static quantity or constant form, but is also a dynamic process. In the same way, the ancients saw the imago Dei in man not as a mere imprint, as a sort of lifeless, stereotyped impression, but as an active force . . . The four transformations represent a process of restoration or rejuvenation taking place, as it were, inside the self, and comparable to the carbon-nitrogen cycle in the sun, when a carbon nucleus captures four protons . . . and releases them at the end of the cycle in the form of an alpha particle. The carbon nucleus itself comes out of the reaction unchanged, 'like the Phoenix from the ashes'. The secret of existence, i.e., the existence of the atom and its components, may

well consist in a continually repeated process of rejuvenation, and one comes to similar conclusions in trying to account for the numinosity of the archetypes.[32]

Anticipating the next chapter, we can think of the self as a cosmic entity that emerges in human life and renews itself endlessly in its rotations through the psyche. Perhaps it relies on human individuals to become conscious of itself, to incarnate in the three-dimensional world of time and space, and also to rejuvenate itself and extend its existence. It subsists in the universe beyond the psyche. It uses our psyches and the material world, including our bodies, for its own purposes, and it continues after we grow old and die. We provide a home where it can emerge and reside, yet in our pride and ego inflation we take far too much credit for its genius and beauty.

9

Of Time and Eternity
(Synchronicity)

From his first attempts to explore the human soul and to map it and its boundaries, Jung was fascinated by what happens on the borders. This was his temperament—he loved to push at the edges of the already known. His first major study was a dissertation on mediumistic trances and the wondrous accounts of long-dead personages by his young cousin, Helene Preiswerk. This was a psychological investigation of the relation between normal and paranormal states of consciousness.[1] Subsequent works on word association and the theory of complexes studied the boundaries between conscious and unconscious parts of the psyche. Pressing further into the territory of the unconscious, Jung found another borderland. This one lay between personal and impersonal contents of the unconscious, between the territory of the complexes and that of the archetypal image-and-instinct combinations. In his consequent investigations of the self, he found a point of transgression at the boundary between psyche and nonpsyche. Since the archetype *per se* is psychoid and does not strictly belong within the confines of the psyche's

199

boundaries, it bridges between inner and outer worlds and breaks down the subject-object dichotomy.

Ultimately this curiosity about boundaries led Jung to state a theory that attempts to articulate a single unified system which embraces both matter and spirit and throws a bridge between time and eternity. This is the theory of *synchronicity*. An extension of the theory of the self into cosmology, synchronicity speaks of the profound hidden order and unity among all that exists. This theory also unveils Jung the metaphysician, an identity he often denied.

Patterns in Chaos

Jung's few writings about synchronicity explore the meaningful order in seemingly random events. He notes—as many others have too—that psychic images and objective events are sometimes arranged in definite patterns, and this arrangement occurs by chance and not by virtue of a causal chain of preceding events. In other words, there is no causal reason for the pattern to appear. It comes about purely by chance. So the question arises: Is this chance event of patterning completely random or is it meaningful? Divination follows this idea that certain chance events have meaning. A certain bird flies overhead, and the soothsayer tells the king that the time is right to set out for battle. Or there is the more complicated case of the ancient Chinese oracle called *I Ching* or *The Book of Changes*. This oracle is consulted by throwing coins or yarrow stalks to determine a pattern of numbers that is then related to one of sixty-four hexagrams. By studying that hexagram, one can determine a pattern of meaning in events of the present moment and an emergent pattern that will take shape in the future. From this one can take counsel. This oracle is based on the principle of synchronicity. The assumption is that there is a meaningful order behind the chance outcome of coin tossing, a burning question, and events in the external world. People who try the *I Ching* are often surprised by its uncanny accuracy. How can one explain these meaningful arrangements and patterns that are not created by known causes?

Even closer to Jung's analytic practice and psychological theory is a phenomenon he notes with fascination, namely that psychological compensation occurs not only in dreams but also in nonpsychologically controlled events. Sometimes compensation arrives from the outside world. A patient of Jung's had a dream of a golden scarab beetle. While discussing this dream symbol in his study, they heard a sound at the window and found that a local Swiss version of this beetle *(Cetonia aurate)* was trying to get into the room.[2] From instances like this, one infers that the appearance of archetypal images in dreams may coincide with other events. The compensatory phenomena cross over the commonly accepted boundaries between subject and object and manifest in the object world. Again, the puzzle for Jung was how to account for this in his theory. Strictly speaking such events are not psychological, and yet they have a deep connection to psychological life. Archetypes, he concludes, are *transgressive*,[3] that is they are not limited to the psychic realm. In their transgressivity, they can emerge into consciousness either from within the psychic matrix or from the world about us or both at once. When both happen at the same time, it is called synchronistic.

References to the *unus mundus* (the unified cosmos) and to the notion (if not the exact term) of synchronicity are scattered throughout the *Collected Works* and in other less formal writings like letters, but Jung did not express his thoughts fully on this subject until fairly late in life. In 1952, he and the Nobel Prize–winning physicist Wolfgang Pauli jointly published *Naturerklärung und Psyche*, (translated into English as *The Interpretation of Nature and the Psyche*), which was an attempt to elucidate the possible relations between nature and psyche. It was significant that Jung published this work with a Nobel Prize–winning scientist and not with a philosopher, a theologian, or a mythologist. Of all of Jung's theoretical work, this piece on synchronicity is subject to the most gross distortion. Jung wanted to avoid being seen as a mystic or a crank, and it is clear that he worried especially about exposing this part of his thinking to the eyes of the scientific, modern public. Pauli's essay, "The Influence of Archetypal Ideas on the Expression of Scientific Theories of Kepler," investigates the archetypal patterns in Kepler's scientific thought and in a sense prepares the way for Jung's more adventuresome contribution, the essay "Synchronicity: An Acausal Connecting Principle."[4] This work on synchronicity adds to Jung's psychological theory the notion that a high degree of continuity exists between psyche and world, such that psychic images (which also include the kernels of abstract scientific thoughts, like those of Kepler) may also reveal truths about reality in the reflective mirror of human consciousness. The psyche is not something that plays itself out in human beings only and in isolation from the cosmos. There is a dimension in which psyche and world intimately interact with and reflect one another. This is Jung's thesis.

Developing the Idea of Synchronicity

In a letter to Carl Seelig, the Swiss author and journalist who wrote a biography of Albert Einstein, Jung writes about his first inkling of synchronicity:

> Professor Einstein was my guest on several occasions at dinner . . . These were very early days when Einstein was developing his first theory of relativity. He tried to instill into us the elements of it, more or less successfully. As non-mathematicians we psychiatrists had difficulty in following his argument. Even so, I understood enough to form a powerful impression of him. It was above all the simplicity and directness of his genius as a thinker that impressed me mightily and exerted a lasting influence on my own intellectual work. It was Einstein who first started me on thinking about a possible relativity of time as well as space, and their psychic conditionality. More than thirty years later this stimulus led to my relation with the physicist Professor W. Pauli and to my thesis of psychic synchronicity.[5]

Einstein's theory of relativity must have captured Jung's imagination even if he did not understand the details of it or the mathematical proofs for it. It is interesting to note, too, that famous physicists played a part in this theorizing at its beginning and the conclusion. This association to modern physics gives the proper historical context for Jung's theory of synchronicity.

The relationship between Jung and the luminaries of modern physics is a story that has yet to be told fully. In addition to

Einstein and Pauli, there were also many other significant figures in modern physics who inhabited Zürich in the first half of the twentieth century and gave lectures or taught at the Polytechnic University where Jung was a professor of psychology in the 1930s. Zürich was a veritable hotbed of modern physics in the first half of this century, and it would have been nearly impossible to ignore the stimulating ferment these intellects created. There was a definite impression afoot that the nature of physical reality was being fundamentally rethought, and Jung early on—as indicated by his letter about Einstein—began thinking about the similarities between modern physics and analytical psychology. Jung's essay on synchronicity was doubtless the result of countless discussions with these people during the thirty or more years preceding its final form and publication.

It must be recognized that the theory of archetypes and the self and the theory of synchronicity were combined to weave a single fabric of thought. This is Jung's unified vision referred to in the Introduction of this book. To grasp the full scope of the theory of the self, one must consider it within the context of Jung's thinking on synchronicity; to grasp his theory of synchronicity one must also know about his theory of archetypes. This is one reason why few other psychologists have followed Jung's lead into the theory of archetypes. It becomes metapsychological to the point of metaphysics, and few psychologists feel comfortable in all the areas required to embrace this full theory—psychology, physics, and metaphysics. It is an intellectual range that few modern thinkers can hope to match. Academics are especially shy of stepping beyond the confines of their departmental specialty. The theory of synchronicity lends to Jung's view of the self as a feature of radical transcendence over consciousness and the psyche as a whole, and it challenges the common boundarylines drawn to separate the faculties of psychology, physics, biology, philosophy, and spirituality. Psychology is traditionally supposed to limit itself to what goes on in the human mind; but with his theory of the self and synchronicity, Jung's analytical psychology challenged this arbitrary segmentation. When Jung was once asked by students where the self ends and what its boundaries are, his reply is supposed to have been that it has no end, it is unbounded. To understand what he meant by this remark, one must realize that he was considering the implications of synchronicity for the theory of the self.

Jung was understandably ambivalent about putting forward an idea of the magnitude that synchronicity entails. Ever the cautious and conservative Swiss, Jung tried generally to rest his case on purely psychological arguments, his area of undisputed expertise. With the theory of synchronicity, however, he went out on a limb. Here the psyche by itself would not support him. Nevertheless at the age of seventy-five, he must have felt he had earned the right to indulge himself in this kind of cosmological speculation. He was ready to go into print with one of his wildest notions, the unity of the self and Being. Is this so different from saying that the self and God are one? He took the risk of sounding like a prophet, or worse yet, a crank.

Synchronicity and Causality

The essay itself is difficult and certainly deeply flawed by a misguided effort at statistical analysis of a piece of research carried out on married couples by a colleague. In my review of this work, I will limit myself to the theoretical sections. Jung begins by commenting on the notion of causality and the laws of probability, and he notes the universal human tendency to project causality. Almost inevitably people ask the question, Why did it happen? One assumes that every event is caused by something that preceded it. Often a causal relation of this sort is present, yet occasionally it may not be. In psychology, for instance, causality is particularly difficult to ascertain because nobody can know for certain what causes us to do, think, and feel as we do. There is conscious motivation, and there is unconscious motivation of psychic contents and impulses. There are many theories that try to explain emotion and behavior causally, but our projections undoubtedly lead us to find more causation in the realm of psychological phenomena than is really there. Or we may attribute events to the wrong causes, finding out later that we were mistaken.

We might jump to the conclusion that a man beats his wife because he was beaten as a child or because he saw his father beating his mother regularly. He behaves this way because of childhood experiences, or because his parents influenced him in that direction. He "takes after his father," or "his mother complex" is responsible, we might say with great confidence in our psychological acuity. This may be a good first approximation, but such reductive analyses surely do not exhaust the full range of possible causes and meanings. There is also a final cause, for instance, which leads people to do something in order to achieve a goal or to gain some measure of adaptation to life. Perhaps this man is trying to gain power and control over his wife, intending by that to achieve more mastery over his own future. Psychological causation can lead backwards into history or equally well forward into the future. And then there are the chance events, being in the right place at the right time. It's hard to explain why some people are so lucky or unlucky, and we often end up praising them for the things they did not do and blaming them for the things they could not avoid. There is almost infinite space for projection and speculation.

We think in cause-and-effect terms because we are human, not because we live in a scientific age. In every period and every culture, people think causally, even if they assign causes to events that our scientific knowledge contradicts. Today we might say that someone is a psychopathic monster because he was severely abused as a child, while in the Middle Ages the view was that the Devil made him do it. Different reasons are given, but the thinking is the same. To challenge causal thinking itself, Jung recognizes, is to go against the grain of common sense. So why do it? Because there are events that cannot be covered by all the theories of causality.

In questioning the ultimacy of cause-and-effect reasoning, Jung discovered that modern physics was an ally, for physics had discovered some events and processes for which there are no causal explanations, only statistical probabilities. Jung mentions, for example, the decay of radioactive elements. There is no causal explanation for why one or another specific radium atom decomposes when it does. The decay of radioactive elements can be predicted and measured statistically, and the rate of decay is steady over time, but there is no explanation for why it happens when and as it does. It just happens. It's a "just so" thing. This discovery of an uncaused event opens a gap in the causal universe. It is not only that science has not yet figured out how causality works here, but rather that in principle the rule of causation does not apply. If there are events that are not created by a preceding cause, how can we think about their origins? Why do they happen? What accounts for their occurrence? Are these events random and purely accidental?

Jung recognizes probability as an important factor in accounting for many events. But there are series of apparently random events that show a pattern beyond the scales of probability, such as runs of numbers or other extraordinary coincidences. Gamblers live and pray for these runs of luck that cannot be explained. Jung wants to stay away from highly intuitive or occult concepts like elective affinities or correspondences, which have been proposed by some seers and visionary philosophers such as Schopenhauer. Instead he prefers to approach this difficult subject scientifically, empirically, and rationally, just as many years earlier he had tackled the mystery of occult mediumship empirically and scientifically in his doctoral dissertation. Jung was thoroughly committed to a scientific approach to understanding.

It is tempting to read Jung's work on synchronicity, however, in more biographical terms. In his views about individuation in the second half of life, Jung holds that people (in the Western world, at least) should try to bring their rational ego-consciousness into contact with the non-rational collective unconscious while not sacrificing the ego's rational position. Jung also believed that the major psychological task in the second half of life is to formulate a *Weltanschauung* or worldview, a personal philosophy of life. And this should include both rational and irrational elements. In this essay on synchronicity we can see Jung using his rational Western scientific ego to explore the world of magic and the rare, inexplicable phenomena that occur in the collective unconscious. He is trying to formulate a symbol, in the form of a concept, that can hold the two realms together in a tension of opposites. While the issues he is dealing with here are similar to those often taken up in religion and philosophy, Jung is trying to bring his scientific rational method and worldview to bear upon phenomena whose mystical, religious, and quasi-magical nature usually excludes them from scientific discussion. For his own personal reasons, but also for our scientific culture as a whole, he is trying to forge a link between the two dominant cultural foci of the West, science and religion. He is trying to hold this tension without one-sidedly favoring either element. His theory of synchronicity is the symbol that will attempt to contain this pair of opposites. This is the personal piece of this work.

Jung was fascinated with J. B. Rhine's experiments in extrasensory perception (ESP) at Duke University. He was impressed because they demonstrated, using probability theory, that ESP cannot be explained causally. The experiments showed that humans can cross the seemingly absolute boundaries that limit us to a single time-space continuum. This reminded Jung of Einstein's theory of relativity and also of dreams he had observed where distant events were imaged during or before they took place. Rhine's experiments offered new empirical evidence for what Jung had already concluded, namely that the psyche is not limited absolutely by the boundaries of time and space. Causality, which assumes an absolutely sealed time-and-space continuum, cannot explain these events. Jung indicates that no energy is transmitted in Rhine's ESP experiments; there is only a "falling together" in time of thought and event. A card is turned over in one room, an image appears in a person's psyche in another room, and these coincide more often than is statistically probable. Jung uses the term "synchronicity" in print for the first time in this essay: "it cannot be a question of cause and effect, but of a falling together in time, a kind of simultaneity. Because of this quality of simultaneity, I have picked the term 'synchronicity' to designate a hypothetical factor equal in rank to causality as a principle of explanation."[6]

Synchronicity and Archetypal Theory

In 1954, two years after the appearance of the synchronicity essay, Jung published a revised version of his definitive theoretical paper "On the Nature of the Psyche." In a major supplement, he links the theory of archetypes to the principle of synchronicity. This is important because it ties these two pieces of his thinking together and forms a single unified theoretical statement. Jung uses the phrase "objective psyche" to discuss the view that the unconscious is a realm of "objects" (complexes and archetypal images) as much as the surrounding world is a realm of persons and things. These inner objects impinge on consciousness in the same way that external objects do. They are not part of the ego, but they affect the ego, and the ego must relate and adapt to them. Thoughts, for instance, occur to us, they "fall into" our consciousness (in German, *Einfall*, literally something that "falls into" consciousness, but also an "inspiration"). For Jung, the intuitions and thoughts that appear from the unconscious and are not the products of deliberate efforts to think but are inner objects, bits of the unconscious that land on the surface of the ego occasionally. (Jung sometimes liked to say that thoughts are like birds: They come and nest in the trees of consciousness for a little while and then they fly away. They are forgotten and disappear.) The deeper one goes into the objective psyche, moreover, the more objective it becomes because it is less and less related to the ego's subjectivity: "It is, at one and the same time, absolute subjectivity and universal truth, for in principle it can be shown to be present everywhere, which certainly cannot be said of conscious contents of a personalistic nature. The elusiveness, capriciousness, haziness, and uniqueness that the lay mind always associates with the idea of the psyche applies only to consciousness and not to the absolute unconscious."[7] Unlike consciousness, the unconscious is regular, predictable, and collective. "The qualitatively rather than quantitatively definable units with which the unconscious works, namely the archetypes, therefore have a nature that *cannot with certainty be designated as psychic*"[8] (Jung's italics).

In earlier chapters I noted that the archetypes are to be considered psychoid rather than purely psychic. In this passage Jung

states this explicitly: "Although I have been led by purely psychological considerations to doubt the exclusively psychic nature of
the archetypes, psychology sees itself obliged to revise its 'only
psychic' assumptions in the light of the physical findings too . . .
The relative or partial identity of psyche and physical continuum
is of the greatest importance theoretically, because it brings with
it a tremendous simplification by bridging over the seeming
incommensurability between the physical world and the psychic,
not of course in any concrete way, but from the physical side by
means of mathematical equations, and from the psychological
side by means of empirically derived postulates—archetypes—
whose content, if any, cannot be represented to the mind."[9] In
other words, Jung sees large areas of identity between the deepest
patterns of the psyche (archetypal images) and the processes and
patterns evident in the physical world and studied by physicists.
So, ironically enough, it turns out that the *participation mystique*
of first stage, primitive psychology is not so far from reality after
all! The psyche, defined by Jung as whatever contents or perceptions are capable in principle of becoming conscious and being
affected by the will, includes ego-consciousness, complexes,
archetypal images, and representations of instincts. But archetype
and instinct per se are no longer psychic. They lie on a continuum
with the physical world, which at its depths (as explored by modern physics) is as mysterious and "spiritual" as the psyche. Both
dissolve into pure energy. This point is important because it suggests a way to conceive of how the psyche is related to soma and
to the physical world. The two realms, psyche and the material
world, can be bridged by mathematical equations and by "empirically derived postulates—archetypes."[10] Neither the material
body nor the psyche need be derived from the other. They are two
parallel realities, rather, that are synchronistically related and
coordinated.

Mind and Matter

The relation of mind to matter intrigued Jung endlessly. He
thought it very curious for instance that, on the basis of mathematical thought alone, a bridge could be built that would stand up

to the rigors of nature and human traffic. Mathematics is a pure product of the mind and appears nowhere in the natural world, yet people can sit in their studies and generate equations that will accurately predict and capture physical objects and events. Jung was impressed that a purely psychic product (a mathematical formula) could bear such a remarkable relationship to the physical world. On the other side, Jung proposes that the archetypes also serve as direct links between the psyche and the physical world: "Only when it comes to explaining psychic phenomena of a minimal degree of clarity are we driven to assume that archetypes must have a non-psychic aspect. Grounds for such a conclusion are supplied by the phenomena of synchronicity, which are associated with the activity of unconscious operators and have hitherto been regarded, or repudiated, as 'telepathy', etc."[11] Jung is generally cautious about ascribing causality to the archetypes in connection with synchronistic phenomena (otherwise he would fall back into a model of causality, with the archetypes being the causes of synchronistic events), but in this passage he does seem to connect them to "operators" that organize synchronicity.

Synchronicity is defined as a meaningful coincidence between psychic and physical events. A dream of a plane falling out of the sky is mirrored the next morning in a radio report. No known causal connection exists between the dream and the plane crash. Jung posits that such coincidences rest on organizers that generate psychic images on one side and physical events on the other. The two occur at approximately the same time, and the link between them is not causal. Anticipating his critics, Jung writes: "Skepticism should . . . be leveled only at incorrect theories and not at facts which exist in their own right. No unbiased observer can deny them. Resistance to the recognition of such facts rests principally on the repugnance people feel for an allegedly supernatural faculty tacked on to the psyche, like 'clairvoyance'. The very diverse and confusing aspects of these phenomena are, so far as I can see at present, completely explicable on the assumption of a psychically relative space-time continuum. As soon as a psychic content crosses the threshold of consciousness, the synchronistic marginal phenomena disappear, time and space resume their accustomed sway, and consciousness is once more isolated in its subjectivity."[12]

Synchronistic phenomena appear most often when the psyche is operating at a less conscious level, as in dreaming or musing. A state of reverie is ideal. As soon as one becomes aware and focuses on the synchronistic event, time and space categories resume their sway. Jung concluded that the subjects in the Rhine experiments must have dimmed their consciousness as they became interested and excited by the project. Had they tried using their rational egos to figure out probabilities, their ESP results would have dropped, for as soon as cognitive functioning takes over, the door closes to synchronistic phenomena. Jung points out, too, that synchronicity seems to depend greatly on the presence of affectivity, that is, sensitivity to emotional stimuli.

In his writings, Jung offers both a narrow and a broad definition of synchronicity . The narrow definition is "the simultaneous occurrence of a certain psychic state with one or more external events which appear as meaningful parallels to the momentary subjective state."[13] By "simultaneous" he means an occurrence in about the same time frame, within hours or days, but not necessarily at exactly the same moment. There is simply a "falling together in time" of two events, one psychic and the other physical. On the psychic side, it could be a dream image or a thought or intuition. (This mysterious correlation between psyche and the object world is the more narrow definition of synchronicity. There will be a more general definition later in this essay.)

Often synchronicity occurs, as noted above, when a person is psychically in an *abaissement du niveau mental* (a lower level of conscious awareness, a sort of dimming of consciousness) and the level of consciousness has dropped into what is today called an alpha state. This means also that the unconscious is more energized than consciousness, and complexes and archetypes are aroused into a more activated state and can push over the threshold into consciousness. It is possible that this psychic material corresponds to objective data outside the psyche.

Absolute Knowledge

One intuitive leap that Jung makes, which is nevertheless based on a good deal of confirming evidence in his experience, is that the unconscious possesses what he calls a priori knowledge: "How could an event remote in space and time produce a corresponding psychic image when the transmission of energy necessary for this is not even thinkable? However incomprehensible it may appear, we are finally compelled to assume that there is in the unconscious something like an a priori knowledge or an 'immediacy' of events which lacks any causal basis."[14] This would allow for the possibility that intuitively we can know things that we have no rational way of knowing. Deep intuition can provide knowledge that is indeed really true and not just speculation, guesswork or fantasy. For Jung, the unconscious defies the Kantian categories of knowledge and surpasses consciousness in the range of possible knowing. In other words, in the unconscious we know many things that we do not know that we know. These could be called unthought thoughts or unconscious a priori knowledge. It is this notion that takes Jung into the furthest reaches of his speculations about the unity of psyche and world. If we know things that are beyond our conscious possibility of knowing, there is also an unknown knower in us, an aspect of the psyche that transcends the categories of time and space and is simultaneously present here and there, now and then. This would be the self.

Jungians sometimes comment that in the unconscious there are no secrets: Everybody knows everything. This is a way of talking about this level of psychic reality. Even putting aside for the moment the people who are extraordinarily gifted in intuition—like some medical intuitives who have proven an amazing rate of accuracy in diagnosis of people they have never known or seen—many people have the experience of dreaming about others in a way that gives them information to which they do not have conscious access. Of course they might not know that a particular dream is accurate. Sometimes we dream other peoples' dreams. Sometimes other people dream our reality. As an analyst who hears a lot of transference dreams, I can verify that some of them (not by any means all) are accurate far beyond the amount of knowledge my patients consciously have about me. Once a patient's dream even told me something about myself that I did not know consciously at the time. She dreamed that I was exhausted and needed a rest. I was not aware of this until I took time to reflect, and then coming down with a case of flu shortly thereafter, I realized that her unconscious had picked up my physical condition more accurately than even I could read with my own consciousness. One can compare this unconscious knower in people to the Eye of God, a notion that nuns formerly used to scare schoolchildren in their attempt to induce strict obedience to the church's teaching. It is not only what you do but even what you think—in fact, it is what you *are*—that God sees and keeps a running account of. This is a projective version of the same idea that some kind of absolute knowledge exists in the unconscious.

To think about this issue of a priori knowledge further, Jung considers the psychological meaning of numbers. What are they? Suppose that we "define number psychologically as an archetype of order which has become conscious."[15] There are, of course, ancient views that cosmic structures of being are based on numbers and on the relations of numbers to one another. Pythagorean doctrines, for instance, taught such views. Jung takes a similar approach, only with more modern notions of mathematics as fundamental structures of psyche and world. When these basic structures of being are imaged in the psyche, they come up as circles (mandalas) and squares (quaternities) typically, to which the numbers one and four are related. The movement from one (the beginning), through the intervening numbers two and three, to the number four (completion, wholeness) symbolizes a passage from primal (but still only potential) unity to a state of actual wholeness. Numbers symbolize the structure of individuation in the psyche, and they also symbolize the creation of order in the non-psychic world. So human knowledge of numbers becomes knowledge of cosmic structure. Insofar as people have a priori knowledge of numbers, by virtue of their cognitive abilities and intelligence, they also have a priori knowledge of the cosmos. (Interestingly, ancient Greeks like Empedocles believed that the gods think in mathematical terms and that humans who were mathematical geniuses were godlike, indeed were as good as gods themselves. With this conviction, Empedocles threw himself over the top of Mt. Etna and into the active volcano below.)

If number represents the archetype of order become conscious, it still does not answer the question of *what* is ultimately responsible for this state of order. What underlies number and images of order? What is the archetype of order *per se*? There must be a dynamic force operating behind the scenes that creates the order apparent in synchronisitic phenomena and reveals itself in number and image. Jung is working his way toward a new cosmology, a statement about the principle of order not only for the psyche but also for the world. It is to be a statement that is not primarily mythological in the religious or imaginal sense, but rather one that is based on the scientific world view of modern times. This leads him to the broader definition of synchronicity.

A New Paradigm

Toward the end of his paper, Jung introduces the far-reaching idea of including synchronicity—along with space, time, and causality—in a paradigm that can offer a complete account of reality as it is experienced by humans and measured by scientists. In one sense, what Jung is doing here is inserting the psyche into the full account of reality by saying that "the meaningful coincidence between a psychic event and an objective event"[16] must be considered. This adds the element of meaning to the scientific paradigm, which otherwise proceeds without reference to human consciousness or to the value of meaning. Jung is proposing that a full account of reality must include the presence of the human psyche—the observer—and the element of meaning.

We have already seen in earlier chapters the tremendous importance that Jung assigned to human consciousness. In fact, he saw the meaning of human life on this planet to be tied to our capacity for consciousness, to add to the world a mirroring awareness of things and meanings that otherwise would run on through endless eons of time without being seen, thought, or recognized.

For Jung, the raising into consciousness of patterns and images from the depths of the collective psychoid unconscious gives humankind its purpose in the universe, for we alone (as far as we know) are able to realize these patterns and give expression to what we realize. Put another way, God needs us in order to become held in awareness. Humans are in a position to become aware that the cosmos has an ordering principle. We can note and register the meaning that is there. But Jung also keenly wants to emphasize that he is not just trying to do speculative philosophy here. That would be traditional and old-fashioned, and would belong to a premodern level of consciousness. He is striving for Stage 5 and even Stage 6 consciousness (see chapter 8) and so is working empirically and scientifically. Synchronicity is not primarily a philosophical view, he wants to argue, but a concept based on empirical fact and observation. It can be tested in laboratories.[17] Only a cosmology of this sort will be acceptable in the contemporary world. Nostalgia for traditional belief systems is to be found in many quarters of our world today, but for the present and future, and for the highest levels of consciousness, the paradigm cannot be mythological. It must be scientific.

As the basis for a new world view, the concept of synchronicity and its implications work because they are easy enough to understand intuitively and to incorporate into one's everyday life. Everyone is aware of lucky things happening, and of unlucky days when nothing seems to go right. Clusters of events that are related through meaning and image but unconnected causally can be readily experienced and verified by one and all. But to take this concept seriously as a scientific principle is not at all easy. It is revolutionary. For one thing, it requires an entirely new way of thinking about nature and history. If one is to find meaning in historical events, for example, the implication is that the underlying archetype of order is arranging history in such a way as to produce some further advance of consciousness. This does not mean progress as humans would like to think of it, but rather an advance in understanding reality. The understanding may amount to recognition of the terrible side of reality as well as the beauty and the glory of it.

This was Jung's driving notion in writing *Aion*. Western religious and cultural history over the past two thousand years can be seen as a pattern of unfolding consciousness about an underlying archetypal structure. There are no accidents in the meandering and vicissitudes of historical process. It is going somewhere, producing a specific image that needs to be mirrored and reflected in human consciousness. There is a light side and a dark side to this image. This same mode of reflection can be applied to an individual's life history as well as to collective history, and indeed the two can (and indeed should be) seen in relation to one another and joined in a meaningful way. Each of us is the carrier of a bit of the consciousness that is needed by the times in order to advance consciousness of the underlying motifs unfolding in history. Individual dreams of an archetypal nature, for instance, may be in the service of the times, compensating for the one-sidedness of culture, and not only of the individual's consciousness. In this sense, the individual is a cocreator of the reflection of reality that history as a whole reveals.

The mental leaps required to think of culture and history in terms that include synchronicity are considerable, particularly for narrowly rationalistic Westerners who are committed strictly to the principle of causality. The Age of Enlightenment left a legacy of facticity without meaning. The cosmos and history, it is supposed, are arranged by chance and by the causal laws that govern matter. Jung recognizes the challenge. He was himself, after all, steeped in the Western scientific world view. "The idea of synchronicity with its inherent quality of meaning produces a picture of the world so irrepresentable as to be completely baffling. The advantage, however, of adding this concept is that it makes possible a view which includes the psychoid factor in our description and knowledge of nature—that is, an a priori meaning or 'equivalence'."[18] Jung presents a diagram that he and the physicist Wolfgang Pauli worked out.

On the vertical axis lies the space-time continuum, and on the horizontal there is the continuum between causality and synchronicity. The most complete account of reality, it is claimed here, includes understanding a phenomenon by considering four

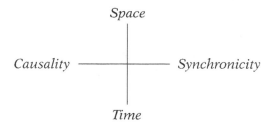

factors: where and when the event happened (the space-time continuum), and what led up to it and what it means (the causality-synchronicity continuum). If these questions can be answered, the event will be grasped in its fullness. There might be debate on any and all of these points; certainly on the question of an event's meaning there is bound to be a great deal of difference and dispute. Interpretations are endlessly generated, especially regarding significant events like the explosion of the first atomic bomb, for example, not to mention much more personal events like the birth or death of someone in the family. There is room for widely diverging opinions here. There is also, of course, a large range of opinion about causality. Jung's point is that the answer to the question of meaning requires more than only an account of the causal sequence of events that led up to the event in question. He argues that synchronicity must be considered in arriving at an answer to the question of meaning. From the psychological and the psychoid side of things, one has to investigate the archetypal patterns that are evident in a constellated situation, for these will provide the necessary parameters for taking up the question of synchronicity and deep structural meaning. With respect to the appearance of the atomic bomb on the stage of world history, for instance, the exploration of meaning would have to include the world constellating factor of the Second World War and the polarization of opposites which that war so violently generated. One would also have to include contemporary humankind's dreams of the atomic bomb in the analysis. What does the atomic bomb add to one-sided human consciousness about the structures of Being?

In order to bring the theory of archetypes into play in relation to synchronistic events that transgress the boundaries of the psychic world, Jung was forced to expand upon his notion of the nonpsychic nature of the archetype. On the one hand, it is psychic and psychological, since it is experienced within the psyche in the form of images and ideas. On the other hand, it is irrepresentable in itself and its essence lies outside of the psyche. In this essay on synchronicity, Jung introduces the idea of the archetype's property of *transgressivity*. "Although associated with causal processes, or 'carried' by them, they [the archetypes] continually go beyond their frame of reference, an infringement to which I would give the name 'transgressivity', because the archetypes are not found exclusively in the psychic sphere, but can occur just as much in circumstances that are not psychic (equivalence of an outward physical process with a psychic one)."[19] The archetype transgresses both the boundaries of the psyche and of causality, although it is "carried" by both. Jung intends transgressivity to mean that the patterns which occur in the psyche are related to patterns and events that lie outside of the psyche. The feature common to both is the archetype. In the case of the atomic bomb, the archetype of the self is revealed in history inside and outside of the psyche by the event of its explosion, in and through the world historical context in which it appeared, and by millions (my guess, although there has been some research on this) of dreams that have featured the bomb.

This idea of the archetype's transgressivity cuts in two directions. First, as I have been discussing, it affirms that there is underlying objective meaning in the coincidences that fall together in psyche and world and strike us as intuitively meaningful. On the other hand, it creates the possibility that there is meaning where we do not intuitively see it, when, for instance, accidents take place that strike us as merely due to pure chance. In both cases, this type of meaning goes beyond (transgresses) the chain of linear causality. Is our birth into a particular family only due to chance and causality, or could there be meaning here as well? Or suppose that the psyche is organized and structured not only causally, as is usually thought of in developmental psychology, but also synchronistically. This would mean that personality development takes place by moments of meaningful coincidence (synchronicity) as well as by a pre-ordained epigenetic sequence of stages. It would also imply that the instinct groups and the archetypes become wedded and activated both causally and synchronistically (meaningfully). An instinct like sexuality, for example, might become activated not only because of a causal chain of sequential events (genetic factors, psychological fixations, or early childhood experiences) but also because an archetypal field is constellated at a particular moment and a chance encounter with a person turns into a lifelong relationship. In this moment, something of the psychoid world becomes visible and conscious (the *syzygy*, the soul mate pair). The constellated image of the archetype does not create the event, but the correspondence between inner psychological preparedness (which may be totally unconscious at the time) and the outer appearance of a person, inexplicably and unpredictably, is synchronistic. Why such connections take place seems a mystery if we reflect only upon causality, but if we introduce the synchronistic factor and the dimension of meaning we come closer to a more complete and satisfying answer. In a random universe, this falling together of need and opportunity, or desire and satisfaction, would be impossible, or at least statistically improbable. These unforgettable mysteries that are embodied in synchronistic events transform people. Lives are turned in new directions, and contemplation of what lies behind synchronistic events leads consciousness to profound, perhaps even to ultimate levels of reality. When an archetypal field is constellated and the pattern emerges synchronistically within the psyche and the objective non-psychic world, one has the experience of being in Tao. And what becomes available to consciousness through such experiences is foundational, a vision into as much of ultimate reality as humans are capable of realizing. Falling into the archetypal world of synchronistic events feels like living in the will of God.

Cosmology

The essay on synchronicity begins with and indeed focuses mostly on what Jung calls the "narrow definition" of synchronicity, that is, the meaningful coincidence between a psychic event such as a dream or thought and an event in the non-psychic world. But Jung also considers the broader definition. This has to do with acausal orderedness in the world without special reference to the human psyche. This is a "wider conception of synchronicity as an 'acausal orderedness'"[20] in the world. This becomes Jung's cosmological statement. Synchronicity, or "acausal orderedness," is a principle underlying cosmic law. "Into this category come all 'acts of creation', a priori factors such as the properties of natural numbers, the discontinuities of modern physics, etc. Consequently we would have to include constant and experimentally reproducible phenomena within the scope of our expanded concept, though this does not seem to accord with the nature of the phenomena included in synchronicity narrowly understood."[21] From the viewpoint of the general principle of synchronicity, our human experience of acausal orderedness, through the psychoid factor and the transgressivity of the archetype, is a special case of much broader orderedness in the universe.

With this cosmological picture I place the finishing touch on Jung's map of the soul. His explorations of the psyche and its borders led him into territory that is normally occupied by cosmologists, philosophers, and theologians. His map of the soul must however be placed within the context of this wider perspective, for this is what provides the most extensive reach of his unified vision. We human beings, he teaches, have a special role to play in the universe. Our consciousness is capable of reflecting the cosmos and bringing it into the mirror of consciousness. We can come to realize that we live in a universe which can best be described using four principles: indestructible energy, the space-time continuum, causality, and synchronicity. Jung diagrams this relationship as shown below.

The human psyche and our personal psychology participate in the order of this universe most profoundly through the psychoid level of the unconscious. Through the process of psychization, patterns of order in the universe become available to consciousness and eventually can be understood and integrated. Each person can witness the Creator and creative works from within, so to speak, by paying attention to image and synchronicity. For the

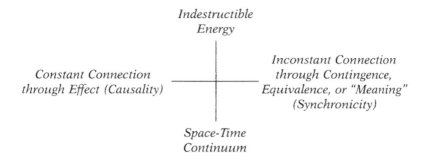

archetype is not only the pattern of the psyche, but it also reflects the actual basic structure of the universe. "As above, so below," spake the ancient sages. "As within, so without," responds the modern soul explorer, Carl Gustav Jung.

Notes

Introduction

1. Jung, *Collected Works*, Vol. 6.
2. Jung, *Coll. Wks.*, Vol. 1, pp. 3–88.
3. Jung, *Coll. Wks.*, Vol. 3, pp. 1–152.
4. Henri Ellenberger, *The Discovery of the Unconscious*, p. 687.
5. Jung, *Memories, Dreams, Reflections*, pp. 182–83.

1. Surface (Ego-Consciousness)

1. Jung, *Coll. Wks.*, Vol. 4, par. 772.
2. Jung, *Coll. Wks.*, Vol. 9/ii, par. 1.
3. Ibid.
4. Jung, *Coll. Wks.*, Vol. 8, par. 382.
5. Jung, *Memories, Dreams, Reflections*, p. 32.
6. Many animal species do seem to have considerable, though peculiar and puzzling, communications abilities and resources. To our knowledge, however, these are but slight compared to even the most reduced human capacity to learn languages and to function in a linguistic universe. No doubt many of their nonverbal communications abilities have yet to be discovered.
7. Jung, *Memories, Dreams, Reflections*, p. 45.
8. Jung, *Coll. Wks.*, 9/1, par. 3.
9. Ibid.
10. Ibid.
11. Ibid.
12. Ibid.
13. Ibid.
14. Jung's fundamental identity as a scientist underlies his admission that the theory of archetypes is a hypothesis. To do otherwise would have been to engage in mythmaking and visionary pronouncement, the basis for religion rather than for science. Jung's writings are occasionally treated as dogma, but they should not be, since he bases himself on an empirical method and claims the role of scientist rather than prophet.

15. Jung, *op. cit.*, par. 5

16. William James, *Principles of Psychology*, Vol. 1, pp. 291–400.

17. Jung, *op. cit.*, par. 6.

18. Jung, *Coll. Wks.*, Vol. 6, p. v.

19. Jung borrowed this phrase from the French anthropologist Levy-Bruhl to describe the ego's most primitive relation to the world and to the surrounding group or tribe. *Participation mystique* refers to a state of primitive identity between self and object, whether the object is a thing, a person, or a group. Charismatic political leaders like Mao Tse Tung sought to cultivate this state of consciousness among their people. "One China, one mind"—meaning Mao's mind—was the Chinese dictator's slogan during the disastrous cultural revolution.

20. Jung, *op. cit.*, par. 9.

21. Ibid.

22. Romans 7: 15–18.

23. Jung, *op. cit.*

2. The Populated Interior (The Complexes)

1. The Word Association Experiment was a test invented by Galton and revised by the German psychologist Wilhelm Wundt, who introduced it into continental experimental psychology in the late nineteenth century. Before Jung and Bleuler adopted it, it had been used mainly for theoretical studies on how the mind associates words and ideas (see *Coll. Wks.* 2, par. 730). Following the lead of Bleuler and the inspiration of Freud's work on the importance of unconscious factors in mental life, Jung tried to turn the test to practical use in the psychiatric clinic while also continuing to use the results from it for theorizing about the structure of the psyche.

2. For details about this research, see Ellenberger, *The Discovery of the Unconscious*, p. 692ff.

3. For a fascinating discussion of Freud's use of the terms complex and core complex, see Kerr, *A Most Dangerous Method*, p. 247ff.

4. Jung, *Coll. Wks.*, Vol. 2, par. 8.

5. Ibid, pars. 1015ff.

6. Jung, *Coll. Wks.*, Vol. 8, pars. 194–219.

7. The various strands of opinion in this discussion have been published in *Lingering Shadows*. These arguments have been reviewed by Anthony Stevens in his book *Jung*, where he strongly takes the position that Jung was not guilty of anti-Semitic and pro-Nazi behavior. The contrary view has been presented in a number of papers by Andrew Samuels.

8. Jung, *op. cit.*, par.198.

9. Ibid.

10. Ibid.

11. Jung, "New Aspects of Criminal Psychology," in *Coll. Wks.*, Vol. 2, pars. 1316–47.

12. Joseph Henderson has been the strongest exponent of this view in Jungian terms. For a detailed discussion of the cultural unconscious and its various aspects, see Henderson's "Cultural Attitudes and the Cultural Unconscious" in *Shadow and Self*, pp. 103–26.

13. This point has been greatly elaborated in the important paper by Hans Dieckmann, "Formation of and Dealing with Symbols in Borderline Patients."

14. Jung, *Coll. Wks.*, Vol. 8, par. 201.

15. Ibid.

16. Ibid.

17. Ibid., par. 202.

18. Ibid.

19. Ibid.

20. Ibid.

21. Ibid., par. 204.

22. Ibid.

23. Ibid.

3. Psychic Energy (Libido Theory)

1. William McGuire (ed.), *The Freud-Jung Letters*, pp. 6–7.

2. Jung, *Memories, Dreams, Reflections*, p. 164.

3. In Jung, *Coll. Wks.*, Vol. 8, pars. 1–130.

4. McGuire, *op. cit.*, p. 461.

5. Jung, *Psychology of the Unconscious*, pp. 142–43.

6. McGuire, *op. cit.*, p. 460.

7. Jung, *Psychology of the Unconscious,*, pp. 144–45.

8. Ibid., p. 156.

9. Jung, *Memories, Dreams, Reflections*, p. 167.

10. Jung, *Psychology of the Unconscious*, p. 480.

11. Jung, *Coll. Wks.*, Vol. 5.

12. Jung's views on the value of regular work are interesting in this regard. The work ethic is actually an emancipator, in his view, from the bondage to the incest wish. "The destruction of slavery was the necessary condition of that sublimation [of incestuous sexuality], for antiquity had

not yet recognized the duty of work and work as a duty, as a social need of fundamental importance. Slave labor was compulsory work, the counterpart of the equally disastrous compulsion of the libido of the privileged. It was only the obligation of the individual to work which made possible in the long run that regular "drainage" of the unconscious, which was inundated by the continual regression of the libido. Indolence is the beginning of all vice, because in a condition of slothful dreaming the libido has abundant opportunity for sinking into itself, in order to create compulsory obligations by means of regressively reanimated incestuous bonds. The best liberation is through *regular work*. Work, however, is salvation only when it is a free act, and has in itself nothing of infantile compulsion. In this respect, religious ceremony appears in a high degree as organized inactivity, and at the same time as the forerunner of modern work" (*Psychology of the Unconscious*, p. 455). This is a version of the notion *Arbeit macht frei*, used so despicably by the Nazis in their work camps where precisely slavery was institutionalized. It is when work is freely chosen and accepted as a duty to life that the transformation of libido can take place. When one freely chooses a vocation and voluntarily sacrifices a great deal of pleasure and sensual gratification for the sake of learning and practicing it, the transformation of libido has been successful.

13. George Hoganson discusses this issue of authority extensively in his book *Jung's Struggle with Freud*.

14. Jung, *Coll. Wks.*, Vol. 8, pars. 6ff.

15. Ibid., par. 5.

16. Ibid., par. 58.

17. Ibid.

18. Ibid.

19. A therapist who took this finalistic energic viewpoint might justifiably be seen as impersonal and unempathic. There would be little attention paid to causative factors like childhood traumas or conflicted and abusive relationships in the past. The focus would be on tracking the flow of energy from ego to unconscious (regression) to new adaptation (progression) and on analyzing away attitudes and cognitive structures that might prevent or block the flow of libido from finding its natural gradient or pathway. It is a much more cognitive approach. The empathic analyst, on the other hand, would look for past reasons for the present difficulty and would show understanding for how the past has created the problems in the present. Jung in general felt that the Freudian approach was of the causal-mechanistic, empathic variety while his own approach was more the finalistic-energic, impersonal type. The analyst who dissects the psyche with a view to analyzing the movement of energy and facilitating its flow toward the goal of balance and equilibrium is using the impersonal method. Extroverts, in Jung's typological understanding, are usually more attracted to causal theories, while introverts favor a

finalistic approach that is more abstract. Many contemporary analysts try to combine them.

20. The difference between Adler and Freud was an important element in Jung's struggle with Freud, and his continuing efforts to understand the interpersonal dynamics entered into his theory of psychological types as well. One reason Jung was drawn to investigate personality differences in terms of psychological type had to do with understanding the difference between the theoretical positions of Adler and Freud. Both theories had a lot to offer and both seemed correct in many ways. Yet Jung, who differed from both Freud and Adler, concluded that Freud's theory was fundamentally extroverted in the sense of assuming drives that seek pleasure and release via objects, while Adler's was introverted because it saw people as basically in search of establishing ego control over objects. Jung saw the power need described in Adler's theory as basically the need of introverted individuals to control the object world rather than relate to it and derive pleasure from it. Introverted people are more motivated by the drive for power and control over threatening objects than by the search for pleasure. Extroverts, on the other hand, are oriented by the pleasure principle and these people conform to Freud's psychological perspective. Both Freud, who sees human beings as basically extroverted and driven by the pleasure principle, and Adler, who sees us as introverted and driven by the need for power, offer true explanations of human behavior, but each man approached the psyche from a different perspective and in a sense was describing a different type of individual.

21. Jung, *op. cit.*, pars. 79–87.

22. Ibid., pars. 88–113.

23. Jung, *Letters*, Vol. 2, p. 624.

24. Jung, *Coll. Wks.*, Vol. 8, pars. 818–968.

4. The Psyche's Boundaries (Instincts, Archetypes, and the Collective Unconscious)

1. This area—the collective unconscious—has caused academic psychology to shy away from Jung and to call him a mystic. Only in recent times have the tools become available, in the form of biological research techniques particularly on the brain and on the relation of brain chemistry to mood and thought, to tackle the far-reaching hypotheses put forward by Jung many decades ago. Much recent research on the biological bases of human behavior is tending to confirm Jung's views that we inherit a great deal of the mental and behavioral patterning that had been considered learned and the result of nurture, not nature (see Satinover, Stevens, Tresan). For Jung, the archetypes are like instincts, in that they are given with our genetic makeup, inborn.

2. In fact, Jung has been seen by some writers (for example, Philip Rieff) as an antiquarian throwback to the 18th century, when amateur scholars and scientists simply collected odd bits of information about everything in the world and created libraries and museums that showed little understanding of what they were housing. Needless to add, Rieff is a diehard Freudian.

3. Jung, *Letters*, Vol. 1, p. 29.

4. Ibid., p. 30.

5. Ibid., p. 29.

6. Jung, *Coll Wks*, Vol. 4, par. 728.

7. Jung, *Memories, Dreams, Reflections*, p. 161.

8. Ibid.

9. Jung, *Coll. Wks.*, Vol. 8, par. 400.

10. Ibid.

11. Ibid., par. 401.

12. Ibid., par. 402.

13. Ibid., par. 367.

14. Ibid., par. 368, citing Bleuler.

15. Ibid., par. 376.

16. Ibid., par. 377.

17. Ibid.

18. Ibid.

19. Ibid., par. 379.

20. Ibid.

21. Ibid.

22. Ibid.

23. Ibid., par. 398.

24. Ibid., par. 404.

25. Ibid.

26. Ibid., par. 405.

27. Ibid., par. 406.

28. Ibid.

29. Ibid.

30. Ibid.

31. Ibid., par. 407.

32. Ibid., par. 408.

33. Ibid., par. 415.

34. Ibid.

35. Ibid., par. 416.

36. Ibid.

37. Ibid.

5. The Revealed and the Concealed in Relations with Others (Persona and Shadow)

1. For a fuller discussion of Jung's views on the subject of evil, see *Jung on Evil*, edited and with an extensive introduction by Murray Stein.

2. Jung, *Coll. Wks.*, Vol. 6, par. 799.

3. Ibid.

4. Ibid.

5. Ibid., par. 687.

6. Ibid.

7. Ibid., par. 798.

8. Ibid.

9. Ibid.

10. Jung, *Coll. Wks.*, Vol. 13, par. 70.

6. The Way to the Deep Interior (Anima and Animus)

1. Jung, *Memories, Dreams, Reflections*, pp. 185–88.

2. Ibid., p. 186.

3. Taken from Jung's "Visions Seminar," as quoted in *Memories, Dreams, Reflections*, p. 392.

4. Jung, *Coll. Wks.*, Vol. 6, par. 801.

5. Ibid.

6. Ibid.

7. Ibid., par. 801.

8. Ibid.

9. Ibid., par. 802.

10. The view was reported in *The New Yorker*, Sept. 9, 1996, p. 34 as the presidential candidates were preparing for the coming election.

11. Jung, *op. cit.*, par. 804.

12. Ibid.

13. Ibid.
14. Ibid.
15. Ibid.
16. Ibid.
17. Ibid.
18. Jung, *Coll. Wks.*, Vol. 17, par. 338.
19. Jung, *Coll. Wks.*, Vol. 9/2, par. 26.
20. Ibid., par. 41.
21. Ibid., par. 42.
22. Ibid.
23. Jung, *Coll. Wks.*, Vol. 16, par. 521.
24. Jung, *Coll. Wks.*, Vol. 9/ii, par. 29.

7. The Psyche's Transcendent Center and Wholeness (The Self)

1. Jung, *Memories, Dreams, Reflections*, pp. 170–99.
2. Ibid., p. 378.
3. Ibid., p. 379.
4. Jung's account of this remarkable incident is found in *Memories, Dreams, Reflections*, pp. 189–91.
5. Op. cit., pp. 195–97.
6. Ibid., p. 199.
7. Jung, *Coll. Wks.*, 9/2, pars. 57–58.
8. Ibid., par. 59.
9. Ibid.
10. Ibid.
11. Ibid., par. 60.
12. Ibid.
13. Ibid., pars., 351–57.
14. Ibid., par. 351.
15. Ibid., par. 357.
16. Ibid., par. 355.

8. Emergence of the Self (Individuation)

1. Jung, *Coll. Wks.*, Vol. 8, par. 778.
2. Ibid., par. 550.

3. Jung, *op. cit.*, par. 769.

4. Jung, *Coll. Wks.*, Vol. 9/1, pp. 290–354.

5. Jung, *Coll. Wks.*, Vol. 13, pp. 199–201.

6. *Modern Man in Search of a Soul* was the title of a famous book published by Jung in 1933.

7. Jung, *The Psychology of Kundalini Yoga.*

8. The volume, which appeared in 1952, was entitled *Naturerklärung und Psyche.* (Studien aus dem C.G. Jung-Institut Zürich, 4).

9. Jung, *Coll. Wks.*, Vol. 13, pars. 248–49.

10. Jung, Coll. Wks, Vol. 10, pp. 437–55.

11. Jung, *Coll. Wks.*, Vol. 9/1, pp. 275–89.

12. Ibid., pp. 290–354.

13. Ibid., par. 520.

14. Ibid., par. 221.

15. Ibid., par. 522.

16. Ibid., par. 523.

17. Ibid., par. 525.

18. The beautiful color plates of this series are inserted in *Coll. Wks.*, Vol. 9/1, following p. 292.

19. Ibid., par. 538.

20. Ibid.

21. Ibid.

22. Ibid.

23. Ibid., par. 544.

24. Ibid., par. 548.

25. Ibid., par. 545.

26. Ibid., par. 548.

27. Ibid., par. 550.

28. Ibid., par. 549.

29. Ibid., par 556.

30. Jung, *Coll. Wks.*, Vol. 9/2, par. 410.

31. Ibid., par. 355.

32. Ibid., par. 410.

9. Of Time and Eternity (Synchronicity)

1. He was also interested in evidence for the existence of ghosts and poltergeists, certainly borderline phenomena. And then there was the

peculiar relation he noted between psyche (inner) and object (outer), as in the "catalytic exteriorization phenomenon" he remarked upon in Freud's presence when they heard a loud report from a wooden bookcase in Freud's study. He reports on this in *Memories, Dreams, Reflections*, p. 155.

2. Jung, *Coll. Wks.*, Vol. 8, par. 843.

3. Ibid., par. 515.

4. This essay is found in *Coll. Wks.*, Vol. 8, pp. 419–519.

5. Jung, Letters, vol. 2, pp. 108–9.

6. Op. cit., par. 840.

7. Ibid., par. 439.

8. Ibid.

9. Ibid., par. 440.

10. Ibid.

11. Ibid.

12. Ibid.

13. Ibid., par. 850.

14. Ibid.

15. Ibid., par. 870.

16. Ibid., par. 850

17. Ibid., par. 960.

18. Ibid., par. 962.

19. Ibid., par. 964.

20. Ibid., par. 965.

21. Ibid.

Glossary

anima   The archetypal images of the eternal feminine in a man's unconscious that forms a link between ego-consciousness and the collective unconscious and potentially opens a way to the self.

animus   The archetypal images of the eternal masculine in a woman's unconscious that forms a link between ego-consciousness and the collective unconscious and potentially opens a way to the self.

archetype   An innate potential pattern of imagination, thought, or behavior that can be found among human being in all times and places.

archetypal image   A psychic pattern, mental or behavioral, that is common to the human species. Archetypal images are found in the dreams of individuals and in cultural materials such as myths, fairy tales, and religious symbols.

compensation   The self-regulatory dynamic process whereby ego-consciousness and the unconscious seek homeostatic balance, which also fosters individuation and the progressive movement toward wholeness.

complex   A feeling toned autonomous content of the personal unconscious, usually formed through psychic injury or trauma.

ego   The center of consciousness, the "I."

ego-consciousness   The portion of the psyche made up of easily accessed thoughts, memories, and feelings at whose center is the ego, the "I."

extroversion   An habitual attitude of consciousness that prefers active engagement with objects to the close scrutiny of them.

imago   The psychic representation or image of an object, like a parent, not to be confused with the actual object.

individuation   The process of psychic development that leads to the conscious awareness of wholeness. Not to be confused with individualism.

instinct   An innate, physically based source of psychic energy (or libido) that is shaped and structured in the psyche by an archetypal image.

introversion   An habitual attitude of consciousness that prefers introspection and the close scrutiny of relations with objects.

libido   Interchangeable with "psychic energy" and having affinities with the philosophical concept of "life force." Libido is quantifiable and can be measured.

neurosis   An habitual attitude of rigid one-sidedness in ego-consciousness, which defensively and systematically excludes unconscious contents from consciousness.

persona   The psychic interface between the individual and society that makes up a person's social identity.

projection   The externalization of unconscious psychic contents, sometimes for defensive purposes (as with the shadow) and sometimes for developmental and integrative purposes (as with the anima and the self).

psyche   An inclusive term covering the areas of consciousness, personal unconscious and collective unconscious. The collective unconscious is sometimes referred to as the **objective psyche** because it is not personal or individual.

psychoid   An adjective referring to the boundaries of the psyche, one of which interfaces with the body and the physical world and the other with the realm of "spirit."

psychological type   The combination of one of two **attitudes** (extroversion or introversion) with one of four **functions** (thinking, feeling, sensation, or intuition) to form a distinctive habitual orientation of ego-consciousness.

psychosis   A state of possession in which ego-consciousness is flooded by the unconscious and often seeks to defend itself by identifying with an archetypal image.

self   The center, source of all archetypal images and of innate psychic tendencies toward structure, order, and integration.

shadow   The rejected and unaccepted aspects of the personality that are repressed and form a compensatory structure to the ego's self ideals and to the persona.

synchronicity   The meaningful coincidence of two events, one inner and psychic and the other outer and physical.

transcendent function   The psychic link created between ego-consciousness and the unconscious as a result of the practice of dream interpretation and active imagination, and therefore essential for individuation in the second half of life.

unconscious   The portion of the psyche lying outside of conscious awareness. The contents of the unconscious are made up of repressed memories and material, such as thoughts and images and emotions, that has never been conscious. The unconscious is divided into the **personal unconscious**, which contains the complexes, and the

collective unconscious, which houses the archetypal images and instinct groups.

wholeness The emergent sense of psychic complexity and integrity that develops over the course of a complete lifetime.

References

Burnham, J.S. and McGuire, W. (eds.). 1983. *Jelliffe: American Psychoanalyst and Physician*. Chicago: University of Chicago Press.

Clark, J.J. 1992. *In Search of Jung*. London and New York: Routledge.

Csikszentmihalyi, M. 1990. *Flow*. New York: Harper and Row.

Dieckman, H. 1987. On the theory of complexes. In *Archetypal Processes in Psychotherapy* (eds. N. Schwartz-Salant and M. Stein). Wilmette, IL.: Chiron Publications.

———. 1988. Formation of and dealing with symbols in borderline patients. In *The Borderline Personality in Analysis* (eds. N. Schwartz-Salant and M. Stein). Wilmette, IL.: Chiron Publications.

Ellenberger, H. 1970. *The Discovery of the Unconscious*. New York: Basic Books.

Erikson, E. 1968. *Identity, Youth, and Crisis*. New York: Norton.

Fordham, F. 1953. *An Introduction to Jung's Psychology*. Baltimore: Penguin Books.

Fordham, M. 1970. *Children as Individuals*. New York: Putnam.

———. 1985. *Explorations Into the Self*. London: Academic Press.

Hannah, B. 1976. *Jung, His Life and Work*. New York: G.P. Putnam's Sons.

Henderson, J. 1990. Cultural attitudes and the cultural unconscious. In *Shadow and Self*. Wilmette, IL.: Chiron Publications.

Hogenson, G. 1994. *Jung's Struggle with Freud*. Wilmette: Chiron Publications

Jacobi, J. 1943. *The Psychology of C.G. Jung*. New Haven, Conn.: Yale University Press.

James, W. 1902. *Varieties of Religious Experience*. New York: Longmans, Green, and Co.

———. 1950. *The Principles of Psychology*. New York: Dover.

Jung, C.G. Except as below, references are to the *Collected Works (CW)* by volume and paragraph number.

———. 1961. *Memories, Dreams, Reflections*. New York: Random House.

———. 1973. *Letters*, vol. 1. Princeton: Princeton University Press.

———. 1974. *The Freud/Jung Letters*. Princeton: Princeton University Press.

———. 1975. *Letters*, vol. 2. Princeton: Princeton University Press.

———. 1977. *C.G. Jung Speaking*. Princeton: Princeton University Press.

———. 1983. *The Zofingia Lectures*. Princeton: Princeton University Press.

———. 1991. *Psychology of the Unconscious*. Princeton: Princeton University Press.

Kerr, J. 1993. *A Most Dangerous Method*. New York: Knopf.

Maidenbaum, A. (ed.). 1991. *Lingering Shadows: Jungians, Freudians and Anti-Semitism*. Boston: Shambhala.

McGuire, W. (ed.) 1974. *The Freud/Jung Letters*. Princeton: Princeton University Press.

Noll, R. 1989. Multiple personality, dissociation, and C.G. Jung's complex theory. In *Journal of Anaytical Psychology* 34:4.

———. 1993. Multiple personality and the complex theory. In *Journal of Analytical Psychology* 38:3.

———. 1994. *The Jung Cult*. Princeton: Princeton University Press.

Rieff, P. 1968. *Triumph of the Therapeutic*. New York: Harper and Row.

Samuels, A. 1992. National psychology, National Socialism, and analytical psychology: Reflections on Jung and anti-semitism, Pts. I, II. In *Journal of Analytical Psychology* 37:1 and 2.

———. 1993. New material concerning Jung, anti-Semitism, and the Nazis. In *Journal of Analytical Psychology* 38:4, pp. 463–470.

Satinover, J. 1995. Psychopharmacology in Jungian practice. In *Jungian Analysis* (ed. M. Stein), pp. 349–71. LaSalle, IL: Open Court.

Stevens, A. 1982. *Archetypes: A Natural History of the Self*. New York: William Morrow and Co.

Stein, M. (ed.). 1995. *Jung on Evil*. Princeton: Princeton University Press.

Tresan, D. 1995. Jungian metapsychology and neurobiological theory: auspicious correspondences." In *IAAP Congress Proceedings 1995*. Einsiedeln: Daimon Verlag.

von Franz, M.L. 1971. The inferior function. In *Jung's Typology*. Dallas: Spring Publications.

Wehr, G. 1987. *Jung, A Biography*. Boston: Shambhala.

Index

CPSIA information can be obtained
at www.ICGtesting.com
Printed in the USA
LVHW081341010419
612539LV00031B/761/P

9 780812 693768